Forever Dobie

Forever Dobie

THE MANY LIVES OF DWAYNE HICKMAN

Dwayne Hickman
and
Joan Roberts Hickman

A BIRCH LANE PRESS BOOK
Published by Carol Publishing Group

Copyright © 1994 by Dwayne Hickman and Joan Roberts Hickman
All rights reserved. No part of this book may be reproduced in any form,
except by a newspaper or magazine reviewer who wishes to quote brief
passages in connection with a review.

A Birch Lane Press Book
Published by Carol Publishing Group
Birch Lane Press is a registered trademark of Carol Communications, Inc.
Editorial Offices: 600 Madison Avenue, New York, N.Y. 10022
Sales and Distribution Offices: 120 Enterprise Avenue, Secaucus,
    N.J. 07094
In Canada: Canadian Manda Group, P.O. Box 920, Station U, Toronto,
    Ontario M8Z 5P9
Queries regarding rights and permission should be addressed to
Carol Publishing Group, 600 Madison Avenue, New York, N.Y. 10022

Carol Publishing Group books are available at special discounts for
bulk purchases, sales promotions, fund-raising, or educational
purposes. Special editions can be created to specifications. For
details, contact Special Sales Department, Carol Publishing Group,
120 Enterprise Avenue, Secaucus, N.J. 07094

Manufactured in the United States of America
10 9 8 7 6 5 4 3 2 1

Library of Congress Cataloging-in-Publication Data

Hickman, Dwayne.
    Forever Dobie : the many lives of Dwayne Hickman / by Dwayne
Hickman and Joan Roberts Hickman.
        p.   cm.
    "A Birch Lane Press book."
    ISBN 1-55972-252-5
    1. Hickman, Dwayne.   2. Actors—United States—Biography.
3. Television producers and directors—United States—Biography.
I. Hickman Roberts, Joan.   II. Title.
PN2287.H49A3   1994
791.45'028'092—dc20
    [B]   94-18115
                                                            CIP

To Albert

CONTENTS

ACKNOWLEDGMENTS

Writing a book about your life can be insightful, embarrassing, depressing, exhilarating, and thought provoking. Over the years, whenever I've experienced what appeared to be a catastrophic situation, I would be reminded by some well-meaning friend that in a few years I'd be able to look back on the problem and laugh at it. Well, after spending the past year reviewing, reliving, and having nightmares about my experiences, I can report that, with only a few exceptions, I have found the humor and forgotten the pain.

In March of 1993 I got a call from Mickey Freeman, a publicist friend of forty years, asking me if I would be interested in writing a book about my life. Although my wife Joan and I work as writing partners on film and television scripts, I wasn't sure that we wanted to write a book, especially one that featured me as the subject. I have always been a very private person and I wasn't really comfortable with the idea of opening up my life to the general public. Joan and I discussed it and decided to decline the offer. Ever persistent, Mickey called a few weeks later, gently prodding us to reconsider; we did, and before we knew it we had a publisher and Joan and I began the task of writing my life story. There were days we cursed Mickey and days we praised him for getting us into this project. In the end, we must thank him because we discovered that we really enjoyed the process of writing a book and may even do it again.

Supersalesman and literary agent Bill Birnes has provided the push, fire, and excitement for this project. He has been our adviser and front-line warrior, making the impossible possible. He and his talented wife and partner, Nancy, provided all the answers to our thousand and one questions and never failed to give encouragement and support.

Joan and I wrote this entire book in longhand on yellow legal pads while sitting on our bed. As you can see, our "information superhighway" is more like a two-lane country road! Without the help of our ever faithful typist and friend, Fel Andrews, this project would have been an editor's nightmare. We couldn't have progressed past page one without Fel, who not only corrected our spelling errors and punctuation, but cheered us on. Our editor, Kevin McDonough, patiently guided us and we are grateful for his valuable input and enthusiasm.

We appreciate Carol and Tom Sneed who supplied missing family photos and John and Stacy Hickman for digging up pictures I hadn't seen in twenty-five years.

My old friend Aron Kincaid came to the rescue with terrific movie stills; Michael Fitzgerald and Rosemary DeCamp also provided priceless photos.

Our special thanks to Gabe Bandy for his photographs and PIC Photo Labs, who worked miracles getting all the photos processed and reproduced.

It's difficult enough trying to remember what happened last week, much less thirty years ago. Bob Denver and Sheila James Kuehl helped to fill in the missing pieces and, as always, gave their support.

Faced with the arduous task of writing a book, the input of others who have traveled this road and know all the potholes and pitfalls can be invaluable. Many-times-published film critic Leonard Maltin provided much encouragement, and our dear friends Terry and Pamela Shoop Sweeney also shared their insight, wisdom, and war stories.

We are especially grateful to Jean Franklin and Sandy Marrow for taking wonderful care of our young son Albert. This book was written during his nap times, trips to the park, and while he watched *Winnie the Pooh* and *Barney*. Working at home with a toddler underfoot provides some incredible adventures...but those stories will have to wait until our next book!

We would have been lost without Margaret Roberts, Albert's grandmother, who kept a watchful eye over him as we "AMTRAK'd" from D.C. to New York to meet with our publisher. We felt very guilty leaving him, but he was having such a good time with his grandmother he hardly knew we were gone.

During the writing of this book we lost Joan's wonderful father, Tom Roberts, and we survived the 6.8 earthquake that hit Los Angeles on January 17, 1994. We feel that our guardian angels were watching over us during those difficult times. Events such as these help us to keep priorities straight as to what is really important in life and what is not.

If I have learned anything from this recounting of my life, it would be to keep a positive outlook, even when it seems impossible to do so; and above all, maintain a sense of humor.

Joan and I thank you, the reader, and hope that you enjoy my life as much as I have.

Forever Dobie

• ONE •

RELUCTANT STAR

"HI, MY NAME IS DOBIE GILLIS!" I first said those words in 1958. I was sitting before a papier-mâché replica of Rodin's *Thinker* statue in a park set on Stage B on the backlot of Twentieth Century-Fox studios. That backlot was sold off years ago to build a shopping center and office buildings, now called Century City, and I did my famous monologue where Bullock's Department Store now stands. I figure that I sat somewhere between women's shoes and the escalator. I had no idea that thirty-five years after uttering those immortal words, I'd be walking along the street and people would still shout, "Hi, Dobie!" "Aren't you Dobie Gillis?" or "Hey, Dobie, I love that show!" During those years I've survived marriages, divorces, children, and career changes, but the one constant thing in my life has been Dobie.

Most people don't realize that I had a career as an actor in movies and television before "Dobie Gillis"; in fact, I made my acting debut in 1940. I was born in Los Angeles on May 18, 1934, so I was only six years old. I made twenty-one dollars that year as an extra in a movie at Twentieth Century-Fox...the same studio where I would later turn into Dobie Gillis.

1

But I'm getting ahead of myself.

The first member of our family who tried to break into show business was my mother, Louise Ostertag. She had moved to Los Angeles from Kansas City, Missouri, with her parents, Mary Ellen and Louis Ostertag. She was their only child; beautiful, petite, and perfect for the "moving picture" business in the mid-1920s, or so her mother thought. Louise Ostertag, movie extra, changed her name and became budding screen star Louise Lang. After meeting my father, Milton Hickman, she gave up her not so illustrious career as an extra and they were married in 1929. They moved in with her parents, which didn't make for the most harmonious living conditions, and in 1931 had their first child, my older brother, Darryl Gerard. I came along in 1934, Dwayne Bernard, and my sister, Deirdre Celeste, was born in 1940. Darryl, Dwayne and Deirdre; I will never understand what could have possessed—and I do mean possessed—my mother to give such bizarre names to her children. Darryl, so I was told, was named after Darryl Zanuck, the cofounder of Twentieth Century-Fox. My name was similar to my brother's, so we have spent most of our lives correcting people who call Darryl "Dwayne" or Dwayne "Darryl." All my life I wanted to be a Robert or a John or a Michael; instead I ended up a "Dobie."

My first childhood memories centered around moving. It seemed that our family uprooted every year or so and never for any apparent reason. Like a band of gypsies, after about ten months, the packing boxes would appear and the house would be torn up. Off we would go, with the car laden with boxes like an old mule; then we'd drive, sometimes less than a mile, to our next "temporary camp." It never made any sense to me, but like all kids, I was held hostage to my parents' strange behavior.

I was a quiet and very shy kid, while Darryl was aggressive and outgoing. I followed Darryl around as he led us in games of cowboys and Indians. If the cowboys won, I was an Indian; if the Indians won, I was a cowboy. Darryl had an active imagination and sometimes his games became a little too realistic. Once, when we were small, a man came to our front door and asked our mother if she had two little boys. She smiled with great pride and replied, "Oh yes, I certainly do." "Well," the man said, "You'd better get out here quick because the big one has just hung the little one from a tree." We also played "Burn the cowboy at the stake."...I don't need to tell you who played the cowboy. It's a wonder I grew up at all.

Darryl was acting as far back as I can remember. As the story goes, our father was getting started in the insurance business in the mid-1930s. He was trying to sell a policy to a lady named Ethel Meglin, who ran a "kiddies' school" where children were taught to sing and dance. She said she'd buy a policy if Dad would enroll one of his kids in her school. Darryl was the oldest, so he was nominated.

He was a natural. Darryl could sing and dance at the drop of a hat. He was a cute kid with wonderful instincts, so it wasn't really a surprise that his career took off in 1939 when he landed a role with Bing Crosby in the movie, *The Star Maker*.

As Darryl began to work, my mother spent all her time with him at the studio. Louise Lang, movie extra, was now playing the greatest role of her life as Louise Hickman, Darryl Hickman's stage mother. While she was busy coaching Darryl, my grandmother was home taking care of me and my little sister.

Occasionally my mother would have to drag me along to the studio and before I knew it I was being pushed along, reluctantly, in my brother's footsteps. The idea of having her two boys in the movies was her dream come true; for me it was a nightmare. I was so shy and self-conscious that I constantly tried to hide behind the scenery for fear I would have to be in a scene.

In 1940 Darryl made *The Grapes of Wrath*, and it was in this movie, at the age of six, that I made my unceremonious debut as an actor. I was an extra in a crowd scene and tried to bury myself between the biggest kids I could find so that no one would see me. And it was in this movie where I made my first money as an actor, twenty-one dollars for two days' work.

No matter how much I would protest, I couldn't convince my mother that I had absolutely no ambition to be an actor. So every time Darryl starred in a film, my mother continued to drag me along as part of the package.

The next movie I tried desperately to stay out of was *Men of Boys Town* at MGM, with Spencer Tracy and Mickey Rooney. Darryl had a good part and I was, as usual, an extra. In one scene, all the junior extras were told to form a line. As the little star wannabes quickly fell into place, I tried to slowly back up, hoping to melt into the dark stage. Suddenly a heavy hand landed on my shoulder. I looked up into the stern face of the assistant director, who had the unpleasant job of corralling all these little extra kids. I reluctantly took my place in line as he proceeded to give us our direction for the next scene. He told us that it would be easy; all we had to do was to run wild, like we did on a playground. We were supposed to come in from all different directions, then jump over the hedge in the middle of the set and fall into line. All the kids were crazy with excitement...all except me. I was the youngest and smallest of the group. Not only was I afraid of being trampled to death by this unruly mob but even if I survived, I couldn't possibly jump a hedge that was nearly as tall as I was. I glanced plaintively at my mother, who gave me one of her looks, so I realized she wouldn't save me. No, this was going to be "every boy for himself." I quickly sized up the situation and I made my plan. When Norman Taurog, the director, called "Action!" my worst fears came true. The boys went crazy, shoving, yelling, running like stampeding horses as they leaped over the hedge. As the mayhem broke out I quickly dropped to my knees and crawled around to the other side of the hedge and proceeded to do what I did best...I hid. When the director called "Cut!" my mother ran over to me. If she had seen my little survival maneuver I would be in big trouble. To my amazement and relief, she threw her arms around me and said, "I'm so proud of you...Now you see, there was no reason to be afraid." I just looked at her and smiled. I never did tell her the truth.

It was during this year, 1941, that the Hickman tribe was once again on the move. This time it was out to the San Fernando Valley to a small two-bedroom house. I really loved it out there. Unlike in the city, the weather was warm and desert dry, and with fields of orange groves and wide open spaces, it was the perfect neighborhood for bike riding and playing.

I attended St. Charles Elementary School for the first and second grades and was taught by an army of nuns. Just the thought of them still makes me break out in a sweat.

During the few times that I worked, my mother would take me out of school and I would have to attend the movie school on the set. Each child was required to have three hours of instruction a day. It was rarely three consecutive hours because of the filming schedule, so the kids would grab fifteen minutes here, another twenty minutes there, throughout the day. It was an impossible way to try to educate a child, but education wasn't the goal of the studio... getting the picture finished on time was the goal, and nothing was going to get in the way of that.

The class was held in what they called a "knockdown," which was constructed by attaching four flats together to form a room. When class was over, or they needed to move the schoolroom, the crew would come along and simply knock down the flats and move them to another site. One teacher, known as a welfare worker in those days, taught all the children, ranging from the first to the twelfth grade.

When I had to return to the nuns I would present them with a certificate that I had indeed been given my lessons. I dreaded coming back to school. The nuns always snatched the certificate out of my hand, looked it over, and snorted. They gave me the "fish-eye" and sent me back to class. The nuns had little patience with show business or the movie-set schools. Every time I returned from a day on the set the nuns seemed to grill me extra hard. It was miserable for me all the way around. I hated being in the movie, then I came back to the nuns, who seemed to punish me for doing something I didn't want to do in the first place.

It was during those two years at St. Charles that I shared the first and second grades with Bing Crosby's twin sons, Phillip and Dennis. Gary, the oldest, was Darryl's age, and

Lindsey, who was the youngest, was too young for school. Phillip, Dennis, and Gary were driven to school by their family's uniformed driver. These boys were a real handful!

As their 1941 Buick station wagon pulled up to the front of the school, you could see all three boys fighting with one another inside the car. Their long-suffering driver would duck as wild punches were thrown...along with books, shoes, baseballs, and anything else the Crosby kids could get their hands on. As they spilled out of the car, they never missed a beat as they continued to push and shove their way across the playground and into the school. Just like a snowball that careens down a hill, growing larger and more powerful, the Crosby mass of fighting, flailing, spitting, scratching, arms and legs rolled across the playground, sucking up any un-suspecting child in their path. By the time they reached the door, a battery of nuns, armed with the official nun weapon, a two-inch pack of wooden rules, braced themselves as they formed a wall of defense between the Crosby cyclone and the defenseless God-fearing children inside. Unlike the rest of us, the Crosby kids were unfazed by this fortress of nuns.

I always found the nuns very scary. Maybe it was that black flowing habit and their enormous headpiece. I always won-dered if that headpiece was hiding a bald head. The idea of seeing a bald nun was pretty frightening, and probably a sin. I could never figure out how the nuns always knew what was going on. It was like they had eyes in the back of their habit. They seemed to have a special radar that could spot a gum-chewer at fifty yards, and if you were talking in line, they could fly in from nowhere, grab you up, and spirit you off to the principal's office where you were never seen or heard from again. Maybe that's where the idea for Sally Fields' *Flying Nun* came from. Anyway, I always tried to keep a low profile with the nuns...and the Crosby boys. Both of them scared me and since I had plenty of experience being intimidated by my older brother, I didn't need to look for any more misery.

One day the nuns ordered us to form a line so we could march out to the playground. As usual, I tried to stay far away from Phillip and Dennis, the twin troublemakers. But as fate would have it, I was sandwiched between the two of them as we stood in line. They started horsing around and I stood like a stone statue, my eyes frozen forward, not daring to move for fear a nun would think I was part of this rowdy pair. As I dared to look up, to my horror, a furious nun had taken flight and was heading straight for us. I say "us" because I was literally caught in the middle. Phillip and Dennis were so busy reaching across me and throwing punches at one another, they never saw the heavily armed "flying nun" heading our way. The sister yelled, "Phillip, Dennis, stop this right now!" Never thinking for a moment that they would obey, she let the wooden rulers come crashing down. What neither the sister nor I had realized was that Phillip and Dennis had ceased fighting as soon as she spoke. Unfortunately, the rulers were already descending at the speed of light, and came crashing down on me, the silent statue of a boy, caught in the middle. From the moment the rulers made contact, my arm seemed to double in size as a huge red knot began to grow. I started to cry, and so did the poor sister, as she grabbed me up in her arms, profusely apologizing. The class stood by, horrified. Suddenly, the silence was broken by Phillip and Dennis laughing uncontrollably at my misfortune. That was too much for the sister. She grabbed them out of line and they disappeared from class for the rest of the day. We all speculated that they would probably come back contrite. What we didn't realize was that even the torture of the Holy Inquisition could not cower a Crosby. That afternoon they were back on the playground, fists flying, as they battled their way back to their car, where their beleaguered driver rounded them up and drove them home. No one could understand how America's favorite performer, Bing Crosby, who had played benevolent priests and Bob Hope's happy-go-lucky road partner, could have such miserable, unruly kids. It wasn't until years later that we learned that the Crosby boys' father, the ever popular pear shaped crooner, was really "Daddy Dearest."

During that year, Darryl was making a movie, *Jackass Mail*, with Wallace Beery. Beery was a big burly man, coarse and tough, and his booming voice scared me to death. Beery was famous for being difficult to work with, going out of his way to be as obnoxious and aggravating as possible. One of his most famous costars was Marjorie Main, and although they worked together on several pictures, he and Marjorie hated one another. She had a fear of germs and wore white gloves to protect herself. This germ-fetish was all the bait that Beery needed to spit and slobber all over her whenever he had the chance. The more she became upset, the more the spit flew from her thoroughly exasperating costar.

While I was visiting Darryl on the set one day, Beery must have realized that he had frightened me with his overbearing manner because he came over and offered me a doughnut. I wasn't too sure of this boisterous, gnarled-face man, but I took the doughnut anyway. He picked me up, set me on his knee, and proceeded to tell me stories about his childhood as an elephant boy in the circus. I was fascinated as he told me about feeding and caring for the elephants and traveling around the country. When he wanted to, he could be warm and pleasant.

Several years later I worked with Wallace Beery on *Bad Bascomb*. In the movie, Margaret O'Brien and I played little Mormon children who were crossing the country with our families on a wagon train. In one scene, Margaret and I hid under a wagon and watched as Beery tried to sing a song around the campfire. He was having a hard time remembering his lines, and after two takes he stood up, swore loudly, and walked off. The set fell silent, then the assistant director yelled, "Lunch, be back in one hour!" One hour later everyone reported back to the set; everyone except Beery. Apparently he had decided to call it a day and had gone home. No one said a word, because Wallace Beery had a well-earned reputation for being the kind of guy you didn't mess with.

Beery drove a 1942 Cadillac. Because we were in the middle of World War II, chrome wasn't available, so it was what they called a "blackout" model. If you had one today it would be worth a fortune. Beery drove like a maniac. He would pull onto the MGM lot at full speed, never bothering to slow down. He was such a menace that the guard at the gate would get Beery's call time and then make sure the entrance was cleared of any pedestrians, because no one was safe when Beery roared onto the lot. Although he had been nice to me, I never pushed my luck and stayed out of his way.

Nearly two years had passed since we had moved to the Valley. Wanderlust hit my parents again, so out came the boxes and up went the "For Sale" sign. It was no time at all before we were loading up the car and heading back to Hollywood. Apparently my father's drive to work had become too much for him, so my folks decided we had to move back into town. This was before Los Angeles had freeways and Cahuenga Boulevard was the only road that connected Hollywood and the Valley. I hated the idea, but no one asked my opinion, so once again I squeezed myself into the car as we took off for our new house.

Actually, the only thing new about this house was the fact we had never lived in it before. Besides that, it seemed to me to be the darkest, oldest, and most depressing place I had ever seen. If home seemed depressing, my new school, Immaculate Heart of Mary, didn't give me any relief either. My new teacher, Sister Stanislaus, was an old nun, whose reputation as a tyrant had been passed down for generations. She must have been close to seventy years old, but she was still an imposing figure since she stood about six feet tall and weighed nearly 250 pounds. Her face had a strange distorted look with what appeared to be a bad nose job. She also had a strong medicinal smell, like she used Mentholatum as her perfume. Sister Stanislaus's favorite prop was a baseball bat, which she carried with her everywhere. She would hold it straight in the air and that meant all the children had to form a straight line directly under the bat. If you deviated from her plan, the bat was conveniently there to persuade you to follow her orders. If you were stupid enough not to get the message, the bat would knock some sense into you. I never got the bat, but I still have a scar on my right hand from Stanislaus's backup weapon, her infamous metal-edged yardstick.

I was writing on the blackboard when someone in the class started snickering. I guess she thought I had provoked the outburst because, out of nowhere, her yardstick came crashing down across my hand. Unfortunately, the metal edge sliced my knuckle open and I stood crying and bleeding in front of everyone. Sister Stanislaus was unmoved by the injury she had inflicted. She ordered me to go to the school nurse, then report back to class at once. I did exactly as I was told and while the nurse bandaged my hand I said a prayer of thanks that Stanislaus hadn't used the bat on me.

As I headed back to class, Sister Clementcia, a nun that was so homely she scared you, came up behind me and told me to remove my hands from my pockets immediately or I would be sent to the principal's office. That seemed to be Clementcia's job, to patrol the halls and prevent boys from walking or standing with their hands in their pockets. No doubt she figured they were doing something sinful. It wasn't that I looked for trouble, actually I was very quiet and tried to stay out of everybody's way, but when you are under the watchful eyes of the nuns you find yourself being punished for anything they imagine you are doing. Sometimes you even get punished for something they think you're thinking about doing. They really struck fear in all of us.

One day several of us were standing by the schoolyard fence pulling at some weeds that had grown through from the vacant field next to the school. Suddenly Sister Stanislaus flew into a rage, swinging her bat and screaming for us to report to the principal's office. As we marched into the school to meet our fate, we were so frightened we were shaking. Later, when we stood in front of the principal, a hundred-year-old nun with the face of a gargoyle, one of my partners in crime, Barney Massemino, started trembling. Sweat poured down his face as the principal asked the name of the nearest public school to his house. Barney could hardly form the words as he told her. Then she asked me. I was so scared I apparently had gone deaf, because she shouted the question again and then jumped up and told me that my smart aleck attitude wouldn't be tolerated. Who was being a smart aleck? I was so upset I thought I was going to be sick right there on her desk. Somehow I finally choked out the name of the nearest school to my house. That question about the nearest public school was the standard line the nuns used on what they thought were delinquent students.

That was their way of telling you that you would be expelled from Catholic school and your parents would have to enroll you in...God forbid, public school. Not only would you lose out on a fine education, you'd also lose your soul to the devil. The principal informed us that she would decide our fate the next week. So, for the entire weekend all I could think about, day and night, was my impending punishment. I went to confession, pleaded for forgiveness for pulling the weeds, and prayed until I fell asleep from exhaustion. As it turned out, the principal never mentioned it again.

As if school wasn't enough pressure, my grandmother came up with the great idea that I needed to have a talent, something that I could excel in so that Darryl and I could both be little stars.

By this time my brother was twelve and enjoying a successful childhood movie career. He sang and danced like a miniature Al Jolson and he could play a dramatic scene so convincingly there wouldn't be a dry eye in the audience. Dancing around in a "Beanie" hat, he'd belt out one of the current hit songs of the day and with sparks flying from his tap shoes, my mother would watch as tears of pride welled up in her eyes. I would watch him too, cheering him on and thankful that everyone was watching him and leaving me alone. From my point of view it was the perfect arrangement. I could go along and play with my friends and just be a kid while gladly leaving all the show business stuff to my more outgoing and obviously more talented older brother. But what seemed like the ideal situation to me and to my mother, who reveled in Darryl's accomplishments, was making my grandmother more angry by the moment. She felt sorry for me because my mother devoted so much time to Darryl's career and because I seemed to be so eclipsed by my extroverted brother. Grandmother decided that I needed to develop a talent, so, as she often told me, I wouldn't be left at the post. Since she took care of me, she decided to become my protector, defender...and "manager." For most children the idea of being showered with one's grandmother's undivided attention sounds like a dream come true. Unfortunately, my grandmother was not the stay-at-home-and-bake-cookies type of granny. No, this woman was opinionated, strong-willed, and unbending. It was more like being under the thumb of a tyrannical Mother Superior.

One day Grandmother pulled me aside for one of her "talks." Actually, she talked and I obediently nodded in agreement. This day she informed me that I needed to have an accomplishment, some great talent, or I would never amount to anything and worst of all Darryl would get all the attention. The more she talked about her plans for me, the more excited she became. As I watched her I thought it was so silly. I was nine years old and I didn't need to accomplish anything except to survive the nuns at school and to stay out of the way of my older brother. I was happy being a kid and doing kid stuff. I was thrilled that Darryl got all the attention and I didn't want to compete with him or anyone else. Even as a kid I didn't think that it was necessary to have some great accomplishment. None of it made any sense to me, but I knew that it would be dangerous business to voice any of these feelings to Grandmother. She felt I needed a talent and announced, with great excitement, that she had decided that I was born to play the trumpet.

Now the fact that I had never expressed any interest in music or the trumpet and, in fact, had never even held a trumpet, made little difference to my strong-willed grandmother. Once she had made up her mind, I was going to play the trumpet whether I wanted to or not. Grandmother and Sister Stanislaus had a lot in common.

And so it started. Grandmother's little darling would be groomed to be a famous trumpet player. There would be no more time for frivolous things like playing baseball or just hanging out with friends; after all, I had a lot of work ahead of me if I hoped to catch up with my brother's many achievements.

So, after fighting with the maniacal nuns all day for my survival, twice a week after school my grandmother would drive me to my trumpet lesson. Louis Maggio, who was a wonderful musician, was my teacher. It must have been painful and nerve-wracking trying to teach disinterested children to play musical instruments. Although I cared nothing for the trumpet, I took to it easily and became quite good, and within a year I was playing in the Los Angeles Junior Symphony Orchestra. Of all his students, Mr. Maggio felt that I held the most promise, which was one of the reasons he became so upset with me when I didn't practice. At one lesson he became so irate he jumped up and yelled, "If you don't practice I'm not going to waste my time teaching you!" Since I didn't want to practice and I didn't want to waste Mr. Maggio's time, I took him literally. The idea of quitting the trumpet and the Junior Symphony was fine with me. Not only did I dislike the trumpet, but it was painful for me to play, because at that time I was wearing braces and in order to play and not cut my lips I had to put adhesive tape over my braces.

It never occurred to Mr. Maggio or my grandmother that I might find this uncomfortable; all they were concerned about was making sure I became the next Harry James. The idea of being Harry James intrigued me too, but not because of his trumpet playing. It had more to do with being married to a beautiful, sexy blonde like Betty Grable, but I was smart enough not to share that information with my grandmother. Anyway, after Mr. Maggio chastised me and threatened not to give me any more lessons, I stood up, put my trumpet in the case, and started to leave. He went crazy, demanding to know what I was doing. I explained that I was just doing as I was told; I didn't want to practice and didn't want to waste his time. "Stupid, impertinent boy, sit down and play!" he shouted. I was totally confused. In my desire to be free of the trumpet forever I had taken Mr. Maggio at his word, never dreaming for a moment it was an idle threat to scare me into practicing. He would have to do a lot more than that to scare me. After all, I was dealing with a lot tougher characters than him every day at school...and some of them carried weapons like baseball bats and rulers.

Even though I was busy with school, trumpet lessons, and the Junior Symphony, my mother still tried to make sure that I kept my meager movie career going. Between my grandmother and her I hardly had five minutes to call my own. By the way, it was about this time that I started collecting unemployment insurance. I know it sounds strange for a kid going to elementary school to be given money for being out of work, but apparently there had been some court case in California questioning the validity of such a claim and the court ruled that a child, regardless of age, who had a history of working, could be just as unemployed as an adult. So, once a week, after school, my mother or grandmother would take me down to the unemployment office where I would stand in line sandwiched between a sea of out-of-work adults. When it was my turn I'd approach the counter, which was so high above my head I had to step back in order to see the person behind the window. It never failed that every time I stood before this employee of the State of California, he or she would glare at me, shout a few questions about my claim, then begrudgingly hand me a check. I don't know if they shouted at me because they assumed I was a child so I wouldn't understand the question unless it was so loud they could be heard outside the building, or that they wanted to intimidate me into not coming back. Either way, their plan didn't work and I faithfully returned week after week. I'd walk out of the building and immediately hand over my check to my mother or grandmother, then I'd return home to practice the trumpet. What a life!

It wasn't long before I landed a small role playing one of the kids in the town in a John Wayne western, *Tall in the Saddle*. On one particular day I had several scenes that required costume changes. When you were an extra you either changed in a bathroom or corner of the stage or a trailer that was usually parked halfway across the lot. It was anything but star treatment. Since both of my scenes were back to back, a quick change was required, so my mother grabbed me up and started heading toward a large dressing room. She looked around, then opened the door and pushed me inside. I told her the dressing room didn't belong to us and she told me to hurry up and change and we would be out of there before anyone knew. I didn't feel good about it, but I started to change my clothes as quickly as I could. I took off my trousers and my mother, kneeling in front of me, was trying to stuff my foot into my next costume. Suddenly the door flew open. My mother and I looked up and gasped. This huge figure filled the doorway...it was John Wayne. He looked totally shocked to see a woman and a mortified little boy standing in his white jockey shorts, changing clothes in what was supposed to be his very private dressing room. My mother stammered something about being finished in a moment, and John Wayne said, "Okay, let me know when you're through." Then he shook his head like, "What the hell is going on," and walked out.

I finished changing as quickly as I could and my mother and I hurried out of the dressing room. John Wayne was talking to someone and he had his back to us. My mother turned to me and said, "Honey, go tell Mr. Wayne he can go in his dressing room now." I looked at her in total disbelief. My mother actually expected me to go talk to John Wayne when it was her harebrained idea to use his dressing room. When I started to object I got one of her looks as she pushed me toward, what seemed to me to be the biggest and tallest man in the world. As I approached John Wayne I started to speak, but he didn't hear me, which was not surprising, since he towered over me by about four feet. I pulled at his pant leg and he turned around. I was so embarrassed as I looked up at the star. Suddenly, I thought, why should I take the rap for this, so I pulled myself together and said, "Mr. Wayne, my mother sent me to tell you that you can use your dressing room now.... It was her idea, Mr. Wayne. I told her I didn't want to go in there, but she made me do it." He looked down at me and chuckled, "Forget it, kid...it won't be the last time a woman will make you do something you don't wanna do." At the time I didn't really understand what he meant. It wasn't until years later that the full impact of his wise words hit home. John Wayne was very nice about the entire incident. My mother had broken a cardinal rule and she knew it. It wouldn't have been the first time a headstrong stage mother had overstepped her bounds and gotten her child fired. My mother was smart enough not to push her luck again.

A few months later, I worked with Fred MacMurray in *Captain Eddie*, the story of World War I ace, Eddie Rickenbacker.

My brother Darryl played Eddie as a kid and I played Louis, one of Eddie's younger brothers. Someone on the lot spotted me during the picture and signed me up to do an MGM musical short film about children from around the world singing their native Christmas carols; it was similar to Disneyland's "Small World" exhibit. We would be performing with the former band singer turned movie star, Frank Sinatra.

All the kids were dressed in their native costumes standing in fake snow. In typical California fashion, the temperature was in the nineties as we all tried to make believe we were shivering in the holiday cold. Frank felt sorry for the hot, sweaty kids dressed in their heavy winter costumes, so on a break, he took the kids outside and bought them Popsicles and ice cream cones from a vendor parked across from the soundstage. Then he sat down and told us stories about his life growing up in Hoboken. We all sat, transfixed, eating our ice cream and listening to Sinatra's boyhood tales. We were too young to care about his singing and bobbysox sex appeal. To us Frank Sinatra was just one of the guys.

Since the movie with Sinatra was filmed at MGM I was attending "movie school" with some of their top child actors. As I look back, it was a cross between "Stepford Village" and "Alice in Wonderland" where special children went to a special schoolhouse and were constantly crossing the line between reality and make-believe. Dressed in exotic costumes, stars like Elizabeth Taylor, Jane Powell, and Roddy McDowall would drop in between scenes to study a little math or history. As a child actor one of the first things you become aware of is who is a big star and who is just another kid actor. Everyone knew their place and I certainly knew I was not in the same galaxy as an Elizabeth Taylor or Roddy McDowall, so I stayed to myself or hung out with the other "unknown" child actors. For one big room full of children it was amazingly quiet. Everyone was very well behaved and mature beyond their years. It was more like a classroom of miniature adults than average everyday kids. Since I wasn't under contract to the studio, the moment I completed a movie I was out of "Wonderland" and back in a "regular" school with "regular" kids where I felt more comfortable.

While I was at MGM I was chosen to test for a movie at Twentieth Century-Fox for a new film that was to be directed by the famous Russian actor and director, Gregory Ratoff. I'll never forget the test scene. I was supposed to be sitting at the breakfast table excitedly telling my parents a story. Simple enough, right? Wrong! It was a disaster. I still wasn't comfortable acting and I was still a very shy kid. Gregory Ratoff was a fat, loud, bombastic Russian who dramatically talked with his hands and spit in your face as he yelled directions at you. Ours was a deadly combination. I was trying my best to be cheerful and excited during the scene, but apparently I wasn't giving enough to my Russian director. In the middle of my speech Ratoff started tapping his cane. The louder he tapped, the faster I tried to talk. Suddenly he yelled out, "What's the matter with that kid . . . . When I tap my cane that means, cut." After the third take he threw down his cane and stormed over to me and screamed in my face, "Look, kid, if you want this part, give me some 'enthusiasm'." As he loudly drew out the word "enthusiasm" into twenty-five syllables, his spit flew across the room and I shrunk down in the chair so low I nearly disappeared under the table. This was not the way to get a shy child to perform.

I may not have understood the "Morse Code" Ratoff was tapping out with his cane, but I had figured out that I didn't like this coarse Russian dictator . . . I mean, director. The next take was a disaster. When I finished, Ratoff threw his hands in the air as if to say, "Off with his head," and I was quietly spirited off the stage. My mother was upset I had blown the audition because apparently I was the perfect age, had the right look, and was the first choice for the part. But I was relieved that I wouldn't have to spend any more time around Mr. Ratoff, whom I affectionately called "Attila the Hun."

It had been two years since we had moved from the Valley into the depressing, dark house in Hollywood. When the packing boxes suddenly reappeared, this was the first time I was happy to move. This journey was just a few miles away, to an old Spanish stucco house on Franklin Avenue.

It was shortly after moving that I got the bright idea to become a Boy Scout. One of my new friends was a scout and he got to wear a neat uniform and carry around a canteen and camping stuff. I wasn't going to be satisfied until I was uniformed and outfitted with my own official Boy Scout paraphernalia. My parents figured it would be a good way to meet new friends, so within a week I was going to Boy Scout meetings after school. I was fascinated as the scoutmaster taught us how to build a fire and how to tie special knots. We learned about snakes and poison ivy and how to pitch a tent, and when the scoutmaster found out that I could play the trumpet I was given the honor of blowing the bugle. After several weeks, it was announced that the troop was going on an overnight camping trip in the Hollywood Hills. I was thrilled because I had never camped out overnight.

Our family was not the "sleep outside" type, although we might have been better off, because the few Hickman family vacations we took were disasters. My father would decide that a nice drive to Bakersfield and a night in a motel would be great family fun. For those of you who don't know Bakersfield, California, let me just say that it's very hot, very dusty, and there is nothing to see or do when you get there. But that didn't stop my dad. My brother, sister, and I would pile into the back of the car and in hundred-degree heat, with the windows down and the hot, dusty air blowing on us, my father would drive at breakneck speed toward Bakersfield. I could never figure out why we rushed to get there, because when you got there nothing was going on. After fighting with my brother and sister and sweating for several hours, we'd check into a dreary motel to spend the night. The three kids shared one bed and my parents the other. There was no air conditioning, so I'd lay sandwiched between my hot, sweaty siblings like a pig in a blanket, waiting for the morning, so we could pile into the hot car again and drive like maniacs back to Los Angeles. You can see why the idea of an overnight Boy Scout campout might sound pretty good to me.

The camping trip was on my eleventh birthday, and I was sure my parents had passed on the word about my big day. After arriving at the meeting place, we lined up and the Scoutmaster had me blow the bugle as my fellow Scouts marched up into the Hollywood Hills. The hills, which are above the Hollywood Bowl, are not as tame as they sound. The area had few homes in those days and it was mostly populated by coyotes, bobcats, raccoons, and snakes, some that rattled. When we finally reached our campsite, the scoutmaster assigned each of us a partner and told us to pitch our tents. My partner was an obnoxious kid named Henry, whose family were camping experts. This kid knew everything about the outdoors. He looked at me like I was some sissy city slicker when I told him that I had never slept outside before.

He pitched our tent with the deftness of Daniel Boone, then I peeked inside and the realization that I would be sleeping on the ground finally hit me. When I started to object, the scoutmaster told me to gather up leaves to make a mattress and to start acting like a real scout. I gathered up all the leaves that were left after my partner, Henry, had stripped the area, making his mattress look like a featherbed. The temperature had dropped and the cold night mist had set in. I was suddenly starved, and asked when they were going to serve dinner. Everybody laughed, thinking I was kidding. I figured this would be like a movie location and the food truck would come to bring us our hot meal and my "surprise birthday cake," so naturally I didn't pack any food. Super scout Henry came to my rescue. He shared an extra potato he had brought along and, with great fanfare, showed me how to cook it by burying it in the ground. Later, as Henry devoured the raw potato like it was his last meal, I tried to eat mine, but ended up throwing it into the woods and eating cold beans from a can. The scoutmaster told us it was time for bed and I realized that any hope of a birthday celebration was rapidly disintegrating. Hungry, cold, and depressed, I got into our tent and settled down onto my leaf mattress. Before I could get settled, Henry was out like a light and, to make matters worse, this kid snored like a moose. All night long I lay awake, shivering in the cold and swatting mosquitoes and bugs.

As soon as dawn broke, this scout was packed and ready to go home. I woke up the scoutmaster to say good-bye and to tell him that I had had it and I was going back home to civilization. He was outraged and told me that under no circumstances would I be allowed to leave. I may have been timid, but when I made up my mind, that was it. He told me that I would be punished. I figured what's the worse they could do to a wayward Boy Scout... execution by a firing squad? No, I had made up my mind and I was leaving. As I headed out of camp he yelled, "Hickman, your scouting days are over!" I yelled back, "They were over last night when I ate raw potatoes and nearly froze to death sleeping on the ground!" Then I headed off on my five-mile hike back to civilization. When my parents came home that afternoon they found me in the bathtub eating a sandwich. I informed them that my scouting days were over and it had been the worst birthday I had ever had.

A few months later, I had a first experience with losing a member of the family. While returning home from the movies, my grandmother was hit by a car as she crossed the street in front of our house. My father told us to stay inside while he and the police took care of the situation.

The tragedy was a shock to the whole family and it took my poor mother years to come to terms with the loss of her mother, Mary Ellen, a woman whose presence was larger than life. Our house seemed empty without her. My grandmother had been a dominant influence in my life, and my trumpet playing had been her dream, not mine. The day she died I put my trumpet in the case and never played again.

Her death was very difficult for me. In some ways I was relieved that she was no longer going to be there to mold me into a child prodigy, and at the same time I felt guilty that I had such feelings about someone who had been as much mother as grandmother to me. For all the pressure she had placed on me, and despite her domineering personality, which I never really cared for, she had always been there for me and now I missed her terribly.

I was still trying to cope with the loss when, in 1946, I was cast as Claudette Colbert's son in the movie *The Secret Heart*. She was very kind to me and went out of her way to make me feel special. She'd invite me to have lunch in her dressing room and would give me candy and gifts. Suddenly, this acting business was looking better to me!

After *The Secret Heart* at MGM I started working in a series of B movies at Columbia Pictures about a dog named Rusty. The "Rusty" series, about a boy and his German shepherd, was really the forerunner of the early TV show, *Rin Tin Tin*.

The next movie I worked on was a Western called *Heaven Only Knows*, later retitled *Montana Mike*. It was about an archangel named Michael who is sent to earth to clean up a crooked town and save the soul of a gambler. Bob Cummings starred as the archangel and Brian Donlevy played the gambler. The film opens in heaven with a little angel, played by me, delivering the "Great Book of Life" to Bob Cummings and a group of other angels. The prop book was nearly as big as I was. As the adult angels look through the pages, they realize the name of the wayward gambler has been left out of the book. I pipe up and say, "Only one name...maybe He [God] won't notice." Upon hearing this blasphemy, the adult angels get upset with me. I was supposed to look like I had just put my foot in my mouth. We rehearsed the scene and Bob pulled me aside and gently made some suggestions on how to do a funny reaction. When we shot the scene, I reacted exactly as Cummings had instructed me, and when the director called "Cut!" he came over to me and said, "Great job, and I loved the 'take.'" I looked over at Bob and smiled and he gave me a wink. I didn't know what a "take" was, but I later found out that it was a comedy reaction...a "look."

That wouldn't be the last time Bob Cummings would help me out. Just a few years later I would be working with him on his TV series and he would become my mentor. It was because of Bob and my success on *The Bob Cummings Show* that I would later become Dobie Gillis.

· TWO ·

BOY ABOUT TOWN

THE YEAR 1948 WAS FILLED with challenges and changes. I landed my first big role in a film, I started high school, which would prove more dangerous than difficult, and I performed on stage for the first time.

For a kid whose acting experience consisted of little more than extra work on a few films, I was terrified of performing on stage. As usual, I was rung into the play because my brother, Darryl, had the lead role. The play was called *This Young World*, by Judith Candell, and this production was to be the world premiere. My brother played a bully who terrorized a group of children in a rural schoolhouse, and I was cast as one of the kids he terrorized. This wouldn't be too much of a stretch for either one of us since I had been on the receiving end of my older brother's mischief for years.

I might have enjoyed my first "treading of the boards"—an old theater expression I've never really understood—if I could have performed in some obscure little theater where any public humiliation would have been limited to fifteen or twenty people. Instead, I was taking my first plunge at the prestigious Pasadena Playhouse. The Playhouse brought in serious theatergoers and critics and had the reputation of mounting groundbreaking productions and introducing exciting new talent.

This Young World was directed by a tough-talking woman named Marsella Cisney. If I had ever wondered what it might be like to go to boot camp, once rehearsals started I wondered no more. Ms. Cisney had the personality of a drill sergeant, and she intended to whip her troupe into shape so that they would give the performance of their lives... or die trying.

During one of the early rehearsals I started clowning around with one of the other boys... a mistake neither of us made again. Ms. Cisney stopped the scene we were rehearsing and told me and my partner-in-crime to come "downstage." Thank goodness this kid knew upstage from downstage because I had no idea, so I followed him down to the footlights. If I had known what I was in for, I would have made a hasty exit out the stage door. Ms. Cisney proceeded to lambaste us. She said that we were a disgrace to the theater, were disrespectful to the other actors who took their craft seriously... and if the show failed it would be on our shoulders. After about fifteen minutes of being thoroughly mortified by this dressing down, we mumbled our apologies and returned to rehearsing the play. But apparently Ms. Cisney wasn't through with me, because for the rest of the rehearsal she stopped me and corrected every line I said and every move I made. I must have been a real source of frustration and annoyance to this lady of the theater because, at one point, she yelled, "Dwayne...I'm sick of watching you amble around the stage.... You act like Gary Cooper." As soon as I heard this any feelings of intimidation I had experienced since the start of rehearsals evaporated. Ms. Cisney obviously didn't think much of Gary Cooper's acting prowess, but for a kid who never really considered himself an actor I was thrilled by the comparison. After all, I didn't know how many people had ever heard of Marsella Cisney, but I did know that the whole world knew Gary Cooper, and, like him or not, he was, undeniably, a big movie star.

For the rest of the rehearsals and the run of the play I was like a mute...never saying a word unless it was my dialogue. Although I was no longer intimidated by Ms. Cisney, I tried my best to avoid any more confrontations with her.

Several days later my brother Darryl's agent, Vernon Jacobson, came by the theater to take him to an audition for a movie. Ms. Cisney was furious because he was leaving in the middle of rehearsal. As Darryl walked out, she grabbed his arm and growled, "How dare you leave in the middle of my rehearsal. Who made this appointment?" Darryl said that his agent had; then Ms. Cisney snapped, "You tell your agent he's an S.O.B." My brother stammered a "Yes, ma'am," and hurried up the aisle. The rest of us stood wide-eyed. It wasn't often we heard that kind of talk from a woman, but this wasn't any woman, this was "Sergeant Cisney." At the time I never would have admitted that I didn't have a clue what an "S.O.B." was!

The opening night finally arrived, and I was a nervous wreck along with everyone else. I had one big scene in the play where I try to stand up to my brother as he terrorizes all the kids in the classroom. Darryl's character is shocked that someone would dare to confront him. To show everyone that he is in charge he grabs me and, in a rage, roughs me up. I don't know if it was the excitement of opening night or the heady feeling of being able to knock his little brother around under the guise of acting, but when my brother grabbed me, he nearly tore my shirt off. I was so taken aback that I whispered through my teeth, "You're tearing my shirt...quit it." At that moment I didn't care if I was standing on the stage of the Pasadena Playhouse or appearing on Broadway. All I knew was that my brother was tearing the buttons off my new shirt that my mother had bought me for the play. My unprofessional protests only seemed to fuel his fire because he just started yelling louder and shaking me around like I was a rag doll. Now I was getting mad. I didn't want to be in this stupid play in the first place. The director had been giving me a hard time, and now, in front of a theater full of people, I was supposed to take a beating from my brother. I could have stayed home and gotten the same grief; I didn't need to get it in public. I glared at him and whispered a little louder, "You're hurting me....Knock it off!" then I shoved him and sat down. The shove was not in the script so he and the cast—not to mention the director—were shocked.

After the show, as the cast gathered with the director for notes on the evening's performance, Darryl complained that I had ruined his concentration because I hadn't stayed in character. In fairness to my brother, he was much more caught up in the drama of the scene than I was. Any concentration I had went out the window because he was hurting me and tearing my clothes off. From my point of view Darryl's performance was pretty hammy, and the whole thing was getting a little out of hand.

The show ran for a week, and every night during our scene Darryl would grab me and I'd whisper, "You're tearing my shirt," and on it would go. He never gave in and neither did I. I will never forget sitting in my dressing room and reading the opening night reviews. My brother's reviews were glowing, but the play and I got a less than enthusiastic response. One of the critics seemed to go out of his way to inform the world that, unlike my brother, I was "disappointing in the role and had little impact." There I sat, a thirteen-year-old kid staring at his first stage review and feeling miserable. I thought about all the rehearsals and how I had been pushed into something I didn't really want to do, but I had tried my very best.

Then something strange happened. I say strange because all my life I had always tried to stay out of the line of fire and make as few waves as possible. But as I looked at what I felt was unfair criticism by this reviewer I suddenly got angry. "Who the hell is this guy anyway?" I remember the moment because it was the first time I realized that I had a real sense of self. I was determined that nobody was going to make me feel bad about myself and I didn't care what this critic or anyone else thought. After all, wasn't I the kid the director had compared to the famous Gary Cooper? He had certainly had his share of lousy reviews. That night my survival instinct kicked in, and from that time on it has never left me.

By the time the play was over I had gained more than stage experience, I had gained life experience. As it turned out, Ms.

Cisney was prophetic about Gary Cooper. Just a few years later I began dating his daughter, and the famous star had his own opinions about my acting ability. But for now the play was over and in two days I would celebrate my fourteenth birthday. My first experience on the stage was only the beginning; the next few years were going to be very interesting.

Shortly after my birthday our family made its final move. My parents, with the help of my brother, who had been working constantly, purchased a beautiful home in the Los Feliz section of Los Angeles. It was an enormous Spanish-style house with a separate three-car garage and chauffeur's quarters. The Los Feliz area represented "old money" and was the home of many silent-film stars, directors, judges, and bankers. Our new home, with its grand staircase and plush grounds, created the impression that the Hickmans had either made a lot of money or some wealthy uncle had died and left them a small fortune; neither scenario was true, of course. Somehow we scraped the money together, and my mother finally had her dream house. Thank God the yearly moves were over.

As we were settling in, I landed my first big role in a movie, playing the villainous kid who cut off Dean Stockwell's hair in *The Boy With Green Hair*. It's called a classic now, but at the time no one thought it would be remembered as anything but a strange antiwar movie. The memory of World War II was still very fresh, and fighting for your country was one's patriotic duty. Anyone who questioned waging war against the enemy was suspect. *The Boy With Green Hair* was making a social statement about war and its effect on children. The director, Joseph Losey, was highly criticized for making an antiwar film, and not long after it was made he was blacklisted. He moved to England and he continued his career there. At the time I was thrilled to have the part but I was so scared that I had so much to do that I really wasn't aware of all the flap about the movie. A lot of child actors who had far more experience had auditioned for the film, but I was given the role and my first opportunity to really show off my acting ability. I was very nervous because I wasn't sure how much ability I really had. Dean Stockwell was the star and a very hot young property. He was a handsome, sensitive child and a wonderful actor, so it wasn't a surprise that he was always in great demand. I had read the script several times before we started shooting and I still didn't really understand the story. It seemed pretty silly that anybody would have green hair, and when I saw Dean with his bright green wig standing around between scenes and hanging out like the rest of us, it seemed even more ridiculous. The kids in the movie made fun of Dean's character because his green hair made him different, and they ridiculed my character because I wore thick eyeglasses.

Instead of sympathizing with Dean's green hair problem, I decided to vent all my frustrations on him and cut off all his hair. My character was not very sympathetic, but it was fun to play once I got over my initial fears. My next big hurdle was learning how to walk wearing the eyeglasses. The lens were very thick and distorted everything. Half the time I was trying not to stumble when I had them on, and then I had to pretend to stumble when they were taken away from me.

There were a lot of boys in the movie with whom I had worked over the years. As we were having lunch one day outside the stage, one of the boys, Teddy Infuhr, and his mother asked me to join them. I moved over to their table and was eating my lunch when suddenly Mrs. Infuhr started yelling, "Yoo-hoo, Cary... Cary..." I looked up and realized, to my horror, that Mrs. Infuhr was yoo-hooing Cary Grant. Mr. Grant was minding his own business, walking across the RKO lot. Dressed in a navy blue suit, he looked every inch the movie star. He was either lost in thought or had just decided to ignore this strange woman yoo-hooing at him, but Mrs. Infuhr, with a tenacity that would make any stage mother proud, wasn't about to give up. As he was about to pass our table, she yelled, "What's the matter, Mr. Cary Grant... are you such a big shot movie star you don't remember your friends?" I was so mortified I wanted to dissolve right into my chair. I felt a hot wave of nervous perspiration break out all over my body as Cary Grant turned toward us and, with a frozen smile, said, "Oh, hello there... Have a nice day," and never pausing a moment, he continued on his way. I had quickly dropped my head down and ducked behind my sandwich for cover, but Mrs. Infuhr didn't miss a beat. She turned to me, beaming, and said, "I told you he remembered us...He was in Teddy's movie, *The Bishop's Wife*.

Now, that was, of course, a major exaggeration. But, in fairness to Mrs. Infuhr, most stage mothers saw their child as the star, no matter how small their part, and felt the Spencer Tracys, Cary Grants, Clark Gables, and the like were supporting players to their little darlings. The truth was, *The Bishop's Wife* was a wonderful Christmas movie about an angel named Dudley, played by Cary Grant, who comes to earth to help a bishop, David Niven, set his priorities straight while he is building a new church and losing touch with his wife, Loretta Young. Teddy had a couple of scenes with a dozen other boys, so it wasn't any surprise Cary Grant didn't recognize them. From that day on I stayed away from Teddy and his mother and ate lunch by myself.

While I was filming *The Boy With Green Hair*, my mother and I stopped for lunch at a little diner in Hollywood called the Nite Lite. They had the best hamburgers in town and I always thought it was a great treat to go there. Mom and I were sitting in a booth eating our lunch when a nice-looking man with slicked-back hair, sporting a pencil mustache and wearing matching khaki-colored shirt and pants walked in. As my mother looked over, he flashed her a smile and sat down at the counter. My mother blushed scarlet and whispered to me excitedly, "Do you know who that man is?" I mumbled something about him looking like a mechanic and she rolled her eyes. "Dwayne, that man is Howard Hughes!" Well, even I had heard of the famous Howard Hughes. When I looked up, she said, "Don't stare at him." What good was being in a diner with Howard Hughes if I couldn't even look at him? I took a bite of my hamburger and decided to try to sneak another look. I raised my head and nearly choked. Howard Hughes was walking over to our table. He turned to my mother and said, "Excuse me, but I believe this young man here is in one of my movies." Mother said something like, "Oh yes...*The Boy With Green Hair*. Then Hughes said to me, "I saw some film on you . . . You're doing a great job." I thanked him, then he tipped his hat, walked out of the diner, and drove off in a dirty, ten-year-old Chevrolet. He was famous for borrowing someone's old car and driving it around so that he wouldn't be recognized, but he rarely fooled anyone. Who could miss that tall, famous man with movie star looks and charm. My mother and I were thrilled that he had noticed my performance, especially since he owned RKO where the movie was being filmed. If that wasn't enough to give my mother and me something to talk about for the next month, the waitress informed us that Mr. Hughes had paid for our lunch. My mother's feet never touched the ground as we left the Nite Lite. For years, my mother told everyone that she and Howard Hughes had had lunch one day.

It wouldn't be the last time my path would cross with the eccentric billionaire. Twenty years later I would be working for him in Las Vegas, but at this point, that was nearly a lifetime away. Now I had more important things to think about, like passing my entrance exam into high school.

Darryl was already attending Cathedral High, a Christian Brothers school in downtown Los Angeles. The family's first choice was Loyola High, but the Jesuit priests who ran the school wouldn't allow Darryl to be absent from his classes to perform in movies, so my father went to the Christian Brothers at Cathedral to plead Darryl's case. They took a more lenient attitude, so he was enrolled there. When it came time for me to enter high school, I took Cathedral's entrance exam and scored so high they gave me a four-year scholarship. Because the school served the downtown area, it pulled in a lot of rough kids from the inner city. The students were not like today's kids who carry automatic weapons to school; they were a postwar version of tough street kids who wore pegged jeans, white T-shirts, and slicked-back hair. They were the trendsetters for young Marlon Brando and James Dean in the 1950s.

I never felt comfortable at Cathedral and never felt like I fit in because I was a quiet, studious kid. I had a few friends and played on the tennis team, but in a school made up of kids from the inner city, I had more in common with the Christian

Brothers than my fellow students. The Christian Brothers took one look at me and knew that I didn't have a chance with these tough street-smart guys and they saved my life, literally. They gave me a job working in the school store where they would lock me behind a caged door and I would sell candy and supplies. This was the only place at school I felt safe. I had good reason to be nervous about my classmates, especially after one very unpleasant experience involving my first car. I was sixteen, and like every kid who had just learned to drive, I couldn't wait to get a car. I dreamed about cars, and to this day remember the ones Clark Gable, Gary Cooper, and Errol Flynn drove. You name the star; I knew their car. In case you're interested, Gable was a real car lover, and over the years I saw him driving several beauties. One was a 1950 Jaguar convertible; another was a beautiful Mercedes 300S. Gary Cooper also drove a Mercedes 300S, a Jaguar, and a Bentley Continental. One time I saw the dashing and handsome Errol Flynn driving down Hollywood Boulevard in a green 1941 Cadillac Fleetwood. Even as a kid, I knew I wanted to grow up and drive exotic cars like all the movie stars.

My first car wasn't quite as elaborate as Gable's or Cooper's or Flynn's, but it was a honey in my eyes. I had saved my money from all my movie jobs and bought a beat-up 1940 Ford. I worked on it and had it painted a metallic brown, and every weekend I would wash and wax my car, then take a drive around town. One Saturday I was driving down Hollywood Boulevard, and as I stopped for a light a motorcycle pulled up next to me. I had been sailing along the boulevard at a pretty good clip and I was sure it was a policeman ready to give me a ticket. I stared straight ahead, figuring if I didn't look over he wouldn't notice me. Suddenly I heard, "Hey kid." My heart sank, this was it. As I turned to face my fate, the guy on the motorcycle said, "Nice car, great color." I stammered a thank-you as the light changed and the motorcycle sped off, leaving me sitting at the stoplight, dazed. The motorcycle driver was no policeman, it was Robert Taylor! I couldn't believe it, Robert Taylor actually complimented me on my car. For the rest of the day I rode around feeling like "one of the guys," and secretly hoping to run into another star so I could show off my metallic brown beauty. You can imagine how upset I was when I came out of class one day to find that some of my fellow classmates had taken a switchblade and carved their initials on my beautiful car. As I look back now, I realize they were probably jealous, but that episode didn't endear them to me. I figured if they would do that to my car they might also do it to me, so I gladly continued my job behind the cage in the school store.

It was hard enough being pulled in and out of class when I was in grammar school, but once I reached high school it became even more difficult. Since none of my classmates at Cathedral were involved in show business, every time I went off to do a movie it only made my life more unpleasant when I returned. I felt like I was being bounced between two different worlds. One day I'm working at the studio with movie stars and the next day I'm sitting in a classroom next to a kid who looked like he'd kill me for my lunch money.

One of my acting jobs during this time was playing Jeanette MacDonald's son in a Lassie movie at MGM called *The Sun Comes Up*, which was the famed singer's last film before she retired. Roddy McDowall had done the first Lassie picture *Lassie Come Home*, and it had been such a big success that a string of movies followed featuring the talented Collie. Hollywood soon found out that a movie about a boy and his dog was a sure family favorite. Years later, *Lassie* became *Benji*, who then became *Beethoven*. Television picked up on the same idea with *Rin Tin Tin* and, of course, the *Lassie* series, which ran for many years.

In *The Sun Comes Up* my mother, Jeanette MacDonald, was a noted opera singer making a comeback after her husband's death. I was her teenage son who had his faithful companion, Lassie, and because I had several scenes where we played together, it was important that I seem comfortable with the dog. So before the filming began, I went out to the studio and worked with the famous dog trainer, Rudd Weatherwax, and Lassie. The first thing I noticed about Mr. Weatherwax was that his pockets were laden down with dog treats. I soon learned that each time Lassie performed a trick Mr. Weatherwax would dig into his pocket and give her a reward, and by the end of the first day I too was laden down with treats. When I returned home that evening and emptied my pockets I found two dog biscuits left over from our day's work. I felt kind of sad because I didn't have a dog of my own to share the treats with. It wasn't that our family didn't love dogs, we did, and we had many of them over the years. Our problem was they all ran away. I could never understand it. Just as our new pet was housebroken and we were used to one another, it would wander off, never to be seen again. Since it happened with every dog we owned, it started to become embarrassing when friends and neighbors would inquire about our pets and we would answer sheepishly, "Oh...well...he's not here any-more." My parents became so self-conscious about it, a mor-atorium was called on all pets in the Hickman household. I never took it personally. I figured our runaway dogs just reflected our family's gypsy lifestyle, but at least for the next few weeks I could enjoy Lassie.

Everyone knows Lassie as the devoted Collie who was endowed with super strength, super smarts and super abil-ities, and on top of all these qualities, she would love and protect her master at any cost. Hard to believe that one dog, even Lassie, could have so many admirable traits. Maybe the reason it was hard to believe was because...well, it wasn't true. Lassie, the wonder dog, didn't exist; Lassie, the five wonder dogs, they existed. I was amazed when Rudd Weather-wax trotted out five identical Collies that all answered to Lassie. He explained that each dog had a special talent: one Lassie could jump high and fetch, one could swim in a rushing river, another could paw at the door and cry with such a catch in its throat that it would bring a tear to your eye, and another could smile and turn its head and bark in the signature Lassie response. The biggest surprise was that Lassie was played by both male and female dogs, but since Lassie was never seen doing what dogs naturally do, no one would ever be the wiser. I worked with all the Lassies and I hate to say this, but the Lassies I met just weren't the warm and friendly dogs they pretended to be. I realize Lassie is like an American hero or heroine, as the case may be, but I have to be honest and the truth is...Lassie had a lousy personality...all five of them.

The Sun Comes Up was filmed at MGM, a studio that always took great pride in doing everything first class. When I was cast in the role I was asked to bring in my navy blue suit. I told them I didn't have a navy blue suit, in fact, I didn't know any kid my age who owned a navy blue suit. I was sent down to wardrobe where my measurements were taken for my first custom-made suit. I was supposed to be the son of a very affluent opera singer, so no expense was being spared on my wardrobe. Unfortunately, at the end of the movie my luxurious apparel and I were parted, as all my clothes joined the vast stock of costumes in the MGM wardrobe department. It seemed to me to be such a waste. Who would come along and fit into my custom-made suit and shirts? They didn't care about my logic; they only cared about keeping the wardrobe.

Aside from giving up my beautiful clothes, the entire experience of working on *The Sun Comes Up* was terrific. Jeanette MacDonald was still very much a star, and the tone of the set reflected her personality—warm, friendly, first-class, and very professional. The first day that I reported to work I was sent over to my dressing room. I approached this small colonial-style "house" on wheels and discovered that this star dressing room was mine. Inside, the walls were wood paneled, and it was nicely furnished. I felt like a real movie star, especially when I saw the nameplate on the door, "Mr. Hickman." Mister Hickman! No one had ever called me that. This acting business wasn't such a bad life after all. The director of the picture was Richard Thorpe, a classy gentleman, who always dressed in a suit, tie, and hat. He was soft-spoken and a wonderful director, especially with child actors. He was the image that Louis B. Mayer wanted his studio and his employees to project—refined, professional, and dignified. You rarely heard any swearing on the sets; L. B. Mayer had a big thing about that. Funny, because behind closed doors he was known to shriek obscenities and occasionally even beat people up, but on the outside everything remained genteel.

In *The Sun Comes Up* my character dies in the first half hour of the picture. After my mother finished her first comeback concert, we are waiting for the car to take us to the after-theater party. Lassie jumps out of the car, into the traffic, and as I run after her, I am hit by a truck and killed. As we prepared for the big scene, Richard Thorpe walked around studying the set. He scratched his head with good humor, and said to me and the camera crew, "Well, I think I shot something like this before. . . . Let's see if I can remember what to do." He brought me in and had me stand in front of a large screen. The process they were using was called rear screen projection and, in this case, the truck would appear on the screen behind me, then I would stand in front of the screen, making it look like I was standing in front of the truck. As the truck appeared to get closer and closer, I was to turn around at the last moment, give a terrified look, then the floor would collapse under me, making it appear as if I fell under the speeding truck. Actually, I made a soft landing onto a bed of mattresses. After each rehearsal Mr. Thorpe would check to see if I was hurt and if I felt comfortable with the direction. We shot the scene in just a few takes, but it was fun and exciting and I could have done it all day. Richard Thorpe went on to direct more famous pictures, everything from *Ivanhoe*, with Robert Taylor, Elizabeth Taylor, and Joan Fontaine, to *Jailhouse Rock*, with Elvis Presley. Years later, his son, Jerry Thorpe, produced the television series *Kung Fu*.

During the filming of the movie I was sent down to the studio barber shop on several occasions to get my hair trimmed. Many times you would shoot some of your scenes, then not work again for a week or two. To make sure that you looked the same as the last day that you worked, the makeup man would take your picture. When you returned to work, one of the first things that would happen was you'd be sent to the studio barber shop to get a trim so your hair would match the way it looked several weeks earlier.

On one of my visits I walked into the barber shop as Clark Gable was getting a trim. The rest of the chairs were filled with studio executives, "nobodys" as far as I was concerned. I picked up a magazine and pretended to read, because all I really wanted to do was watch Clark Gable get his hair cut. He stood up, checking himself in the mirror, then turned to the barber and said, "Looks good, thanks a lot," then he walked out. I immediately jumped up and sat in Gable's chair. It was still warm from where he sat and I tingled all over as the barber gave me my trim. When he finished, I stood up, checked myself in the mirror, turned to the barber and said, just like Clark, "Looks good, thanks a lot," then I walked out. I felt like I had a lot in common with Clark Gable, the world's biggest movie star. We were both working on the same lot, both acting in a movie and, of course, we both shared the same barber!

As the movie progressed, I had several more uneventful haircuts, then, on my final trip for a trim, I witnessed an episode that soon became a famous story around Hollywood. I was sitting, minding my own business, waiting for a chair to open up and hoping to see my buddy Clark again, when a guy came in and took a seat next to me. All the chairs were filled with men getting haircuts, some getting shaves, some sitting back with a hot towel over their face. A baseball game was on the radio, and since it was turned up fairly loud, no one really had any choice but to listen to it. Apparently the guy sitting next to me wasn't a big baseball fan because, after a moment or two, he got up and loudly announced that he was sick and tired of listening to the ballgame, then he walked over and changed the station to music. A voice came from under a steaming towel and said, "I was listening to that game, turn it back on." I noticed that no one else said a word; they just stood there frozen, giving one another worried looks. The guy wouldn't be swayed. He said to the voice under the towel, "I'm sick of listening to these damn ballgames. Listen to them on your own time." Suddenly, the man under the towel sat straight up and angrily jerked the towel off his face. I couldn't believe my eyes and I thought the loud mouth was going to have a heart attack, as the man said to him, "I was listening to that ballgame, and this is 'my time' because this is *my* studio. Turn the ballgame back on....Now!" Then he laid back down, and the barber put a new hot towel over Louis B. Mayer's face.

The guy quickly turned the ballgame back on, then profusely apologized to one of the most powerful men in Hollywood, and slunk out of the barber shop. I had just witnessed a guy single-handedly destroy his career because he had a big mouth. It was a lesson I never forgot. As a chair opened up I sat down and got my trim. No one said a word until Mr. Mayer left, then the place exploded with that nervous energy that comes after you've witnessed someone's most embarrassing moment. All I wanted to do was get out of there and go back to the soundstage. The story circulated around town for years about the guy who got into it with L. B. Mayer about a baseball game. The guy had his fifteen minutes of fame, but it cost him his job.

My next movie, *The Happy Years*, was set in an 1890s boys' prep school and brought me together again with Dean Stockwell. It was directed by William Wellman, who was known as "Wild Bill." Wellman, one of Hollywood's biggest directors, rightly earned his reputation as a tough, hard-driving man's man who was larger than life. *The Happy Years* wasn't his most famous picture by far. He had directed such classics as the original *A Star Is Born*, *Beau Geste*, with Gary Cooper; *The Ox-Bow Incident*, with Henry Fonda; *Battleground*, with Van Johnson; and later *The High and the Mighty*, with John Wayne. "Wild Bill" came off as a very gruff guy, but I had an opportunity to get to know him a little better when, a few years later, I dated one of his daughters, Kitty. Despite his king-size personality, he was a very charming man who entertained us by the hour with his "Hollywood war stories." He loved to describe, in graphic detail, his many run-ins with the studio hierarchy and his never-ending battles with the establishment. No matter how abrasive and tough he tried to be, he always had a twinkle in his eye and a soft spot in his heart.

When I think about my work as a child actor and the opportunity that I had to be around movie stars like Clark Gable, Errol Flynn, Cary Grant, and Gary Cooper, I realize how fortunate I was. Although I never cared about acting as a child I always got a thrill out of seeing my favorite stars. As I fell in and out of love with Katharine Hepburn, Lana Turner,

Judy Garland, Hedy Lamarr, and a host of other beauties I'd pass on the lot or sit next to in the commissary, I didn't realize that these were the "golden years" of the motion picture business and that I was, in a small way, a part of the most glamorous time in the history of Hollywood. Because I had been going to the studio since I was about five, I took for granted that the town would always be the same. I didn't realize that I was experiencing the end of an era and the beginning of another.

During my junior year in high school I did my first acting on television in a series called *Public Defender*, in which I had a terrific role, playing a troubled kid who is a pyromaniac. When I would go out on auditions I would always see the same group of child actors. We were not necessarily the same type but were all about the same age. One day I ran into Danny Mummert and his mother at a casting session. When Mrs. Mummert discovered that I had a car and was driving myself to auditions, she decided that "Little Danny" and I should go together. The reason I called him "Little Danny Mummert" was because he looked exactly like Tiny Tim in *A Christmas Carol*, a thin, sickly, pasty-white kid who walked with a cane. Every time "Little Danny" had an audition, Mrs. Mummert would call my mother and ask if I was going and if I could please give her "Little Danny" a ride. Despite my objections, I would reluctantly pick up "Little Danny" for our audition. After helping him out of the car and into the casting office, I would go in for my audition and be finished in about two minutes. Then I would help "Little Danny" into the casting director's office and wait for a half hour as he auditioned. When we drove home I'd ask him how it went and he'd give me a weak Tiny Tim smile and say, "Oh, great, I got the part." The next several auditions turned out the same way. I felt sorry for the kid, but this was getting ridiculous.

After waiting one afternoon for an hour as "Little Danny" auditioned and, of course, got the role we were both up for, I said sarcastically, "I guess you'd like me to drive you to work." To my surprise, he said that he was hoping I would ask because he had to report to the set at 6 A.M. and he didn't want to bother his mother. As I handed "Little Danny" his cane and helped him to his front door, I decided enough was enough. I looked into his little pasty white face and told him that I was very sorry, but I couldn't drive him anymore. He wasn't bothered at all. He thanked me and said that it wasn't a problem because a lot of people wanted to drive him. He went on to say, "It must be hard on you when I get all the parts and you never get anything.... I was hoping I'd bring you some luck," then he turned and limped into his house. I couldn't believe it: "Little Danny Mummert" felt sorry for me? Maybe I was making a terrible mistake, but as I drove home I realized it was the right decision. I didn't want to spend the rest of my life being known as "Little Danny" Mummert's chauffeur.

As it turned out, I was moving into that awkward stage most child actors face. I never cared much about acting, and certainly at this point in my life I had no intention of being an actor, so it didn't bother me when my work slowed down. That summer I toiled behind the scenes at Columbia Studios delivering scripts. My boss was a nice woman named Rita O'Connor who ran the stenographic pool. In those days there were no Xerox machines, so there would be a long row of twenty or more women banging away at their typewriters, rushing to get the studio's many scripts typed onto stencils; then the copies would be run off on a mimeograph machine. When the scripts were completed, I would deliver the copies to departments like wardrobe, publicity, and makeup, and, of course, the executive offices. The head of Columbia Studios was the infamous Harry Cohn, whose name struck fear into anyone on the lot. This man was so disagreeable and so mean that, years later at Cohn's funeral, Red Skelton turned and looked around at the hundreds of people at the cemetery and said, "It just goes to show, give the people what they want and they'll turn out every time." So it should come as no surprise that I dreaded delivering scripts to Mr. Cohn's office. Not that I ran into him that often. If I saw him walking toward me on the lot I'd step into the closest office building just to stay out of his way.

Mr. Cohn's office was huge, with high ceilings and paneled walls. Everything in it seemed larger than life. His outer office had not one, but two secretaries, which he felt was the mark of a very important man. When I would deliver a script I would leave it with one of his secretaries, then get out of his office as fast as I could. This one particular day I arrived with his script delivery, but neither secretary was at her desk. I walked into the empty outer office and meekly said, "Hello, hello." Suddenly a voice boomed, "Who the hell is it...? Come in here." I froze....I couldn't move. The voice was coming from Cohn's office, and I knew I was about to come face to face with the most feared, most difficult, and, to me, the scariest man in Hollywood. Again, the voice yelled, "Get the hell in here..." Somehow my feet got the message. The next thing I knew I was standing across the desk from Harry Cohn. The room was so large and he was so loud and overpowering I felt like I was standing in front of King Kong. Any moment I expected to see fire and smoke billow around him. Trembling, I handed him his scripts. He took them and hardly looked up. For some reason I just stood there like a dummy, staring at him. I snapped out of it when he demanded, "What the hell are you doing...? Get out!? Once again, my feet responded and I was backing out of the door so quickly I nearly fell down. All I could squeak out was, "Yes sir.... Sorry, Mr. Cohn." When I got back to the steno pool I couldn't wait to tell everyone about my close encounter with "King Cohn," as he came to be known. When I finished recounting my story, one of the secretaries said that she had seen him earlier in the day and she told me, "You know, when I saw Mr. Cohn, he didn't seem at all like himself.... He almost looked pleasant!" I guess I was lucky I caught him on his good day. God help you on the other 364.

During my senior year at Cathedral High I was trying to figure out what to do with the rest of my life, when I was approached by Brother S. Edward, who was a vocation director. His job was to look for bright, clean-cut young men to recruit into the Christian Brothers. I don't know if it was because of the kindness of the Brothers or that I had seen too many movies with Bing Crosby and Pat O'Brien playing benevolent priests, but suddenly I felt I had the calling. Brother

S. Edward invited me up to Napa, California, to visit the Christian Brothers novitiate. Nestled in the rolling hills of the Napa Valley, the Christian Brothers not only made their famous wine, but had a preparatory school where young men would study to be a Brother. The Christian Brothers were really teachers, not winemakers. I went up for one night to meet everyone and to see basically if this was the place I wanted to spend the next several years training. Everyone was very nice and the grounds were beautiful. Over the years, my father, brother, and I had been on weekend retreats where we would listen to sermons, read, study, and use the time for quiet reflection on life. I always enjoyed the retreats, so I was sure I'd love it there. I was shown to a very large room with high, vaulted ceilings and a small cotlike bed in the corner, where I would spend the night. I got ready for bed and finally found the light switch, which was at the other end of the room, and turned off the light. The room was pitch black as I made my way across the cold Spanish tile floor.

As I lay on the cot I thought about all the famous priests, saints, and popes who had slept in rooms just like this one, for hundreds of years, as they prepared for the priesthood. The silence was broken when I suddenly heard squeaking and flapping noises. I figured birds must have made a nest in the rafters. Just as I was about to return to my pious dreams, something flew into my head with a loud screech. It scared me to death. I jumped out of bed, stumbled across the room, and turned on the lights. I was horrified to see nearly a dozen bats flying around the room. I ran back to the cot and covered my head with the blanket as the bats dive-bombed around me. I never closed my eyes all night as my thoughts switched from saints and the Vatican to Dracula and Translyvania. The next morning I thanked Brother S. Edward, but told him I wasn't sure if the Christian Brothers was quite right for me.

A few weeks later, as I prepared to graduate, I still felt that I wanted to enter the priesthood and, after much thought, I decided that I wanted to join the Passionist Priests. They lived in monasteries and traveled around the country conducting missions and retreats. I applied to the Passionist Preparatory

Seminary in St. Louis. I had graduated from Cathedral High School with honors, and I was immediately accepted into the seminary. With great excitement and fanfare, my proud Catholic parents put me on the plane for St. Louis. During the trip I thought about my exciting new life and how I wanted to spend the rest of my life serving God and the church. I thought of the beautiful pageantry and what I felt was the glamour and idealism of being a priest. I didn't know what I expected the seminary to be, but I was surprised to find that it was just like a boarding school with a lot of rules and regulations.

In the weeks prior to my move to the seminary, I had turned all of my attention to study and spiritual contemplation. There were no dates, no parties, no last-minute flings. I had assumed the personality and conduct of a priest, but once I had arrived and the realization that my freedom to experience life as a normal young man was over, I became obsessed by the desire to have everything a priest must disavow. It was like going on a diet. Before the diet you never think about food, but once you know that you can't eat, food becomes an obsession. All I could think about was dating and driving around town in a car. It didn't even have to be a flashy car or a beautiful date, just an old clunker and a plain girl would have made me ecstatic. Because my attention was on everything except my seminary studies, I found that I couldn't do anything right. If I was supposed to be studying, I was off praying for guidance; if I was supposed to be praying, I was eating or going for long walks. I tried my best, but it was no good, and as disappointed as I was, I knew it would never work out. After two weeks, I bid farewell to the monastic life and returned home.

By now it was mid-September and the school year was underway. I was allowed to take the entrance exam for Loyola University. My scores were very high, and I enrolled as an economics major. I now had great plans to be a stockbroker or corporate tycoon, never an actor; I wanted a real job, something with security.

The university had a drama department and an acting troupe called the Del Rey Players. I had been asked to join them, but I wasn't really interested. With after-school jobs, studying, and dating, I didn't have much time. I did meet two guys from the group that I really liked. One was a fellow named Dick Clair, who later became a writer on *The Carol Burnett Show,* and also created *Mama's Family* and *Facts of Life.* The other guy was Bob Denver. Yep...you got it, I was hanging out with the future Maynard G. Krebs. Neither of us had any idea that about five years later we would become a comedy duo like Abbott and Costello. Actually, we were more like *The Odd Couple! Dobie Gillis* was lurking on my horizon.

In the meantime, I was enjoying school and the usual teenage pleasures. One of the girls I dated was Gretchen Dockweiler, the pretty daughter of a local judge. Her family was very well to do; in fact, she was the only person I ever knew who had a state beach named after her family—Dockweiler Beach, which is south of Venice, California. Gretchen lived down the street from us in Los Feliz, and her family was very close with another well-known neighbor and many evenings she would invite me to join her and her parents for an evening of films at their friend's house. Their friend was Cecil B. DeMille. The DeMille home was actually two large, imposing Spanish houses connected by a breezeway. Inside, the heavy velvet draperies and dark mahogany wood made it look like the house in *Sunset Boulevard* and I expected to see Gloria Swanson as Norma Desmond descend the large staircase. From the moment I crossed the threshold I felt as if I were stepping back to the 1920s. All of his guests would assemble in the DeMille screening room, where overstuffed couches were placed in rows, and down front a huge leather club chair waited for the host. Mr. DeMille would stand at the door for a moment as a reverential hush fell over the crowd. Then he walked to the front of the room, turned to his guests, and made a few remarks about the film we were about to see. I never saw DeMille when he wasn't wearing his khaki jodhpurs, riding boots, white shirt, and tie. Many times he was coming in from work, but on his days off I always wondered why he'd wear that getup around the house. DeMille would sit in his huge leather chair, then, with the wave of his hand, signal to his projectionist to start the film.

When the film was over and the lights came up, the guests were deadly silent. No one dared comment until DeMille gave his opinion. If he turned to the crowd and proclaimed, "Pretty good film," all the guests would suddenly start nodding and murmuring to one another, "Yes, good film" and "I thought so, too." If DeMille gave the movie a thumbs-down, "Not very good, I feel it really missed," the crowd would shake its collective head and repeat, "I felt it missed, didn't you?" One particular film I remember seeing at DeMille's house was *The Big Sky*, a Western starring Kirk Douglas. I liked the movie, but I had been fully indoctrinated, like the rest of the group, to keep my humble opinion to myself. DeMille's judgment on *The Big Sky* was, "Not too bad, but it needed more work." And, as usual, we all agreed. After the screening, all would go down to pay homage to Mr. DeMille as he sat in his chair holding court. Everyone was very effusive with him because they were probably afraid that if they said anything out of line he'd hit them with his riding crop. His fights were legendary, so everyone kept a respectful distance.

At the end of my sophomore year at Loyola, 1954, I needed to earn some money, so I started looking for a summer job. Since I hadn't worked in a movie or on television in a year, I knew I couldn't count on that, so I decided to get a real job. I took the Civil Service test and applied for a job at the Department of Water and Power. I was very excited by the prospect of working at the D.W.P. While I was waiting to hear from them, I got a call from a former agent of mine who asked me if I was interested in going on an audition. I told him that I really didn't care about acting anymore, I was hoping to start a career with the Department of Water and Power. He laughed and said, "What are you planning to do, become a meter reader?" I didn't think he was funny and told him that I was very serious about working for the D.W.P. and I didn't want anything to interfere with me getting the job. He assured me that it was only an audition and I probably wouldn't get the part anyway. Agents are famous for building your confidence, so, with that thought in mind, I agreed to go on the audition for *The Bob Cummings Show*, and anxiously waited for my call from the Department of Water and Power.

THREE

BENNY, BURNS, CUMMINGS, AND ME

DRIVING TO MY AUDITION for *The Bob Cummings Show* I was more worried about getting a job at the Department of Water and Power than landing a part in some television pilot. If I had any idea how this show would change my life I would have been a wreck. I pulled into General Service Studio, parked my car, and strolled over to the show's production office. As I walked along the lot I passed the stage where George Burns and Gracie Allen filmed their hit show and the stage where the Nelson family shot *The Adventures of Ozzie and Harriet*. No one knew at the time that these shows would be part of the Golden Age of television. The actors, directors, writers, and producers were just working on a show and glad to be employed

When I arrived at the Cummings production office, I looked over my scene and waited to go in for my audition. Unlike today, where the waiting room would be filled with twenty actors, all competing for the same role and sitting elbow to elbow with their "rivals," my audition was very civilized. I sat alone, except for the secretary, made small talk, and looked over my lines. Of course they were auditioning other actors, but it wasn't a "cattle call" and the actors were treated with more respect.

The secretary informed me that I could go in, so I walked into the producer's office. There sat Bob Cummings and Paul Henning, the writer and producer of the show. Paul was a wonderful writer who later went on to create *The Beverly Hillbillies*, *Petticoat Junction*, and *Green Acres*.

They asked me to read my scene with Bob. I was to play his nephew, Chuck, and after my audition I reminded Bob that we had worked together when I was a little boy on *Heaven Only Knows*. He smiled and said, "Oh, yes, you were wonderful. I remember you in that scene riding a horse into town and alerting all the townspeople about the bad guys. I was very impressed with you." I was pleased that Bob held me in such high esteem; there was only one problem, it wasn't me. That scene was done by another kid actor, but who was I to argue with Bob Cummings? I graciously thanked him and went on my way. I don't know if it was my reading or his mistaking my identity, but I was called back to read again.

This time I read for Bob, Paul Henning, and the other producer of the show, George Burns. I had grown up listening to George Burns on the radio and here I was auditioning for him. I knew he was a big star, but, oddly enough, I wasn't really feeling nervous or intimidated because I still didn't care if I got the part or not. My goal was to go to college, graduate, and get a nice steady job. Everyone was very pleasant, and because they created such a relaxed atmosphere my reading went very well. In fact, when I left I felt pretty confident that I would get the part.

When I returned home I got a call from the D.W.P. guy. He told me that I had passed the Civil Service exam with flying colors and to come down for an interview the next day. I was overjoyed because I felt for the first time in my life I'd have a real job like everybody else and, with a little luck, maybe one day I'd run the Department of Water and Power. Brushing any thoughts or interest in *The Bob Cummings Show* aside, I excitedly made an appointment to meet with Mr. Miller of the D.W.P.

The next morning I was a nervous wreck as I drove to my interview. Dressed in my best—and only—suit, I tried to look like a junior executive. I waited in the reception room on pins and needles as I tried to read D.W.P. information pamphlets. My appointment was for ten A.M. and as the minute hand of the office clock clicked to the hour I was promptly ushered into Mr. Miller's office. I could tell right away that he was a button-down kind of guy.

He congratulated me on my high score on the Civil Service exam then proceeded to ask me about my work background. I was embarrassed to tell him that my only job experience had been acting in the movies. Mr. Miller gave me a "fish-eye" when I mentioned my movie work… "So, in other words, Mr. Hickman, you've never really had any work experience?" I suddenly got a sinking feeling that my future with the Department of Water and Power was going to be over before it started. My mind started to race, then I blurted out something about occasionally working for my father, cleaning his office on weekends. Mr. Miller's attitude suddenly brightened, "Why didn't you put that down on your application…? Working for your father is wonderful experience… I like a young man with ambition."

At that moment I wasn't going to argue the point that acting in a movie was not exactly a picnic and my work experience in my father's office consisted of emptying two trash cans and vacuuming the rug. It was a job I grudgingly did for a dollar an hour, and ambition had nothing to do with it. Mr. Miller then went on, at length, telling me about his early days at the D.W.P. The interview was winding down and Mr. Miller looked at me, for what seemed like five minutes, not saying a word, then, with great formality he stood up, extended his hand and said, "Welcome aboard, son, you can start work tomorrow." He then informed me that I would make $400 for the summer, and if I did a good job I would be set for life with the D.W.P. I was ecstatic as I shook Mr. Miller's hand and said something about making him proud of me.

Driving home I thought about the last two days and how easy and relaxed everyone had been at my audition for *The Bob*

Cummings Show and how no nonsense and businesslike every-thing was at the Department of Water and Power. No wonder I had been nervous with Mr. Miller; this was a real job with serious responsibilities, not some frivolous television show.

When I got home I raced through the front door bursting with my exciting news, but before I could say a word my mother congratulated me. I excitedly told her that tomorrow morning I would start my job at the D.W.P. and that I planned on this being the beginning of a lifelong career. My mother looked surprised and said that it was great the D.W.P. wanted me, but she was congratulating me about *The Bob Cummings Show*. While I was out securing my future with a real job, my agent had called and told her that I had gotten the part of Bob Cumming's nephew Chuck. I was thrilled. This was my day; everybody wanted me. I immediately called my agent, who told me that I would be paid $200 for the pilot and it would film for two days. I told him that I had just been hired by the Department of Water and Power and was supposed to start work the next day. My agent laughed, "Hey, kid, what are you, a meter reader or an actor?" I still didn't think he was very funny and told him that I'd have to call him back. I knew I couldn't do both jobs. There was no way Mr. Miller would give me time off to do a television pilot, and there was no way I'd have the nerve to ask him. I didn't know what to do. On the one hand I could work for two days and make $200; on the other, I could work all summer and make twice that much and have a future with a steady job where I could work for the next thirty years. After struggling with my dilemma I finally turned to my father, who gave me some great advice which I have tried to follow all my life. "Son, always take the job that has the least amount of work for the most amount of money."

I called my agent and told him to close the deal. He said that he already had because he knew I'd come to my senses! Then I made the call to Mr. Miller at the D.W.P. and told him what had transpired and that I had made my decision to do the television pilot. I was secretly hoping that he would be thrilled with my good fortune and tell me to enjoy the show and the D.W.P. job would be waiting for me. No such luck. The reality was that Mr. Miller did not share my enthusiasm. In fact, he told me that he was very disappointed because he felt that I was "real D.W.P. material" and he feared I was throwing away my future on a silly television show. I have to admit, there have been times in my life when I wondered if Mr. Miller wasn't right! Then he made a last ditch effort, "Dwayne, your father is a businessman; don't you think you should get his advice before you make such an important decision? I informed Mr. Miller that I had gone to my father and his advice was to take the job that was the least amount of work for the most amount of money. There was a long dead silence on the other end of the phone, then finally, Mr. Miller, in a very curt tone, said, "I see. Your father certainly has a very interesting work ethic, one you obviously share. Good day, Mr. Hickman," and he hung up. I stood there holding the phone and wondering if I had just thrown away my future as a budding corporate tycoon.

There are times when making a choice between one thing or another can change your whole life, and *The Bob Cummings Show* was one of those decisions. Had I not done Bob's show, I would never have been offered the role of Dobie Gillis. But at this point, having made my decision, all I cared about was having a summer filled with tennis, girls, and very little work.

Several days later Paul Henning asked me to come by his office to meet Rosemary DeCamp, the actress who would play my widowed mother. She had always been Bob and Paul's only choice to play the role. Lovely, warm, and funny, Rosemary always joked that she had made a career of playing somebody's mother. Those "somebodys" included James Cagney in *Yankee Doodle Dandy*, Ronald Reagan in *This Is the Army* (though he was older than she was) and Sabu in *Jungle Book*. We hit it off immediately, and she took me under her wing. She had been very successful in radio as well as movies, and that experience, plus her attitude of "Just flow with it, kid," made her a great teacher.

It was Friday afternoon and we were to begin shooting on Monday and one major character in the show had yet to be cast. From the beginning Paul Henning had written the character of Schultzy, Bob's adoring, wise-cracking photographer's assistant, with only one actress in mind, one-time child star Jane Withers. He had been in negotiations for several weeks with Jane's agent, and as the time was closing in, Jane's demands were getting bigger. Basically it was becoming the "Jane Withers and Bob Cummings Show." Friday rolled into Saturday and still Schultzy had not been cast. Paul, Bob, and a wonderful guy named Eddie Rubin sat in the production offices watching the hours click by and wondering where they would find a Schultzy. Paul couldn't get the idea of Jane out of his head, yet he knew her demands were out of the question and they would have to pass on her.

Eddie Rubin was the dialogue coach and general assistant and, as it turned out, he saved the day by pulling a Schultzy out of thin air. As Paul and Bob went back and forth about their dilemma, Eddie had heard enough. He suddenly jumped up and said, "I'm going to the bathroom and when I come back I'll have your Schultzy with me." Paul and Bob rolled their eyes and laughed. As Eddie walked out of the office and down the hall to the men's room he couldn't believe his eyes, there standing at the water fountain taking a drink was a plain, kind of wacky-looking girl. Eddie grabbed the unsuspecting woman by the arm and said, "Come with me," then he ran back to the office, burst through the door, and said, "I've got her...I've got Schultzy.... She was at the water fountain." Paul and Bob looked at the girl, who gave them a giggle and a funny, "Hello, guys." Paul shoved a script into her hand and told her to read the scene with Bob. No one had even bothered to ask if she was an actress, but from the moment Ann B. Davis said her first line, the role of Schultzy was hers. Ann was funny, a little kooky, and a one-of-a-kind character who was plucked from obscurity to become a fixture of series television. Eddie Rubin had saved the day and the show.

On Monday morning the entire cast, including our last-minute Schultzy, assembled on Stage 4 to start rehearsing the pilot. The premise of the show had Bob Cummings playing Bob Collins, a professional photographer who spent his working hours surrounded by beautiful models. His widowed sister, Margaret, played by Rosemary DeCamp, and her son, Chuck, played by me, lived with him. Bob's devoted assistant, Schultzy, had a hopeless crush on her boss but never had a chance with all the sexy competition vying for his attention. Chuck hoped to get in on Uncle Bob's action but he wouldn't get much of a chance since his mother kept a close eye on him and her roving bachelor brother.

Basing his character on the noted glamour photographer Paul Hesse, Bob played the typical 1950s man-about-town with a different beauty on his arm every night. Hugh Hefner went on to personify the lifestyle in the 1960s. Bob Collins had two arenas to play in: his office, with faithful Schultzy answering his phones and doing a running commentary on the stream of buxom beauties who filed in, and he had his home, where he lived with his sister and me.

The first day of the show we rehearsed the script and the second day we filmed. Actually it was more like three days because we filmed into the wee hours of the morning in order to complete the show in "just two days." We later joked that "it was a two-day show...even if it took three!" The pilot was directed by Fred DeCordova, who had worked for years with Jack Benny and went on to become the director and producer for *The Tonight Show Starring Johnny Carson*.

I had taken the job figuring I was going to be paid the most money for the least amount of work, but I was in for a big surprise: I never worked so hard in my life. Cummings, Paul Henning, and George Burns were the ultimate professionals, and we rehearsed until the scene was the best it could possibly be. I didn't really have much experience with comedy and Bob Cummings guided me every inch of the way. Halfway through the first day Bob pulled me aside and said, "Chuck"—he always called me "Chuck"; even forty years later he called me "Chuck"—"Chuck, this is your chance to go to school and learn comedy and get paid for it, and I'm gonna be your teacher." I listened to every word he said. I also listened and learned from George Burns, who came down to watch the final dress rehearsal and give his suggestions and notes.

The pilot went smoothly and although I was nervous I tried to take Rosemary's advice and just have fun with it. Ann B.

Davis had even less experience than I, and she was terrific. It was nearly two A.M. when we finished the show, and I had learned so much in two, or rather two and a half days, that my head was spinning. Then suddenly it was over and the bleary-eyed cast said goodbye and we all went on with our lives as if the past two days had been a dream. The whole experience had been so intense, with Cummings correcting and directing me and rehearsing until we were ready to drop, that I was kind of relieved that it was over. I couldn't imagine working at such a manic pace week in and week out.

Within a few days I put the whole experience out of my mind and looked forward to a summer of tennis and dating. But to my surprise, after several years of hardly ever working as an actor I was suddenly landing jobs on various television shows. I auditioned for *The Lone Ranger* and was cast as the innocent younger brother of a gunfighter who was wanted for murder. Although the show was supposed to take place out on the range, in actuality it was all filmed on a sound-stage. Tons of dirt had been brought in to transform the stage into the western range, complete with tumbleweeds, cactus, huge boulders, and, of course, a western town. It was a terribly hard show to work on because the air was thick with dust clouds, the result of horses and stagecoaches roaring through the set. Imagine half a dozen cowboys thundering by on their horses with guns blazing, not to mention the hot lights raising the indoor temperature close to one hundred degrees. The motto was "quick, fast, and cheap." When I finished shooting my scene, the wardrobe man literally snatched the hat off my head and put it on another actor who was getting ready to shoot the next show. If your costume was a little too big or a little too small, you were told not to worry about it, just to "act" like it fit!

My show was moving along right on schedule, mainly because every shot was done in one take, unless the camera-man had a problem or the actor forgot his lines. In the last scene of the show I was supposed to be running from my outlaw brother as I made my way into the hills. I was trying to hide behind a rock when my brother shot me. As he fired the gun I screamed out in pain, and dramatically fell against a boulder. I really threw myself into the moment, perhaps a little more than necessary, because when I hurled myself onto the boulder it scooted across the stage floor about five feet. No one had told me that the rocks were papier-mâché and that one man could easily pick up as many boulders as his arms could hold. The director yelled "Cut!" and walked over and asked me what I thought I was doing. I mumbled something about trying to look like the bullet had gone through my heart and the force of the shot had thrown me onto the rocks. He looked at me like I was crazy, then he shook his head and said, "This isn't some great drama we're doing here, kid; it's *The Lone Ranger* . . . . Now just take the bullet, drop to the ground, and stay off the rocks." I was so mortified I wished it had been a real bullet. When the director called "Action!" my brother shot me and I once again screamed in pain, but this time I dropped to my knees and collapsed in a small heap on the ground and I didn't move or breathe until I heard the director yell "Cut!" The next thing I knew, the wardrobe man pulled off my hat, vest, and holster as quickly as he could and handed them to the next actor. It would be over ten years before I worked on another Western and that would prove to be a much more rewarding experience.

Several weeks later, I was cast in *The Stu Erwin Show* playing the basketball team captain who was the boyfriend of Stu Erwin's youngest daughter, played by a cute kid named Sheila James—that's right, the same actress that would become Zelda Gilroy to my Dobie Gillis. Sheila was very bright, and we had a great time working together. The only problem was that I was totally wrong for the part. To be believable playing a "hot dog" basketball player who is the team's captain required a few things I didn't have . . . height and ability. I was only five-foot-nine, and when they brought in the Culver City High School basketball team as extras, I looked like a midget. I had shot baskets and played a little "one on one," but I had never really gotten into the game, mainly because everyone who played on the team at Cathedral High was well over six feet tall, not to mention the fact that if they didn't like the way you played they'd stuff you, instead of the ball, into the basket.

I suggested that they change the story and make me captain of the tennis team, at least I could show off a little bit, since my tennis game was pretty good, but no luck, it was going to stay basketball. I went into my dressing room and as I changed into my uniform I looked in the mirror and couldn't believe it; the tank top was so big on me that the armholes reached my waist and the number "8" covered my entire body. I looked like the incredible shrinking man. I sent for the wardrobe man because I was too embarrassed to be seen outside of my dressing room. I told him that I needed a smaller size and he looked at me, snickered, and said, "Sorry, but that's the smallest size they have." The assistant director came over and told me that it was time to shoot my scene, and even he stifled a laugh when he saw me. When I walked onto the set, the giants from Culver City High joked about my uniform, then proceeded to put on their best display of fancy footwork. These weren't actors, this was a real team and they played like the Harlem Globetrotters.

As we set up the scene where I "hot dog" around and shoot from center court to make the winning basket I was so nervous I thought I would pass out. I had nothing going for me. I was too short, these guys were too good, and to top things off, I looked like a fool. We rehearsed a couple of times and each time I missed the basket. I knew if I could just get a little closer I could get the ball through the hoop because what I lacked in fancy footwork, I made up for in my free-throw ability. The director called "Action!" and the guys from Culver City started to do the play we had rehearsed but at that moment I decided to take a chance and do the unexpected. Since they had been instructed to do the exact same moves they had re-hearsed, they were not prepared for me to charge up the center of the court toward the basket, which is exactly what I did. I made my way through the sea of flailing arms and squeaking tennis shoes and took my shot. As the ball left my hands I said a quick prayer, then watched it fly through the air. It hit the rim, bounced up, and fell through the hoop. My teammates looked shocked, as did the crew, and the director who called "Cut!" and came over to me. That was great, Dwayne, but I wasn't prepared for your changes.... Let's try it again, the same way." My heart sank. Could lightning strike twice? I made my move up the center and, by some miracle, the ball dropped through the hoop again. Then I heard the words I was waiting to hear, "Cut and print!" The scene was over and, best of all, I could get out of my ridiculous outfit.

As I hurried toward my dressing room, Sheila ran over and congratulated me, then she went on to tell me that everyone had figured we'd have to shoot all day to get that scene...."Boy, you sure got lucky." She smiled and said that she hoped we could work together again. The next time I saw Sheila was four years later, when Dobie met Zelda.

Later that summer I had a small part on *The Loretta Young Show*. Every week gorgeously gowned Loretta would pirouette through those famous French doors and introduce her show. I had the role of a young man being interviewed for a job by Loretta, who played the head of the office. We shot the master scene, then did her close-up. As they set up for my close-up, the director told Loretta she could go to lunch since she wouldn't be on camera and the script girl could deliver her lines to me. She smiled and said, "Certainly not, I want to do Dwayne's close-up," so she said her dialogue off-camera as I played the scene. Her daughter, Judy Lewis, was a friend of mine and I spent a lot of time at their beautiful house off Sunset Boulevard. Loretta has a great sense of humor and always kidded me about the way I bounced when I walked. She would ask me to get up and walk across the living room, then she would laugh hysterically and tell me that I reminded her of Jack Benny.

Shortly before school started, my mother got a call from an acquaintance named Agnes Horrocks, who was the house-keeper for the priests who lived in the rectory at the Immaculate Heart of Mary church. Agnes had a friend who worked as a cook for a wealthy family in Brentwood, a beautiful area of Los Angeles near the ocean. The family had a daughter who was sixteen and her mother was looking for a suitable young man to be her escort. Because they were Catholic, the cook called Agnes at the rectory hoping that she would know of a nice young man. Apparently Agnes felt I would be the ideal choice. I certainly wasn't wealthy, but I had the reputation of being polite and respectable, so Agnes was calling to see if I would be interested in meeting this girl. My mother put me on the phone and, after much protest, I reluctantly agreed to meet her. I must not have sounded very enthusiastic because Agnes started telling me, in glowing terms, what a nice family the girl came from and how lovely she was. I thanked her and started to hang up when Agnes asked, "Dwayne, don't you even want to know the young lady's name?" Embarrassed that I had forgotten such an obvious question, I said, "Of course," and Agnes told me that her name was Maria... Cooper. She went on to say that I had probably seen her father in the movies; his name was Gary Cooper. I was taken aback. This wasn't just any blind date, this was a blind date with Gary Cooper's daughter. I was an enormous fan of his and told Agnes that one of my favorite films was *High Noon*. But that still didn't change the fact that I was nervous about going out with someone I had never seen before. Agnes assured me that Maria was a beautiful young girl and that I would have a great time.

All the arrangements were made and on Saturday night I drove out Sunset Boulevard to pick up Maria. No one likes blind dates, especially one that has been arranged by a cook, a rectory housekeeper, and an overanxious mother. You can imagine the pictures that flashed through my mind as I tried to imagine what Maria looked like. All I kept seeing was a girl that looked exactly like Gary Cooper. I parked my car in the driveway and rang the doorbell of their beautiful mansion. The housekeeper showed me into the living room and introduced me to Maria's mother. Mrs. Cooper, known to her friends as Rocky, was the former Veronica Balfe, the daughter of an extremely wealthy New York family. A debutante and actress, Rocky met the handsome movie star, Gary Cooper, and sparks flew. Their only child, Maria, was the center of their world.

As I walked into the living room, I introduced myself and shook Mrs. Cooper's hand. She motioned for me to sit down and proceeded to ask me a few questions about school and work, then there was an awkward silence. I felt that she wanted to ask me something or that I was supposed to volunteer some information, but I had no idea what else she might want to know about me. Suddenly Mrs. Cooper said, "Uh...Dwayne, what kind of car do you drive?" I told her that I drove a 1953 Plymouth that my father had bought for me last year, then I quickly added that it was new when he bought it, not used. "And how are the brakes on your car? Are they in good working order?" she asked. I assured her that my car was my pride and joy and it was in perfect shape. Looking enormously relieved, she laughed and told me that she had been very nervous about Maria going out in the car. She didn't want to offend me by asking the questions but she had to be sure my car was safe. In fact, she was going to have the butler go out front and look my car over and test the brakes, but she felt comfortable now that we had talked. Then she smiled and said she hoped that she had not offended me. I assured her that I wasn't offended, then Mrs. Cooper called for Maria to join us.

Any reservations I might have had about my blind date flew out the window when Maria walked into the room. A dark-haired beauty, she was the perfect combination of her parents—tall and lean like her father and dark and exotic like her mother. Soft-spoken and shy, Maria was even more nervous about this setup than I was because this was her first date. I received my final instructions from Mrs. Cooper, then I slowly and carefully pulled out of the driveway and headed to Marymount High School and a fully chaperoned tea dance.

In no time at all during our ride Maria and I were chatting like old friends. She told me that her father would be away for a while in Mexico filming two movies back to back, *Vera Cruz*, with Burt Lancaster, and *Garden of Evil*, with Richard Widmark. We arrived at the dance and I did my best to move Maria around the floor and not step all over her feet. I didn't know if she was just being polite or maybe it was self-preservation, but after a few spins around the dance floor, Maria said that she hoped I didn't mind but she didn't really like to dance. I told her that it was fine with me because I didn't like to dance either...in fact I wasn't very good at it. She said, "I noticed," and we both burst out laughing. We spent the rest of the evening talking and meeting her schoolmates. At eleven o'clock I walked Maria to her front door and said good night. She was a lovely girl and we became close friends and continued to date over the next few years.

I had just started my junior year at Loyola when I got a call from my agent. He told me that the pilot I had shot at the beginning of the summer had been picked up by NBC. All I was thinking about was school, so I asked him, "What pilot are you talking about?" He said, *The Bob Cummings Show*, remember?" Embarrassed, I told him that I remembered the show but I was in school now and I was very busy. My agent informed me that I was going to get a whole lot busier because I would be starting work on the show in less than a month. I hung up the phone and my mind started to race; how would I ever be able to carry a full load of classes and rehearse and film a television show at the same time? I had already started my semester and I didn't want my studies to suffer because of some television series. After all, I was trying to get a degree in economics so I could land a steady job after I graduated from college. And if the pilot was any indication of what I could expect, I was in for some grueling work under the guidance of Bob Cummings, who was a perfectionist of the highest order.

I was suddenly flooded with emotions; first I was excited, then I was worried about my education and my future, then I felt like an ingrate, since any actor in the world would kill to have a steady acting job. And then I felt foolish for even questioning my good fortune because I had no money and this show would pay me far more than any college kid could earn during the school year. I didn't get much time to think about my dilemma because the phone rang again and it was the secretary at the production office informing me that I had a meeting the next day with an attorney named Gordon Stulberg. I panicked and asked her what I had done that I would need an attorney. She laughed and told me that "my crime" was that I wasn't twenty-one yet and the court had to approve my contract because I was still a minor. Mr. Stulberg was the attorney who had been assigned to me and he would represent me in court.

This was part of the so-called Coogan Act, which protected the wages of child actors by placing a percentage of their earnings in a trust that would be available to them when they turned twenty-one. The Coogan Act was named after Jackie Coogan, the child star whose parents had squandered every dime he had made in the movies, and that was a considerable sum. Coogan took them to court. The result was protection under the law for all future child actors.

I met with Gordon Stulberg the next day. He explained that I would need to fill out expense forms which he would present to the court. The court would allow me to have enough money to pay my bills, and the rest of my wages would be put into a trust. I was embarrassed to tell Mr. Stulberg that I didn't really have any expenses: I lived at home, so I didn't pay rent, and my folks were paying for college. My only real expenses were the upkeep on my car and money for dates. I asked him what they were going to pay me each week, and he explained that I would make $200 per show, and if the filming took more than two days I would get an extra $50. (Today, I would make about $10,000 a week for my part, but in 1954 that $200 seemed like a windfall.) I quickly realized that if I didn't come up with some expenses real fast I wouldn't be taking home any money and it would all be put into the trust. I would turn twenty-one the following May, but I wasn't going to go without spending money until then. By the time I finished filling out the form, I was paying $300 in rent and another $400 for miscellaneous expenses, leaving only around $50 that would go into the trust. Mr. Stulberg looked over the form and asked me if I was sure of the figures. I swallowed hard and said, "Oh, yes sir."

A few days later we were standing in court in front of the judge as he looked over my expense sheet. I'll never forget how nervous I was as I watched him carefully study the figures. He shook his head and stared at me over his glasses. Suddenly I panicked. What if he didn't believe me? Had I just committed perjury? Could I go to jail...? Just as I was about to confess my crime, the judge looked up and said, "You live at home and go to school, Mr. Hickman? I squeaked out "Yes, sir." Then he said, "Are you trying to tell the court that you pay your parents $300 in rent and your additional expenses are $400.... Are you sure of this? Again, I squeaked out a rather unconvincing "Yes, sir." The judge shook his head and turned to my attorney, "I can't believe you would bring this document before the court, Mr. Stulberg...but since your client will be twenty-one next year this court will approve his expenses..." I was so relieved that it completely went over my head that I had humiliated my attorney in front of the judge. As we walked out of the court, I thanked Mr. Stulberg. He curtly shook my hand and said, "Thank you, Dwayne, that was the most embarrassing moment I have ever experienced in court.... Next time, please get yourself another attorney."

Over the years Gordon Stulberg and I would run into one another and we would always laugh about our day in court. Apparently my little ruse with my expense form didn't hurt him because he went on to become the president of Twentieth Century-Fox, where I would later film *Dobie Gillis*.

A few days later I reported, once again, to Stage 4 at General Service Studio to begin work on *The Bob Cummings Show*. As I drove to work I felt very excited, but I was still a bit overwhelmed by the idea of doing a television series and at the same time trying to juggle my college classes. I pulled in to the studio and the guard stopped me and asked my name. I told him that I was Dwayne Hickman and that I was one of the stars of *The Bob Cummings Show*. He looked down his list of names and finally said, "Oh, yeah, Hickman.... Sorry, you don't have a parking space, you'll have to park on the street." So much for my newfound fame.

It had been four months since we had worked together, and when the cast assembled for our first day we were all very tentative. We had only known each other for a few hectic days; then, after filming, we had all gone our separate ways.

After we shot the pilot, Cummings went on to star in Alfred Hitchcock's *Dial M for Murder*. When I questioned Bob about his costar, Grace Kelly, he gave a very cool response and

told me that the two didn't have the kind of intimate relationship she had shared with Ray Milland, the film's other star. I
got the message and didn't bring it up again.

The cast of the TV show may not have known one another
very well, but by the time lunch rolled around it was suddenly
like we had never been apart. A lot of that easy and relaxed
atmosphere on the set was due to Bob Cummings, Paul
Henning, and George Burns. These three men were very
professional but never took themselves too seriously. We had a
new director for the show, a bright young guy named Rod
Amateau, and our schedule would be the same as the pilot; the
first day we would read the script and rehearse, the second day
we would film. Once in a while our two-day show spilled over
to three as we filmed late into the night. The reason we worked
these late hours was that the overtime was cheaper than
bringing everyone back for another day.

In the 1950s most of the half-hour comedies were still being
shot with only one camera. *The Burns and Allen Show* was
thought to be very innovative because they filmed with two
cameras, and since George Burns was one of our show's
producers, we also used the two-camera technique. When *I
Love Lucy* debuted in 1951, it wasn't long before Desi Arnaz
began using three cameras and brought in a live audience to
watch the show film. Within a few years most of the comedies
on television used a multiple-camera technique.

Unlike today's filming schedule, where a half-hour comedy
would rehearse four days and film on the fifth, we completed a
show in less than half the time and with fewer script changes.
When Paul Henning presented us with a script on Monday
morning, it was polished and ready to shoot. If we were having
a problem with a line or something didn't work, then Paul
would change it, but for the most part the script we rehearsed
Monday was the script we filmed Tuesday.

Today, when a cast gets a script on the first day of
rehearsal, it's more of a rough draft than a finished product,
and the extra rehearsal days don't always make the show
better. The large staff of writers rework the script so much that
most of the jokes disappear and the story becomes flat. It is an

impossible situation for the actors because what they have rehearsed on one day will be thrown out the next morning and they must start all over again. It's like getting a different script every day. The actor never gets a chance to learn the material or polish his performance, and this is one of the reasons why many of today's comedies aren't very funny and don't live up to their potential.

Another element that is essential to the making of a quality show is the rehearsal process. Cummings loved to rehearse, and so did I. It was hard work, but the more we did the scene the more comfortable we became and the more we could perfect our performances. We arrived at the studio around 9:30 A.M., rehearsed until lunch, then again all afternoon until we did a run-through of the show for Paul Henning and George Burns. I was really impressed by George, who could look at a scene and in a moment identify any problem and give you the perfect solution. I'd do my scene, then look over at George, who would always be wearing a hat when he didn't wear his toupée. He'd be puffing on his cigar, then he'd catch my eye and give me a nod of approval, or he'd say, "Listen, kid, don't say the line like it's a joke... Just say the line and keep moving or you'll die where you stand..." I never argued with George's advice.

Many times during these rehearsals there would be another gentleman watching the show. He would sit next to George laughing, thoroughly enjoying the rehearsal. Imagine looking out and realizing that you were playing a comedy scene in front of the two greatest comedy legends in the business...George Burns and Jack Benny.

Benny would wander over from his show and join George as he watched our run-through. They had been the closest of friends for years, and Jack was, without a doubt, George's best audience. All Jack had to do was look at George and he would convulse with laughter. Many times after the rehearsals Jack would come over and compliment me on a scene. That was pretty heady stuff for a kid doing his first series. Interestingly enough, it never really went to my head; it just made me try even harder to listen, learn, and do the very best work I could do.

I was with Jack in a social situation only once. We were both attending a party given by celebrity columnist Cobina Wright. We were all standing around talking and visiting when Jack spotted me and made his way through the crowd. We chatted for a moment about *The Bob Cummings Show*, then he took hold of my arm and told me that he had the most incredible experience that day and he just had to share it with me. I couldn't imagine what it could be but I figured it would be pretty good; after all, he was Jack Benny, a living legend.

Jack squeezed my arm and proceeded to tell me that he had been out driving around and got hungry so he stopped at a restaurant called Tiny Naylor's. He asked if I had ever been there. I had. Then, with great amazement and total sincerity, he told me that he had ordered a cheeseburger and that it was the best cheeseburger he had ever eaten. Then he asked me if I had ever had a glass of their water. A bit confused, I said I was sure I had. Jack squeezed my arm again and said, "Tiny Naylor's has the coldest and best-tasting water I've ever had." At that moment I realized there was no punch line, no great event; nothing had really happened to Jack besides eating a good cheeseburger and drinking a cold glass of water. Here was a man who was fabulously wealthy and one of the most famous entertainers in show business, and the simplest plea-sure in life was a big deal to him. As I got to know Jack, I realized what all his friends knew, that he was not a comedian who told jokes like most comics; he was serious and sincere and a wonderfully kind gentleman who just happened to be very funny.

Several days later, Jack was sitting with George watching our rehearsal, when suddenly George turned to Jack and said, "Had any good water lately?" Jack started laughing uncon-trollably; apparently he had also told George about his Tiny Naylor's experience, and in true Burns fashion Burns turned it into a joke at Jack's expense. We all enjoyed George's sharp humor although at times it could cut a little too close.

During one of the rehearsals a young actor had a guest part on the show, and like a lot of actors doing comedy, he made the same mistake I had and read his line like he was saying the funniest line in the world. George stopped the rehearsal and said, "Kid, if you lay it in like it's a big joke and it fails, you'll look like a fool. Do it real..." The actor started the scene over and once again he laid the joke in. George stopped him again and said, "Kid, I'm gonna tell you one last time.... You read the line like that and an angry lynch mob will come to your house and hang you from the nearest tree." That seemed to get the guy's attention because the next time he read the line, he said it perfectly.

Even Cummings wasn't immune to George's sharp comments. In one show Bob did a scene where he came out of the bathroom without his shirt. Now Bob had a pretty good build, but apparently George wasn't impressed, so he stopped the scene and told Bob that he thought it would be better if he wore a shirt. Bob told him that Paul Henning liked the scene without the shirt. Without missing a beat, George said, "Then tell Paul when he writes the show...not to wear a shirt," then he puffed on his cigar and the entire set broke up. Once again George was right. When we shot the scene Bob wore his shirt. Bob usually deferred to George, but once in a while Bob would disagree and insist on doing it his way. I noticed that when Bob did it his way, George's way was usually better. Bob was a much better actor than George, but George was a great comedian and had an eye for the overall picture.

Bob enjoyed the role of comedy teacher and I was certainly a willing pupil. Many times when Bob and I were doing a scene together he would correct my mistakes without anyone else having a clue as to what was going on. If I started drifting into his light or moving slightly off my mark and covering his face in the camera, Bob would gently pull me into the correct position. After looking at the dailies (a term used for the film that was shot the day before), Bob noticed that I moved my eyes a lot in the scene and no matter who was in the scene with me, I was the only person you looked at. That was enough for Bob. During our next scene together Bob said, "Chuck...if you stand behind me I don't want you to move your eyes; just look at one object." That was great for Bob, but I ended up looking like a statue. It wasn't that I was trying to steal the scene, it was just the way I acted. Bob called it "listening with my eyes" which, by the way, is exactly what he did when he was in a scene.

The more Cummings and I worked together the more our timing and performance became the same. In one show we had a dream sequence where we were playing poker in an Old West saloon. We were filming the scene and I looked at my cards and said through my clenched teeth, "I'll take another card," then Bob said, through his clenched teeth, "Gimme a card and I'll raise you." I started to say my next line and Bob yelled "Cut!" "Chuck...who's going to do Gary Cooper, you or me?" We all laughed as the pupil was obviously turning into his teacher.

During the second year, as I got better with comedy, my part got bigger. In one show I was supposed to be taken with the beautiful blond rich girl, Melinda Applegate, who was played by young Connie Stevens. She was sexy and vivacious, and I had an instant crush on her, but unfortunately she didn't feel the same way. In fact, the models working on the show each week looked at me like I was a kid even though we were all about the same age. These beauties were far too sophisticated for me. In my scene with Connie I tried to do my best, very British, Laurence Olivier imitation. Bob got quite a kick out of it because he had worked with Olivier and, as I found out later, did his own very convincing imitation of a "Brit." When we finished our scene, Bob called me over and said, "Chuck, that was terrific....One day you're gonna have your own show."

When I wasn't rehearsing I'd visit the set of *Burns and Allen* and *Ozzie and Harriet*. *The Burns and Allen Show* was shot with two cameras and was really like a filmed radio show. George and Gracie basically took their enormously successful radio act and put their zany cast of characters on film, and the television show ran from 1950 to 1958. I was crazy about Gracie Allen. She was a delightful lady and not at all the airhead character she played on the show. George Burns was the same on camera as off—smart, funny, and very acerbic. Any actor who worked with George had better be prepared and know what he was doing.

On one of their shows the entire storyline revolved around a character named Dr. Cronkite, whom everyone talked about but no one ever saw. In the final moment of the show the doorbell rings and George opens the door and the man standing there was to say, "Hello, I'm Dr. Cronkite," which would get a big laugh. Unfortunately, the actor playing Dr. Cronkite was a bundle of nerves and during rehearsal blew his line several times. Beads of sweat poured down his face as he profusely apologized to everyone. Finally filming started on the scene. George opened the door and the man froze, nothing came out. The second take he stammered, "Hello...I'm... uh...I'm..." George yelled "Cut!" and again, and again, take after take, the poor guy couldn't say his line. Finally George opened the door and the actor blurted out, "Hello...I'm George Burns," and George said, "No, I'm George Burns and you're fired... We'll pick this up next week with another actor." It happens to every actor sooner or later, and it truly is the actor's nightmare.

The set of *Ozzie and Harriet* was totally different from *The Bob Cummings Show*. Ozzie Nelson, who wrote, produced, directed, and starred in the show with the rest of his family, was very low-key. They shot five days with one camera, while we shot one day with two cameras.

After one of my visits to their set I said to Rosemary DeCamp that *The Ozzie and Harriet Show* seemed so slow compared to our show. Rosemary rolled her eyes and said, "Dwayne, they're not slow, they're real... Our show is hyper and crazy." While Ozzie was calmly saying, "Hi, Rick..., hi David, want some milk and cookies?" Cummings would be flying through the set spitting out lines at ninety miles an hour like, "Schultzy, call the field and tell King to preflight the Beech." That would be some flying reference Bob would throw in, since he was an avid flyer. Translated, it meant, "Schultzy, call the airfield and tell Mr. King to prepare my Beechcraft [plane] for a flight."

I got to know the Nelsons pretty well since David and I were about the same age and, along with his brother Ricky, we would stand around and visit. Ozzie thought it would be fun to have me appear on their show as my character from *The Bob Cummings Show*, so I did a couple of guest shots as David and Ricky's buddy, Chuck MacDonald. Everyone on the set was easy to work with, and I felt like I was actually visiting Ozzie and Harriet in their home because it was so laid back and natural. It was more like a home movie than a TV show, but I must say that I preferred the breakneck, high energy, all-the-stops-pulled-out style of *The Bob Cummings Show*.

After working at this fast pace for more than a season I thought that I could handle anything. That was my first mistake. My second mistake was agreeing to appear in the live television show, "Captive City," for *Lux Video Theatre*. To this day I will never understand why actors would allow themselves to be put through the torturous process of live TV. I was young and very naive when I reported to the large rehearsal hall at NBC in Burbank, where I met the rest of the cast who would also participate in this madness. "Captive City" was a story that took place in a newspaper office and it would star Gig Young, Murray Hamilton (who later became famous in his role as the mayor in *Jaws*), and James Mason, who was the host of the show. Mason had the easiest role because he could read all his lines off cue cards, yet he was still very stiff and uncomfortable. We rehearsed for several days with only part of the script. Each day Gig Young would ask when we would be able to see act three and he was told the act three hadn't been written yet. Then he was quickly assured that he would have it before the show hit the air so he needn't worry. That's easy for the writer because he's not the poor guy standing on the stage when the red light on the camera goes on and he suddenly pops on the screen of a million or more television sets around the country.

My part was not very large. I played a copyboy who would come in and out throughout the story. My heart bled for Gig and Murray. They were never off camera for the entire show. Most of the time their scenes were played sitting behind their desks so their lines were pasted everywhere. Since rehearsal time was short and the script was either not complete or constantly being changed, the actors couldn't possibly rely on their memory. The only way they could get through the show was to write their lines on every prop, piece of furniture and, if necessary, available body part.

During our show Gig had his dialogue written on the papers at his desk and, as he moved around the set, on the backs of chairs. Murray Hamilton used the palm of his hand and sleeve of his jacket.

Finally the dreaded moment had arrived. As we got into our wardrobe and makeup we headed back to our dressing rooms for some private moments where we could look over our lines and say a few impassioned prayers. The minutes were clicking away and I was so stressed I was ready to jump out of my skin. Suddenly there came a knock at the door. It was Vincent Donohue, the director. Vincent was a major Broadway and television director and he had been brought in to fix all the problems and whip these "Hollywood actors" into shape. He turned to me and said, "Dwayne, I have a few changes for you." Before he could finish I nearly flew at him. Hysterically, I told him that there would be no more changes and that I would do the best I could, but to leave me alone! Every good director knows when his actor is about to go over the edge and be a complete loss. Vincent took one look at my wild eyes and knew it was time to quietly back out of my dressing room and just wish me luck.

As we all assembled on the stage and the assistant director started the ten-second countdown, I looked around at Gig, who looked like he hadn't slept in a week and poor Murray, who was having periodontal work and was suffering with tooth pain on top of everything else. Then, of course, there was James Mason, for whom no one felt sorry because he had cue cards. Suddenly the assistant director pointed to us and the red lights on top of the cameras lit up and we were off and running. My heart was beating so hard I couldn't hear a word. Then I heard myself saying my lines. It was like an out-of-body experience. Somehow we got through it.

We performed the show seven to eight P.M. so that it aired live to the East Coast from ten to eleven. In New York the show would be taped and later aired on the West Coast. The show could have been taped in the first place, instead of sent out live. Whenever that was suggested, the powers to be said that it would be too expensive to edit. Actually, I believe they liked the raw-edged excitement of watching the poor actors survive the hour-long, high-anxiety stress test. By 8:05 there wasn't an actor in the building. We all fled as fast as we could, jumped into our cars, and headed into the dark night. I guess we were all afraid that if we hung around a moment longer someone would say, "Let's do it again."

When I returned to *The Bob Cummings Show* I recounted my terrible experience. Rosemary DeCamp laughed and said that she had done several shows and each one was worse than the last. Bob Cummings, who had won an Emmy for "Twelve Angry Men" for *Studio One* and later was also critically acclaimed for *Playhouse 90*'s "Bomber's Moon," summed it up perfectly. He said, "Chuck...doing live television is like shooting an entire movie in one take." I said that it felt like I had been pushed out of a plane at forty thousand feet without a parachute.

Suddenly I realized that I had joined the brotherhood of actors who had lived through those stress-filled, anxiety-ridden, heart-stopping moments of live television that bind bit player and star. It's like living through some terrible experience and being able to share those harrowing moments with a fellow survivor.

I must admit I felt a lot smarter than Bob or Rosemary: I had learned my lesson the first time and vowed never to do live television again!

• FOUR •

THE "BIG APPLE" AND MY ROCK-'n'-ROLL NIGHTMARE

IN FALL 1957 *THE BOB CUMMINGS SHOW* found a new home and a successful time period back on NBC. Originally, the show had aired back on NBC then moved to CBS, where we were opposite *You Bet Your Life*, with Groucho Marx. Then we joined the competition, returning to NBC on Tuesday nights at 9:30 opposite CBS's *The Red Skelton Show*. ABC was a fledgling network that aired religious shows and news programs, so it wasn't yet providing much competition for the two other networks.

The Bob Cummings Show was very popular, and each of the characters had his or her own following. Bob was always a favorite of the female audience and most of the male population was living vicariously through him as he romanced his bevy of voluptuous beauties. Rosemary DeCamp was the character everyone sympathized with because she had to deal with a house full of crazies, and Ann B. Davis as Schultzy was the plain Jane who loved her boss but never had a chance because Bob was too blinded by a beautiful face and a buxom mate. Then there was me, young Chuck, the foolish kid trying to chase in his Uncle Bob's footsteps. I was getting quite a following with the teen audience.

One time, on a trip back to Cumming's home town of Joplin, Missouri, to celebrate "Bob Cummings Day," the entire cast was in a parade with hundreds of fans lining the streets and screaming hysterically as we rode by. As my car turned the corner and started down the main street the announcer introduced me. No sooner had he said "Dwayne Hickman" than a horde of wild, screaming teenage girls ran over and threw themselves on my car. I had never experienced anything like this and I was scared to death. The car was so laden down with the weight of crazed fans that it wouldn't budge. Suddenly, a dozen or more of Joplin's finest pried the women off my car and we sped away. All anyone talked about the rest of the trip was my encounter with my adoring fans. Cummings was not particularly thrilled by the fact that I had overshadowed his big day. Despite a bit of jealousy Bob would watch me and take great delight in his protégé's progress. Quite often he would say, "Chuck, one day you're gonna have your own show."

I had been so busy going to school and working that it wasn't until my encounter with the fans in Joplin that I suddenly realized that I had become a celebrity...and a television star. The whole notion took me aback since I had never really considered myself a serious actor. I had either been the tag-along little brother who got extra parts or an unsuccessful child actor whose career never really got off the ground. If I seemed surprised by all this success and newfound celebrity, my family was even more perplexed by my sudden good fortune. Darryl had always been the famous one in the family, and his status had been well deserved, since he was a terrific actor and had enjoyed great success as a child star. But in his adolescence, like the majority of child actors, his career slowed down and he had trouble finding work. While I was enjoying my newfound fame on *The Bob Cummings Show* Darryl had been drafted into the army and, with a lot of mixed emotions, he was watching his quiet, younger brother, who had always shied away from the spotlight, suddenly come into his own.

For years he'd often tell the story about being in the army, and getting on an elevator one day, as a stranger turned to him and said, "May I ask you a question?" Figuring that he was going to be asked for his autograph he smiled and said, "Certainly." Then the stranger asked, "Are you Dwayne Hickman's brother?" He was totally shocked. He said that while he was away "fighting for his country" his little brother was starring in some frivolous television series. Since Darryl was stationed at Fort Ord, near Carmel, California, every time he told the "elevator story" and got to the part of "fighting for his country," I'd chime in, "Was that the Battle of Carmel? You must have been fighting for dinner reservations!" While all this was said somewhat tongue in cheek and Darryl would react with mock upset, I think, in reality, it was very hard for him. After years of doing serious acting work, suddenly his career had cooled off and while he was stuck in uniform, his kid brother, who never had wanted an acting career, much less stardom, seemed to have it all.

My mother was equally surprised by this turn of events. No one in the family, including my father and sister, who had no interest in show business, seemed to know what to make of my success; so around the house no one said much about it. But in years to come, as my career grew and my celebrity increased, what had started out as a subject my family never discussed and tried to ignore, finally became a wedge that eventually would estrange me from both my brother and sister.

It was during *The Bob Cummings Show* that, for the first time in my life, I really enjoyed acting, but I don't think I ever really believed that I would have a show of my own. The thought of it was overwhelming. I was already exhausted trying to rehearse, film, and attend Loyola University full time. I was working three days a week doing the show and the other two days I tried to catch up at school, taking notes on missed classes and making up tests. Since I rarely went to class I never really got to know any of my classmates. I was also appearing on television every week and in publicity layouts in the popular movie magazines, so no one really knew how to react to me. Any chance I had to be "just a regular college kid" was over. I finally had to drop out of school at the beginning of my senior year, but I promised myself that I would go back to Loyola and get my degree, which I did, nearly ten years later. I might note that no one has ever asked me for, or seemed to care that I had, my Bachelor of Science degree—or any degree for that matter—but at least I had the satisfaction that I completed college.

I had just quit school and was devoting myself full time to the show when Bob called me into his office. He was there with George Burns and Jack Benny. When Bob told me that they wanted to make some changes in the show, my heart sank. I knew he was going to fire me, and if that wasn't bad enough, I would be humiliated in front of George and Jack. To my great relief, Bob informed me that they wanted to give me my own show, a spin-off called *Chuck Goes to College*. I was thrilled. As I got up to leave, Jack Benny said, "Oh, Dwayne, I just want to tell you that I think you have the best comedy timing of any young kid I've ever seen." Before I could reply, George turned to him and said, "He's not such a big deal. He's only doing Cummings, who's doing you.... What timing? And, as usual, Jack laughed hysterically.

Walking out of Bob's office I couldn't believe my good fortune. Flattered, excited, and scared, all I could think about was Bob taking my arm and repeating, "Chuck, some day you're gonna have your own show." My head was spinning. With Cummings, Burns, and Benny's blessing, I knew that *Chuck Goes to College* couldn't fail. (Obviously I still had a lot to learn about television!)

A few weeks later, while *The Bob Cummings Show* was on hiatus for a week, we shot the pilot for my show. Paul Henning wrote an amusing script that had me packing up and leaving my mother and my Uncle Bob and heading out on my own. I would live in a dormitory with several other guys and the stories would revolve around me dealing with school, dating, escapades with my buddies, and more girl chasing, just like my Uncle Bob.

I was the natural character to spin off from the show and

everyone was very pleased with the pilot and sure of its success. Bob was behind the project one hundred percent and decided that he and I would go to New York to promote the sale of the show. When Bob told me about the New York plans, he took on his mentor-father figure personality and described in detail how he was going to expose me to Broadway theater, New York nightlife, and the art of handling the press. Wide-eyed and excited at the prospect of traveling around the Big Apple with Bob Cummings, world traveler and sophisticate, I couldn't wait to begin our journey. My excitement was dampened when Bob happily informed me that we would be flying to New York in a few days. Suddenly my palms began to sweat and I felt my stomach starting to do flip-flops. I asked Bob if he wouldn't like to take a train instead. He looked at me like I was a foolish child and said, "Chuck, no one takes a train when you can fly.... You're not afraid of flying, are you?" I nodded my head yes and found myself being lectured for the next twenty minutes by Bob Cummings, pilot, on the safety of air travel.

I have to admit that Bob made a pretty convincing argument for flying since he knew more about aviation than most commercial pilots. He was the first private citizen in the United States to be given a pilot's license. His love for flying came naturally. His godfather was Orville Wright, who, along with brother Wilbur, practically invented the airplane. Bob's father was a surgeon back in Joplin, and he saved Orville's life after the latter crashed his airplane in the Cumming's field. During Orville's recovery, doctor and patient became fast friends. Wilbur, the more reclusive brother, was never as close to Dr. Cummings as his outgoing brother, Orville. When Dr. and Mrs. Cummings's son was born, the doctor insisted that he be named after his airborne friend, Orville, but his wife stood firm and decided that their son should be a junior. After the birth of his son, Dr. Charles Clarence Cummings filled in the name on the birth certificate...Robert Orville Cummings. When Bob's mother realized what her husband had done she crossed out "Robert Orville" and wrote in "Charles Clarence Cummings, Jr." Over the years, in an attempt to please everyone, Bob's birth certificate finally read Charles Clarence Robert Orville Cummings. It was the perfect name for a man who had so many different personalities.

As a young man, Bob was known as Chuck Cummings. My character was, of course, named after him. He often joked that he and I looked and acted so much alike that he had to remind himself that we were not related.

The morning of our departure I arrived at the airport and nervously waited for Bob at the TWA terminal. He suddenly appeared out of nowhere, took me firmly by the arm, and escorted me onto the plane. As we buckled our seatbelts and began to taxi down the runway, Bob gave me a moment by moment commentary on the pilot's procedures. He was trying his best to make me feel comfortable as I watched the buildings below us grow smaller and smaller. Then I settled back and Bob explained in great detail that the aircraft we were flying was a Constellation, a four-engine prop plane that was the most modern and up-to-date aircraft of its day. It would fly nonstop from Los Angeles to New York City in only nine hours. Today the Concorde can fly from New York to London in about two hours, and a jet flight from Los Angeles to New York lasts only four and a half, but in 1957 our plane was state-of-the-art. Bob told me the owner of TWA was his flying buddy, Howard Hughes, and that a seat was always reserved on every TWA flight for Hughes, just in case he wanted to jump on a plane and fly somewhere.

Cummings kept his airplane at Hughes Aircraft in Culver City. One day Hughes asked to borrow Bob's plane. Bob agreed and watched it disappear into the wild blue yonder piloted by his billionaire friend. That was the last time Bob saw his plane; Hughes apparently forgot where he left it, so he bought Bob a new one. Months later, Bob's plane was discovered in a field in the Bahamas overgrown with vines and grass. Hughes borrowed people's planes in the same carefree manner that he borrowed people's cars.

As Bob recounted his aviation stories with Hughes I decided not to tell him that my mother and I had met him at the

Nite Lite diner and he had bought us lunch. My story some-how lost its excitement compared to Bob and Howard's escapades.

Just as I was starting to relax and feel the circulation return to my white knuckles, Bob announced that he was going to take a nap. No sooner had Cummings drifted off to sleep than we hit some turbulence. Bouncing around the sky, I looked to Bob for some reassurance. He opened one eye and said, "Nothing to worry about, Chuck... I had my engines stall at twenty thousand feet.... That's when you worry.... Now, get some sleep." Then he closed his eye and nodded off as we pitched and tossed our way across the United States. When we landed at Idlewild Airport, later known as Kennedy International, in New York, a very rested Bob Cummings bounced off the plane, followed by his worn-out and weary young friend.

We were met by our agents from MCA who took us to our hotel, the Savoy Plaza on Fifth Avenue at 57th Street, across from Central Park. Bob and I shared a two-bedroom suite and received the star treatment. The next morning we had break-fast, then Bob's interviews started. They would last until noon. We'd then have a luncheon interview at a fancy New York restaurant, then back to the hotel for more interviews throughout the afternoon. It was an exhausting schedule even though all I did was watch, listen, and learn. Bob felt that it was important to see everything that was playing on Broadway, so every night we went to the theater. MCA arranged for tickets, so we had the best seats in the house. We would go to dinner, where Bob instructed me that we would have one cocktail, a vodka martini, then eat a light meal and head off to a show. Just the idea of seeing a show on Broadway was impressive to me. I naturally assumed that if an actor such as Ralph Richardson, Fredric March, or Jason Robards Jr. was in a show, then it had to be great acting and wonderful theater. I was shocked when Bob didn't share my enthusiasm. It seemed like some theatrical sacrilege that he didn't think every show on Broadway was a gem. That's when Bob gave me some wonderful advice. "Chuck... don't be influenced by critical acclaim or popular opinion. Follow your own instincts.... Just because it's on

Broadway doesn't mean its' great.... It's really a case of 'The Emperor's New Clothes.'" Bob's advice was certainly true and I have found over the years that his theory applies not only to show business but to all areas of life. Don't always believe the hype; believe in your own observations and feelings and ninety-nine percent of the time you'll be right.

The next morning I went to Mass at St. Patrick's Cathedral, and when I returned to the hotel Bob suggested we take a walk through the city. It was a beautiful day, and as we strolled along, what I think must have been the length of Manhattan, Bob told me about his life and how he got started in show business. He had attended the American Academy of Dramatic Arts in New York. At that particular time British actors were the rage and this young actor from Joplin, Missouri, couldn't get a job. He got the crazy idea that he would go to England, change his name, and return to the States as a young British actor. As unbelievable as the idea seemed, it worked. Bob paid some London theater owner to put his name on the marquee, and he had his picture taken standing in front of the theater. The name on the marquee was not Robert Cummings, but his British alter ego, Blade Stanhope Conway. With his new name, fake resumé and his picture taken in front of the phony marquee, Bob sent letters to all the New York agents telling them he was arriving in the States and wanted an interview. The ploy worked. Suddenly the out-of-work American actor, Robert Cummings, was the British actor Blade Stanhope Conway, and the toast of New York.

After working for several years and doing quite well, "Blade" joined *Earl Carroll's Vanities* where he played the straight man for a hot young comic named Milton Berle. Although Berle never really believed that his sidekick was British, he never blew his cover. Their friendship lasted all of Bob's life. When British actors fell out of favor, Robert Cummings, American actor, reappeared. Bob had a successful film career, appearing in such movies as *King's Row* with Ronald Reagan, *Saboteur* for Alfred Hitchcock, and, of course, the famous *Dial M for Murder*, another Hitchcock classic.

Bob was a man with many personalities, some of which

could really get on your nerves. He was a taskmaster on the set, rehearsing over and over until the scene was perfect. He was the mentor and teacher, taking me aside and guiding me. He was also Bob the health fanatic. Each week it was a new vitamin or special health food. I must admit, Bob was ahead of his time in this area. During the 1950s when smoking was the popular vice of the day, Bob was telling anyone within earshot how cigarettes would destroy their health. This was not the politically correct attitude since R. J. Reynolds Tobacco Company sponsored *The Bob Cummings Show*. I smoked at the time and Cummings gave me a lecture every time I lit up. He was right, of course, and I eventually quit.

Many of his eccentricities were strokes of genius. Years before anyone ever thought of putting seatbelts in an automobile, Bob outfitted his car with them. He explained that every plane had seatbelts and every automobile should have them as well, since driving a car was, he felt, far more dangerous than flying in a plane.

As we walked through Manhattan, Bob gave his opinions on everything under the sun. When we returned to the hotel, I sat in my suite and thought about this very complex man. Although Bob had wanted to be a mentor to me, I found him to be a severe and harsh taskmaster. He picked on everyone in the cast to varying degrees, but when it came to me, he criticized and corrected every move I made. I don't know if it was because I was so young or because he saw in me the possibility of molding someone in his own image. Whatever the reason, he was relentless. He would pick on me until I thought I'd go crazy; then, just as I was about to explode he'd say, "That's it, Chuck.... Perfect. That's just the energy I was looking for." At that point I'd be so frustrated that I was ready to kill him.

Bob was eccentric, brilliant, vain, funny, and, at times, very distant. I certainly respected his talent, but he never gave me the opportunity to get close to him or build a friendship, and for that I will always be a little sorry.

He did, however, share one personal thing that has stayed with me after all these years. Bob said he had a credo that had been passed on to him from his godfather, Orville Wright. He had always lived by it and now he would pass it on to me. "Chuck, whenever you have a dream or desire, even if it seems outlandish and impossible, if you'll say this credo, and really believe it, your dream can come true..." He stopped and looked at me very seriously and said, "Chuck, are you listening?" I said I was. "Chuck, just say to yourself over and over, 'You can accomplish anything in the world by acting with all your heart as if it's already accomplished.'" Then he had me repeat it several times until I had committed it to memory. I may not have known Bob any better than I had before, but his credo has stuck with me for years, and when I use it I find that it always works.

The next day Bob told me that we were going to visit a doctor friend of his on the East Side of the city before our luncheon interview. As we arrived at the doctor's office I realized that it was not a social visit, but that Bob was there for what he referred to as "a treatment." While waiting for the doctor Bob explained that whenever he was in New York he would come here because this doctor was famous for his youth serums. Bob told me that he received injections from the glands of a monkey and the sperm of a sheep. I just looked at him, waiting for the punch line, then I realized that he wasn't kidding. I knew that Bob was obsessed about staying young and maintaining a youthful appearance. His hair was dyed that strange henna red and he colored his skin so that he always looked tan. During breaks in rehearsal he had a trainer who would not only massage Bob's arms, legs and back, he also specialized in massaging prostates. Bob swore that the prostate massage released some kind of endorphin that helped keep him full of energy. He offered me his trainer's services, but I felt that I had plenty of energy and I passed. I had thought I had heard everything when Bob told me about his massaged prostate, but that paled in comparison to getting injected with monkey glands and sheep sperm. When I pressed him about which glands of the monkey were used he gave a vague answer, then he was called into the examining room. As I waited for him all I could think about was some poor monkey losing his glands for some crazy youth serum. I had a pretty good idea which "glands" they were using. I also couldn't help thinking about the guy who had the job of retrieving the sperm of a sheep. The whole thing was thoroughly distasteful. About twenty minutes later Bob emerged from the inner office with a smile on his face and a bounce in his step. He introduced me to the doctor and said he would be happy to pay for a treatment if I was interested. I declined, saying that at twenty-four I felt that I had plenty of energy and all the youth that I needed. "Uncle Bob" was an amazing and very interesting fellow.

As we prepared to return to Hollywood, Bob had one final interview, but it would prove to be one of his most important. He and I had lunch with columnist Earl Wilson, and as I sat quietly, Bob talked nonstop for nearly two hours. He covered many subjects but mostly promoted our show and my pilot, *Chuck Goes to College*. Earl asked Bob about his work in films and what it was like to work with Alfred Hitchcock. Bob described in great detail *Saboteur*, his first Hitchcock movie and, of course, the popular *Dial M for Murder*. In an offhanded manner, Bob told how "Hitch" was a gourmet and how he loved good food and wine. He chuckled and said that "Hitch" would drink and fall asleep after his meal. "You know how too much wine can make you sleepy?" Earl Wilson nodded and kept taking notes.

The next day, when Wilson's column came out, the headline read, "CUMMINGS SAYS HITCHCOCK DRINKS AND FALLS ASLEEP." I couldn't believe it. Bob had talked for two hours about the show and Earl Wilson printed a throwaway comment that was taken totally out of context. When NBC got wind of the piece they were up in arms, "How could Bob insult this fine director? Didn't he realize that Hitchcock would never hire him again? What most people didn't realize is that Hitchcock wouldn't have hired him again anyway, with or without Wilson's column. Bob had already sealed his fate while he was filming *Dial M for Murder*. Hitchcock was famous for telling the actors exactly how to act in each scene. No one argued with him or ever made suggestions, and if he told you how to read a line you did as you were told. It didn't leave the actor much room for creativity, but the smart ones didn't care. They were just glad to work with him; all except Bob, who kept telling Hitchcock during *Dial M for Murder* that what the story needed was a little comedy and his character could help lighten things up. Bob was lucky Hitchcock didn't have his character murdered instead of the would-be killer Grace Kelly stabbed with the scissors. His suggestions on comedy were met with a very icy reception by the famous director. After the film was finished, Bob could be assured that he would never see, much less work with, Alfred Hitchcock again.

We spent the last day in New York shopping and that night boarded what is now referred to as the "red eye." In those days they had sleeping berths in first class and, just like a train, the berths were stacked one above the other. Bob had the bottom berth and I ended up on top. If I thought I hated flying by day strapped in my seat, that wasn't anything compared to the terror I felt as I lay down on this shelf and buckled the belt across my chest. No sooner had I said goodnight to Bob and laid down than we hit some turbulence. Suddenly it was like being strapped onto a roller coaster that never stopped. I was frightened to death, and judging by the screams and prayers being said by my fellow passengers, I wasn't alone in my fears. The plane was dropping and pitching so violently that had I not been belted in I would have hit the top of the plane as we would suddenly drop several hundred feet. The pitching, tossing, dropping, and bouncing continued throughout the night. The poor stewardess kept running up and down the aisles attending to airsick passengers and bringing the faint of heart, like me, smelling salts. I would have been better off if I had fainted; at least I could have gotten some rest. As it was, I never closed my eyes.

Hours later we made our descent into Los Angeles and finally landed. I unbelted myself and slipped out of my bunk onto very weak knees, as a rested and relaxed Cummings was standing there to greet me. When I commented on our flight from hell, he told me that he hadn't been the least bit concerned and had slept well. I gave him an incredulous look;

no one in his right mind could have slept through that turbulence. As Bob leaned over to pick up his bag I noticed that he had a cut on the top of his head. Apparently during last night's roller coaster ride my sleeping friend has sustained an injury. When I asked him if he had been hurt, he said that it was just a small cut and a stewardess had cleaned it for him with a little alcohol. What Bob didn't realize—and what neither his attending stewardess nor I told him—was that the alcohol had taken all the dye out of that spot on his head. I wasn't suppose to know he dyed his hair, so I didn't see how I could tell him that he had a big white patch on the top of his head without embarrassing him. So I never said a word about it and climbed into my limo and said goodbye. New York and Bob Cummings had been quite an adventure, and I was glad to be home.

We had been back from our East Coast trip a few weeks when we got the word that all three networks had passed on my pilot. Cummings, Paul Henning, and George Burns took it in stride, but I was really upset. Paul told me that I had learned a valuable lesson, "Never count on anything as a sure thing in show business...and especially in television." He went on to say that if a show had a likable star, a good premise, and seemed like the kind of show the public would watch, the networks, in their infinite wisdom, would usually pass on it. Paul said the networks put on what *they* wanted, not what the public wanted. Years later, when I went to work for a network, I realized that Paul's words were as true today as they were in the late 1950s.

With the pilot *Chuck Goes to College* behind me I settled back into *The Bob Cummings Show*. Most of the teen stars on television were starting to follow in Ricky Nelson's footsteps and becoming rock-and-roll singers. Connie Stevens, Tab Hunter, and Edd Byrnes ("Kookie, Kookie, Lend Me Your Comb") were cutting records.

ABC-Paramount Records approached me about launching my rock-and-roll career. Cummings and Paul Henning thought it would be great for the show, so, after being pushed by them and the record company, I reluctantly agreed. After signing my recording contract, I started taking singing lessons with a very patient lady name Sandy Oliver. I didn't have much faith in my singing ability, but I figured that if I took two lessons a week and practiced day and night, somehow my hard work would make up for my lack of talent. My producer at ABC-Paramount was a talented guy named Don Costa. After my singing career died, Don went on to become a very successful composer and arranger, but at this point he was in charge of producing my record. He came up with a rock-and-roll song called "School Dance" that was supposed to be my ticket to fame and fortune.

We were set to record "School Dance" at Capitol Records on Vine Street in Hollywood. The music business was foreign to me, and I never really understood it. The recording session was scheduled for 8 P.M., but when I objected and told Costa that I'd rather record during the day, he looked at me like I was crazy. Apparently musicians are night people. No one recorded during the day.

I got to the recording session early, hoping to practice my song a few times before the orchestra arrived, and by eight the musicians starting wandering in. Most of them were scruffy guys who didn't look like they had the price of a ham sandwich. Each musician picked up his sheet music, which he had never laid eyes on, and after quickly running through it a few times, played it perfectly. I started to panic; I was in fast company and I knew it. We began to rehearse and I was so blown away by the musicians' great sound I missed my cue. They stopped playing and just looked at me like, "Wake up, buddy, this is where you come in!" After a bumpy run-through, Don Costa decided to lay one down. There is an excitement that fills the room when the musicians are hot and the singer takes off and everything comes together; at least that's what I've been told. Nothing anywhere near that happened during the "School Dance" recording session. The musicians were wonderful, but I couldn't get through the song to save my life. After about the fifth take, the musicians were starting to look at one another and roll their eyes. Don Costa was having a fit because we had been in the studio an hour with these highly paid union musicians and we hadn't recorded a note. He called a break and everyone went outside to smoke and gossip with the other musicians who were recording down the hall with Frank Sinatra. It was like a party with his gophers running here and there and his musicians talking and laughing with my musicians.

While they swapped stories about "Ol' Blue Eyes," my guys were bemoaning the fact that they were wasting their time with some dummy kid who couldn't carry a tune. When the break was over, we all reassembled in the studio and I apologetically stumbled through yet another unsuccessful take. I had a terrible time keeping the beat and I just couldn't stay on key. For some reason, Steve Lawrence was in the booth listening to my session. He was probably taking a break from recording one of his albums and needed a good laugh. When I looked up and saw him, he gave me a half-hearted smile and a thumbs-up. I've never been so embarrassed, but, little did I know that my greatest humiliation lay ahead of me. After about the tenth take Don Costa spoke over the loud speaker and told the musicians that it was obvious that I wasn't going to be able to do the song and that they were going to record the music so I could sing to it at a later time. The musicians murmured something like. "It's about time..." and then the orchestra laid down a perfect recording of "School Dance" in one take. Several days later I returned to the studio to do the vocal and it turned out to be an engineer's nightmare because I never completed one whole song. They had to splice together pieces of thirty different takes to come up with the final recording. In case you're not one of the few people who bought "School Dance," let me just say that it was a typical 1950s rock-and-roll song, and if Ricky Nelson or Fabian had made the record it might have been a big hit, but for me it was a bomb.

Since they had dropped a bundle on "School Dance," the record company decided to send me on a low budget—and I do mean low budget—five city tour to promote the record. They had assigned a gruff old guy from New York to accompany me on the trip. Actually, it was his job to drive the car and try to get as much air time as possible on all the local radio stations. The tour lasted a week, but by the third day I was ready to call it quits. The days were long, the motels were dreary, and I didn't have a heart for it. All I wanted to do was go home and try to put this entire episode behind me. My crusty companion and I were really getting on one another's nerves. I knew we were going nowhere with "School Dance," yet every time any radio station in the middle of nowhere wanted a live interview, off we would go, no matter what hour of the day or night. It seemed the only deejays interested in playing my record or interviewing me were working the graveyard shift. As upset and depressed as I was, the poor old guy driving me around must have wondered what his career had come to, being stuck with some kid who couldn't sing a note.

The high point of this grand tour was supposed to be my appearance on the hottest, hippest teen show on television. Dick Clark's *American Bandstand* was the show that helped launch the careers of such artists as Chubby Checker, Frankie Avalon, Buddy Holly, and every hot young singer in the business. Standing backstage watching the other performers, I knew I was in over my head. Any ounce of self-confidence flew out the window as I watched the slick, hip, young heartthrobs talk and joke around. They didn't have a moment's concern about going on stage to sing and trying to stay on key. Singing in a recording studio is one thing, but performing on TV in front of a million or so people is more humiliation than one person can take. Before the show started the assistant director came backstage and posted the running order of the show. I held my breath as I prayed that I would not be the opening act. My prayer was answered, barely; I was the second act on the show. The singer who went on before me was a South Philly homeboy named Frankie Avalon. Handsome and self-assured, Frankie wowed the crowd. Girls screamed and swooned as he danced around, singing his hit song, "De De Dinah." He was so relaxed and in charge I almost forgot that he was lip-syncing the record. I looked at him dressed in his bright red jacket, white pants, and white shoes, then I looked at myself in the backstage mirror in my gray herringbone sport coat, dark gray slacks, and black wing-tip shoes. Frankie looked like a rock-and-roll heartthrob; I looked like a fifty-year-old bank teller.

How would I ever follow him? Frankie finished his song to deafening applause and screams, then he bounced off stage, flashed a perfect pearly white smile, and said, "I warmed them up for you, they're all yours." Sweat began to break out on my upper lip, and before I could think of some hip response I could hear Dick Clark giving me a flowery introduction. Suddenly I was on stage.

Looking out into the sea of screaming excited teens, I thought for a fleeting moment that maybe I had been too hard on myself, maybe I was just as much a teen singing sensation as this slick Avalon fellow. As the music started I tried to bounce around the stage and be loose like Frankie. I was only into the song a few bars when I could tell that I was already a few words behind. I could hear my recorded voice booming across the stage but my mouth was so out of synch that I looked like Charlie McCarthy. My lips kept flapping away but I just couldn't catch up. I also noticed that all the screaming had ceased and the once frenetic teens were just staring at me as I tried to desperately get back in sync, while continuing to bounce around to the beat. I thought the song would never end.

The heat of the lights combined with my nervous, nonstop bobbing around had left me drenched in sweat. Actually it's what performers call "flop sweat." It happens when you're out there trying your best but the act is dying and the audience can't wait until you get off stage. Finally my song was over and I finished to lukewarm applause. Even the ever-pleasant Dick Clark gave me a "Forget it, buddy" look. "School Dance" and I were a big flop. When I got backstage, the other performers smiled and gave me a halfhearted "Nice work." This tour was becoming a torture test. As if this appearance on *American Bandstand* wasn't humiliation enough, I was scheduled to join Dick Clark two days later on the Saturday night version of the show in New York City, but first I was to meet with the president of ABC-Paramount Records in New York.

I had hardly recovered from my *Bandstand* appearance when I walked into the plush offices of Sam Clark. He asked me how the tour was going and I plastered a stiff toothy smile on my face and lied, "Oh, just great, Mr. Clark." He told me that he wanted to listen to my record and, if I didn't mind, get an opinion from this kid singer from Canada who had just had a big hit called "Diana." The "kid" was Paul Anka. Paul walked into the room and Sam Clark hailed him like a long-lost son. Anka hardly glanced my way as Sam put my record on the stereo, a state-of-the-art sound system. There must have been six large speakers around the room, so no matter where you turned you could hear every note and every word of the record. "School Dance" started to play and Paul walked over to one of the speakers and listened intently. Neither Sam nor I were listening; we were both watching Anka for his reaction. I hadn't sung eight bars before Anka slowly began to shake his head from side to side, as if to say "Not a chance." Then, without a word, he turned and walked out. I was mortified. Sam Clark looked at me like I was a bug. I stood there not knowing what to say. The silence was only broken by my pathetic, slightly sharp singing that filled his office. My fate had been sealed with Sam Clark and ABC-Paramount Records.

I had only one more appearance with Dick Clark and then I could escape back to California. This was the nighttime version of *American Bandstand* and I don't know if it had anything to do with my appearance on the daytime version two days before, but this time I wasn't asked to sing. All I had to do was sit in the audience and chat with Dick Clark. As I waited to go on, I thought about the past week and all the interviews, the endless hours spent in the car with my morose and dreary record promoter, the humiliating moments on *American Bandstand*, and, of course, auditioning my record for Paul Anka. As I replayed the moments in my mind, something clicked inside me. It was the same kind of moment that I had experienced years before at the Pasadena Playhouse as a kid when I read my lousy reviews. My survival instincts suddenly kicked in. I looked around and thought, "What's the matter with me? What do I care if I can't sing like the rest of these guys? I'm an actor and a good comedy actor. I wonder how well these guys would do if you handed them a script and told them to go onstage and do the jokes." My pep talk seemed to work, because by the time I was about to go onstage I was totally calm. I was standing backstage when the great Fats Domino came over and introduced himself. Warm, friendly, and very funny, he was having a drink and offered me some of his Scotch. I thanked him but said I didn't care for any, then I said, "Hey, Fats, where were you two days ago when I needed you?" He had no idea what I was talking about. The stage manager came over and told me it was time to join Dick Clark, so during the commercial break I made my way into the audience and sat down. Dick and I were to chat about the record, then do a comedy bit blowing out candles on a birthday cake. The comedy was suppose to come from the fact that as much as we blew on the candles they wouldn't go out. The big moment came, but the bit didn't work because all of the candles went out; not one remained burning. Clark looked stunned, and I made some smart adlib like, "Well, this was really a funny idea." Dick wasn't amused, and since my remark was not in the script, he just looked at me. When the show was over, my grumpy companion drove me to the airport and I flew back to Los Angeles. This was one of the few times in my life that I looked forward to getting on a plane.

I had learned a valuable lesson. Everyone has something he does well. Dick Clark is unsurpassed as host, deejay, and master of ceremonies, but he's no comedian. I was a good comedian and had learned my craft with the best, but I would never be a singer, much less a rock-'n'-roll star.

As I flew home, I tried to put it all in perspective. By the time the plane touched down in Los Angeles, I breathed a sigh of relief that I had survived my rock-'n'-roll nightmare.

· FIVE ·

HOT CARS, COLD GIRLS, AND FAST COMPANY

WHEN I RETURNED FROM MY TOUR, I went back to work on *The Bob Cummings Show.* Even though my recording career had failed, I was still a popular teen actor, and I was always doing publicity layouts with young starlets for the current crop of movie magazines. I had begun to settle into my life as a working actor and found myself enjoying the hard work as well as the benefits. Under Cummings's watchful eye my work was getting smoother and my confidence was growing. For the first time in my life I was earning a lot of money, at least by the late 1950s standards, and I was seeing the distinct possibility that I could have a successful career as an actor. My personal life was also improving as I began dating some of the young actresses who guest-starred on the show, as well as girls outside the business. Kitty Wellman was a young actress whose father was the famous director William Wellman, for whom I had worked as a child in the movie, *The Happy Years*. The Wellmans had a house full of children and lived on a mini-estate in Brentwood, and going to the Wellmans was like visiting the Kennedy family. Everyone was very athletic, and outgoing, and the house was always alive with activity. Kitty and I dated occasionally and I always enjoyed visiting and listening to her father's colorful stories. She later married actor James Franciscus and had several children. We still run into one another from time to time.

While visiting the *Burns and Allen* set, I met an actress named Judi Meredith. We saw each other a few times, but neither of us felt any sparks flying, so we gave up dating but remained good friends. Judi was then seen around town with Frank Sinatra, and several weeks later I got a call from a friend who asked me if I had seen the latest issue of *Photoplay*, the hot movie magazine. He suggested I get down to the nearest drugstore and pick up a copy. When I got to the magazine rack, there on the cover of *Photoplay* was a picture of my friend Judi Meredith and, on either side of her, was me and Frank Sinatra, with the heading: JUDI'S LOVE TRIANGLE. I thought how ridiculous it was that anyone could think that I could possibly be a rival to Frank Sinatra. Apparently, Judi's publicist thought that he could get a lot of mileage out of this fabricated story. It was lucky for Ol' Blue Eyes that Judi never heard me sing "School Dance" or he never would have had a chance!

I started dating a pretty brunette, Kay Diebel, who was a student at Immaculate Heart College. Kay had a fleeting brush with show business but decided to pursue a far more sensible line of work as a dental hygienist. I was crazy about Kay, but unfortunately her feelings toward me were less than enthusiastic.

We had been out several times and on one particular evening decided to double-date with a young actor and his wife, Jerry and Ruth Paris. Jerry, who had been a friend of mine for years, got his first big break on television as the next door neighbor, dentist Jerry Helper, on *The Dick Van Dyke Show*. He later went on to direct many shows, including the series, *Happy Days*, and a couple of *Police Academy* films. Jerry, Ruth, Kay and I decided to have dinner down on the Santa Monica Pier in a local hot spot called Chez Jay's. After a few drinks and a large seafood dinner, one of us got the great idea to go down to Pacific Ocean Park which is now long gone, and ride their enormous wooden roller coaster. We piled into the roller coaster cars and were catapulted out over the dark Pacific Ocean. If one ride seemed fun, four more rides sounded even better. We laughed and screamed as we turned upside down and dropped at zero G's into space.

The evening wound down, Jerry and Ruth waved good-bye and drove home, as Kay and I got into my car and proceeded to drive the winding Sunset Boulevard from the beach all the way to Kay's home in the San Fernando Valley. We hadn't driven very far when my stomach began to pitch and roll. I tried to ignore the fact that my lobster dinner was percolating up and down as I made small talk with my date, but the more I fought it the worse it got. I clinched my teeth and tried some deep breathing. Kay looked over at me and said, "Dwayne, are you okay?" I shook my head "Yes," not daring to open my mouth. "Are you sure...? You don't look very well." That was all I needed to hear. I pulled the car over, jumped out, and got sick. If you want to impress a girl who seems a little aloof, losing your dinner on Sunset Boulevard is not the way to do it. I tried to appear as suave and nonchalant as possible when I returned to the car, but my chances of a relationship with Kay were over. Several days passed and I didn't hear from her, so I called her and said, "I thought you'd at least call and see how I was doing?" She told me that she knew I was all right, then sarcastically suggested I give up riding roller coasters. I hung up and decided that I was hitting my head against a brick wall; after all, next week there would be another girl to date. I didn't see Kay for a couple of years. When we met again, she was married to that hip slick singer from my *American Bandstand* show, none other than Frankie Avalon. Whenever I'd see Kay over the years, she'd always take great delight in reminding me of the night I lost my lobster dinner on Sunset Boulevard.

Maria Cooper and I had remained friends since our first date, when she was sixteen. More platonic than romantic, our relationship continued even though I dated other girls. On one occasion, Maria invited me to be her date at a party her parents were having at their new home on Baroda Drive in Holmby

Hills. Shortly after our first date the Coopers had sold their large home in Brentwood and had given the adjacent acreage to the Catholic church, St. Martin of Tours. Their new home was an architect's dream, with walls of glass from floor to ceiling and a fireplace in the middle of the living room, surrounded by a pool of water. With a roaring fire the reflection of the flames on the water gave the expected dramatic effect.

The party was a black-tie affair, and the guest list was like a Who's Who of Hollywood: Clark Gable and his wife, Kay Spreckles; Cyd Charisse and Tony Martin; Jimmy Stewart and his wife, Gloria; Rosalind Russell and husband Frederick Brisson; and, of course, Gary and "Rocky" Cooper. The women were dressed in elegant evening gowns, and the men were attired in tuxedos. Cyd Charisse wore a breathtaking emerald green gown with a plunging neckline, and I thought she was one of the most beautiful, sophisticated women I had ever seen. The party was going strong, with Gary Cooper playing the bongo drums, and everyone dancing and having a great time. The moat around the fireplace was quite a conversation piece, but, unfortunately, such an architectural masterpiece can be impractical and sometimes dangerous. Around the water was a small hearth that came up from the floor about six inches. It was an accident waiting to happen, and Rosalind Russell was at the wrong place at the right time. She was standing talking to Kay Gable with her back to the fireplace, and as she stepped backward, she tripped over the small hearth and fell into the water. The pool around the fireplace was only about a foot deep, but she was soaked. Fortunately, she wasn't hurt. Cooper and I ran over to fish her out, and it was no easy job because her sequined gown was water-logged and weighed a ton. Always the good sport, Rosalind disappeared with "Rocky" Cooper and, moments later, rejoined the party wearing a pair of "Rocky's" tennis shorts and a blouse. The entire party went on as if nothing happened. When the evening ended and everyone headed home, Rosalind kissed the Coopers good-bye and the maid handed her a plastic bag that contained her soggy, sequined evening gown. The expensive gown was probably ruined, but Rosalind didn't give it a thought.

Several weeks later, in true Cummings fashion, Bob gathered us around the table on the stage to make an announcement. These announcements could be about anything from his critique of the latest movie to vitamins and health food or to his latest brainstorm. On this particular day it was about his decision to do a play called *Holiday for Lovers*. He informed us that his good friend Frank Hale, a very wealthy Palm Beach businessman, had built a beautiful new playhouse and Bob was going to open the theater. He would star in it, of course. Joining him would be an old friend of his, the actress Julie Bishop. He and Julie had worked together in his earlier TV series, *My Hero*. That show lasted only one season, then Bob went on to do our show. Cummings then broke the news that he wanted Ann B. Davis and me to join him. Ann would play the part of the maid, I would be the love interest for the pretty young ingénue played by Oliver Sturgess, and the role of the sexy blond would be played by Lisa Davis. She and I had been out a few times, but I was a kid in her eyes. Lisa was busy dating Michael Rennie, the tall, sophisticated British actor who starred as a spaceman in the science fiction thriller, *The Day the Earth Stood Still*. Since Rennie was in his late forties and I was in my early twenties, it wasn't really a big surprise that Lisa looked at me like I was her kid brother. The play sounded like a fun idea, and certainly anything you did with Bob had the potential of becoming an adventure.

We started rehearsals right away because we had only two weeks before we were to fly to Palm Beach. Our TV show was on a hiatus, so we spent long days at Bob's house in Beverly Hills rehearsing, rehearsing, rehearsing. All the preparation paid off, because by the time we boarded the plane for Palm Beach the show was in very good shape.

We arrived around midnight and headed to the Royal Poinciana Hotel which was next door to the new playhouse. Exhausted, we all headed to our rooms and right to bed. The next morning we all met for breakfast and were given our rehearsal schedule for the next week. The play would open in five days and run for a week. Two weeks in Palm Beach sounds like a working vacation, but when you are in a show with Bob Cummings, it's all work and very little vacation. We rehearsed from early morning to early evening, then we ate dinner and went to bed, so none of us saw the warm Florida sunshine for the first five days. Who had any energy left for an exciting nightlife? And, believe me, Palm Beach, the millionaires' playground, had a very exciting nightlife.

The opening night of the Royal Poinciana Playhouse was one of the big social events of the season. Everybody who was anybody turned out. Names in the audience read like a list from the *Fortune 500* as the Vanderbilts, Fords, Dodges, Whitneys, Rockefellers, and lesser-known millionaires filled the spectacular new theatre.

Backstage, Cummings was nervously running around checking every last detail. He came into my dressing room to check on me. As he stuck his head through the door, I had to stifle a laugh. Bob had overdone his stage makeup so much that he looked like a clown. Dark tan skin, rosy cheeks, red lips, and so much white around his eyes that they nearly popped off his face. He was horrified when he saw me. "Chuck, look at you, where's your makeup?" When I tried to explain that I was fully made up, Bob cut me off and grabbed up a sponge and started working on me. He told me that I would bleach out and look pasty under the hot stage lights, so he started packing the makeup on my already madeup face. By the time he finished I looked as foolish as he did, then Bob checked his watch and ran out to find his next victim. I wiped off as much as I dared and headed for the stage. The play ran without a hitch. We were all so well rehearsed we could have done the play in the parking lot and it would have been a smashing success. After the show, Frank Hale had arranged a reception for the cast and invited the wealthy patrons. For those of us who were not to the manor born, rubbing shoulders with America's wealthy, beautiful people was an eye-opening experience. The Palm Beach crowd was divided into two groups; those who were born into wealth and never had to work a day in their life, known as "Trust Fund Babies," and those who made a career out of hanging around, and if they were lucky enough, marrying one of those fabulously wealthy people. The older women, dripping in diamonds and furs, were escorted by their handsome young husbands, and older wealthy men were sporting sexy young wives wearing designer gowns and flashing lots of cleavage.

Making my way through the crowd, I was introduced to a sexy, leggy ex-showgirl named Greg Sherwood Dodge. She was married to a fabulously wealthy man named Horace Dodge, of the Phelps/Dodge fortune. Horace, who was at least twenty years her senior, was in ill health and at home in bed. He had drunk and nearly partied himself to death; apparently life with Greg was too much for him. She was beautiful and full of fun and seemed to take an interest in me. When she invited me back to her house, I looked at this gorgeous woman in her evening gown, rock-size diamonds, and floor-length fur coat, and suddenly felt very overwhelmed. I didn't want to insult her, so I told her that I'd love to join her and asked if I could bring along a friend. She reluctantly agreed, so I grabbed Lisa Davis, our resident sexpot from the show to be my chaperone. We jumped into Greg's Lincoln Continental and drove off into the warm, balmy night. When Greg turned the car into the crushed shell driveway, Lisa and I just looked at one another in amazement as we pulled up in front of the most incredible estate I had ever seen. The house was an enormous Mediterranean Villa named Casa...something, with a yard that stretched as far as you could see. It was after one A.M. as Greg threw open the front door and led us through the house and out to the enormous pool and guest house. She turned on the stereo full blast, grabbed me, and started dancing around the pool. After a few spins and dips—Greg was leading, I was following—she announced that we should all have breakfast. We trooped into the kitchen where I thought we would throw together some eggs or make a sandwich. Obviously that's not how it's done in Palm Beach. Greg said, "I'll be right back," and went into the housekeeper's bedroom and woke up the woman and her husband, who was the butler, and told them to make breakfast.

Lisa and I were mortified as the bleary-eyed, bathrobed couple proceeded to fix ham, eggs, toast, coffee, and pastry as we retreated to the pool to be served. I profusely apologized to the butler as he brought me my breakfast, but he didn't seem upset; apparently this was business as usual. By now it was after three A.M., and Lisa and I were exhausted. I told Greg I needed to call a cab to get back to the hotel. "Nonsense, my chauffeur will take you back," she said. Within minutes, the bleary-eyed driver appeared and we said good night to Greg and headed back to the hotel.

The next few nights Greg came to the show and after the curtain, Lisa and I would join her as she took us party-hopping. I had always heard about the idle rich, but now I was seeing it first hand. Their days were filled with tennis, sailing, polo, and shopping; then they would rest up for the night's work of nonstop partying. One night we went to a party at the famous restaurant Nino's Continental, where I met an older woman in her late seventies named Dolly. She wore more jewelry than I had ever seen in my life. She had large dangling earrings, bracelets running up both arms, rings on every finger, and a necklace that had the largest diamonds and emeralds I had ever seen. In fact, the stones were so large I was sure that it had to be costume jewelry. Thinking that she must be someone's eccentric aunt, I was shocked to find out that she owned most of La Cienega Boulevard in Los Angeles. That street was known as Restaurant Row, and my new friend, Dolly, informed me that she ate free in all of the restaurants because they were all sitting on her property. She asked if I would like to be put on her board of directors so I could eat free as well, but I politely declined. When I commented on her necklace she told me that it was so heavy it gave her a headache. Then she took it off and handed it to me. She was right, it weighed a ton. Then she said, "What's the point of having all this silly stuff if you don't wear it." I nodded politely, then checked my cheap Timex watch to see how soon I could get out of there and back to the hotel to get some sleep. These people were really beginning to get on my nerves. Two days before our show closed, Greg told me that she wanted to throw a party for me at her home. She promised that it would be just a small affair with a few friends enjoying a little music and dinner. I had seen enough of Palm Beach to know that would mean one hundred people, a twenty piece orchestra, and a twelve-course meal. I thanked her, but begged off.

By the time we boarded the plane to head back to Los Angeles I had experienced enough of the lifestyles of the rich and famous to last me the rest of my life. I think all of us at some point have wished that we were so wealthy that we'd never have to work another day or ever worry about money. But once you have the opportunity to see firsthand the way they live, you quickly realize that it really isn't what it's cracked up to be. Empty days filled with mindless playtime followed by endless nights of partying with hangers-on leaves a person bored and unfulfilled. No one has the satisfaction of accomplishing anything worthwhile or even having a goal to work toward. Instead of envy, I felt very sorry for many of the people I met.

I never saw or spoke to Greg Dodge after leaving Palm Beach. Years later I read that her husband, Horace, had died and she was in bad financial straits; apparently, what had seemed to be an ever-flowing fountain of money had dried up. I felt very sorry for Greg; who, unfortunately, got caught up in a self-indulgence that eventually ruined her life.

With the winter hiatus over and Palm Beach a memory, I plunged back into work on *The Bob Cummings Show*. I had always loved cars and had planned to buy myself something special when my career was established.

When Bob and I had been on our New York trip a few months earlier, I had dropped into a Mercedes-Benz dealership in the heart of Manhattan. The Mercedes was not the popular car it is today, so when a youthful celebrity came in, the owner of the dealership decided that it was a perfect photo opportunity and a great way to market the car toward young people. After I returned home I was sent a copy of the picture of me and the sporty Mercedes 190SL that was going to be used in an ad campaign. For weeks I kept looking at the picture and imagining myself driving around town in the fabulous sports car.

Gary Cooper had been a car enthusiast and when I had admired his Mercedes and told him that I would love to have a car like his, he said that if I kept working in television he was sure that I would. After four years of the TV series I felt that the time had come to take the plunge and I bought my black Mercedes-Benz 190SL with red leather interior. I paid $5,700 for that car, which was a lot of money for an automobile in 1958. But, for me, the purchase of this car represented more than owning a luxury automobile; it represented my hard work, a sense of independence, and a personal pride in what I had achieved on my own.

A few days later I had a date with Maria and when I drove up the driveway, Mr. Cooper was near the garage working on one of his cars. He looked up as this strange vehicle pulled up in front of his house. When I jumped out, a smile broke across his face and he came over to congratulate me and said that he was proud of me for buying the car. "Sometimes you just have to do something special for yourself." Then we went over every inch of it, and as I lifted the hood we both looked at the clean motor and the precision workmanship with almost a hushed reverence.

Everything in my life seemed to be great. My role in *The Bob Cummings Show* was bigger than ever. I was making more money than I had in the past, and as I tooled around town in my 190SL I felt like I was really on my way. I was dating a lot of different girls, including Maria, who was more friend than girlfriend. Up until then I had a few crushes, but I had not met anyone I was really head over heels in love with. That was soon to change.

During rehearsal of one of the shows, I met a cute, blond actress who was playing the role of a nurse. From the moment we met, Dorothy Provine and I clicked. She was funny, charming, smart, and sensitive, and I was crazy about her. We quickly became an item around town, and, as two young stars, we were a publicist's dream. We attended openings and parties and did photo layouts that were splashed across all of the movie magazines. With my work on the series filling up my days and Dorothy's guest appearances on shows keeping her busy, we had to grab every spare minute that we could find. On weekends we'd jump into my Mercedes and drive out to the beach or up the coast to Santa Barbara. I felt like the luckiest guy in the world as I drove along with Dorothy by my side.

The Bob Cummings Show went on its hiatus and I looked forward to a relaxing summer with Dorothy, when I got a call from my manager, Ted Wick. He told me that Leo McCarey was directing a movie starring Paul Newman and Joanne Woodward. It was called *Rally Round the Flag, Boys!* and there was a wonderful role of the young lead that I was perfect for. A few days later the casting director drove me out to the backlot of Twentieth Century-Fox Studio where they were already shooting. As we arrived, McCarey was directing a scene with Joanne Woodward and a three-year-old boy. It was the child's close-up, and his line was, "It's a T-Bird!" and the youngster stumbled through take after take. Watching McCarey work with him, I realized why he had such a wonderful reputation as a children's director. Instead of calling "Cut," after every blown line and starting over with "Action!" McCarey let the film keep rolling as he gently talked the child through the scene. Joanne Woodward was very gentle as well, giving the child his cue again and again and again. The only time they stopped shooting was to reload another magazine of film. Finally, the small boy gave the perfect reading. McCarey yelled "Cut!" and then he hugged the youngster, who happily ran off to play. He had created as little stress and pressure on his pint-size actor as possible.

Leo McCarey had started in the movie business in the 1920s, first as a writer, then as a director. He did many of the Laurel and Hardy films, as well as the Marx Brothers movies, including my personal favorite, *Duck Soup*. His later credits included such classics as *The Awful Truth*, with Cary Grant and Irene Dunne; *Going My Way*, with Bing Crosby; and *An Affair to Remember*, with Grant and the lovely Deborah Kerr.

I approached McCarey, and introduced myself, and the casting director told him that I was being considered for the role of Grady Metcalfe. McCarey chatted with me for a few moments about my work, then he excused himself and went on to direct the next scene. The casting director and I watched as they continued to film, but at this point I was starting to feel very unnecessary and foolish just hanging around. I was really disappointed because I had wanted the part and the oppor-tunity to work with McCarey, so I said good-bye and headed back to my car. As I started to drive away, the casting director came running over, waving his arms and yelling for me to wait. Breathless, he stuck his head in the car window and said, "I talked to Mr. McCarey and he says you're perfect for the part.... You got it!" I was thrilled and a little confused because McCarey hadn't heard me read one word of dialogue. I later found out that he relied on his gut feeling and a sixth sense that he had developed after working with hundreds of actors over the years.

I got a call from one of the producers who wanted to know if I knew how to ride a motorcycle. I told him that I didn't, so I spent the next two weeks working with a stunt driver learning to ride a Harley-Davidson. Every day the stunt man would have me driving all over the backlot until riding that big motorcycle was second nature. My character, Grady Metcalfe, was a rich kid who lived in a small eastern town called Putnam's Landing. His idea of rebelling and being "one of the in-crowd" was to dress in black leather from head to toe and ride a big Harley-Davidson. Marlon Brando was very hot at the time, having starred in *The Wild One*, and he was the current measure of what was cool. I thought that it would be fun to have Grady walk, talk, and act just like his hero, Marlon Brando. It gave the character an added dimension and a bigger than life quality.

Rally 'Round the Flag Boys! was written by Max Shulman, who was famous for his books of short stories, including *The Many Loves of Dobie Gillis*. Fate was steering me toward Dobie, but at that point I had never heard of Dobie Gillis. Max had written a script for *Rally*, but the studio wasn't happy with it, so they hired another writer to rewrite Max. This made him extremely upset and he walked away from the movie. By the time I arrived, Max was long gone, so our paths didn't cross until later that year.

The stars of the show were Paul Newman and his wife, Joanne Woodward. *Rally* would be one of Paul's first comedies. Both Newman and Woodward were New York actors, having trained at the Actors Studio. Strangely enough, I didn't feel nervous or the least bit intimidated. I had been playing comedy for four years with Bob Cummings, and I had created a character in Grady Metcalfe that I felt comfortable with. Bob had been a wonderful teacher, and now that I had an opportunity to work on my own I realized just how much I had learned.

My girlfriend in the movie was played by a sultry blond teen model from New York, Tuesday Weld. It would only be a short time before Tuesday would become Thalia Menninger to my Dobie Gillis, but for now she played Comfort Goodpasture; Max Shulman always came up with great names. Tuesday was only fifteen, yet somehow she seemed more like thirty, and her mother was on the set every day keeping an eye on her worldly and sophisticated daughter.

Tuesday wasn't the only beauty on the set. A gorgeous brunette from England, Joan Collins, rounded out the cast, and I do mean rounded out. She was the most sultry, sexy woman I had ever seen, and although Joan and I were the same age, she seemed much older and more sophisticated. She always dated older men, and every day she would tell me about some studio executive who wanted to sleep with her. I didn't tell her that the thought had crossed my mind, too, but she was far too intimidating for me to do anything about it. Joan had done a lot of film work in England prior to coming to Hollywood, and I had seen her in one of her recent films, *Land of the Pharaohs*, and thought she was breathtaking. She also had a good sense of comedy and, along with Jack Carson, added a wonderful eccentric quality to the movie.

Although Tuesday was much younger, I didn't have much luck with her either. I drove her home a few times and when I suggested that we go out on a date, Tuesday responded with a curt no. Then I made the mistake of pressing her for a reason. She rolled her eyes and said, "For heaven's sake, don't be such a simpleton.... Can't you see that you're too young for me.... And anyway, you act like a farmer." Tuesday always did have an endearing way about her. She was born to play Thalia Menninger. It probably served me right; I was dating Dorothy Provine and shouldn't have been looking around, but you can't blame a guy for trying.

Since I wasn't making any headway with Joan Collins or Tuesday Weld, I must have been diverting all my energy into the movie, and it seemed to be paying off.

One morning in the makeup trailer, Paul Newman came up to me and said that he had seen my work in dailies and it was really terrific. I was thrilled by his compliment and later that day Joanne also offered her praises. Leo McCarey was the kind of director who left you alone and gave you very little direction. The only drawback to this style is that you wonder if what you are doing is working. Apparently it was, and as I look back I'm sure if Mr. McCarey hadn't liked it he would have told me. I was used to working with Cummings, who suggested every move and talked an actor through every scene, always giving immediate feedback.

On the days we didn't shoot, Joan, Tuesday, and I reported to a rehearsal hall to go over the "Putnam's Landing Fourth of July Pageant Indian Dance." The choreographer was the famous LeRoy Prinz, and he had his work cut out for him. For hours he would rehearse the three of us, along with nearly fifty extras. I would practice the steps over and over, but it seemed that I danced about as well as I sang, which meant I was in big trouble. During breaks I would go out and dust off my Mercedes, Joan would be constantly on the phone, setting up appointments and dates, and Tuesday would sit around, bored to death. She told me I acted like a little old man, fiddling with my stupid car. You could always count on Tuesday to tell you what you didn't want to hear.

After a week of rehearsals, Leo McCarey and his cinematographer, the veteran Leon Shamroy, came up to watch us perform. I flailed my arms and bounced on one foot and the other, giving my best imitation of a dancing Indian. We all passed the test, and the next two days we shot the sequence. It was quite a production number, with hundreds of extras performing and fireworks exploding everywhere. As they set up to do my closeup with the exploding fireworks, I told McCarey that I thought this could be very dangerous. Annoyed, he looked at me and said, "Don't worry, kid, if anything happens to you I'll see that you get a Purple Heart." Everyone laughed...I didn't. When Paul Newman wanted to do his own stunt and climb to the top of the mast of a sinking ship, McCarey refused, telling him that he didn't want to have Paul take the risk and hurt himself. Since McCarey didn't show me the same concern, apparently I was expendable!

During one of the complicated camera moves I walked over to Leon Shamroy and jokingly said, "Hey, Leon, if you need any help with the shot, just let me know." He looked at me like I was nuts. I probably was nuts, because Leon was not only considered the best cameraman in the business, but also the meanest grouch who ever lived. The first words every actor heard when they came onto the set was "Stay away from Shamroy!" So I was lucky he didn't jump off the camera and punch me. After *Rally* he went on to film *Cleopatra*, with Elizabeth Taylor and Richard Burton. Years later he came by the *Dobie Gillis* set and seemed almost pleasant.

My experience on *Rally 'Round the Flag Boys!* had been an exciting break from the routine of doing a weekly television series. After a movie, actors usually go their separate ways, and many times you never see an actor or actress again for years. That was not the case for me and Tuesday. We were destined to be together again. Within the next year the "farmer" and the worldly teenage model would be transformed into Dobie Gillis and Thalia Menninger.

· SIX ·

HI!....MY NAME IS DOBIE GILLIS

THE FIFTH SEASON OF *The Bob Cummings Show* was in production and I felt that the series was starting to wind down. I had mixed emotions about the possibility that the show's run could be over. In some ways I was ready for a new challenge and looked forward to possibly doing more film work; then, on the other hand, I felt a little nervous leaving the security of working every week with the same familiar faces.

We were only a few weeks into the season when my manager, Ted Wick, told me about a pilot they were casting at Twentieth Century-Fox, written by Max Shulman, called *The Many Loves of Dobie Gillis*. Ted felt that I would be perfect for the role of Dobie, the all-American teenager. When he submitted my name to Fox, the studio was very interested and contacted my agents. MCA promptly told then that I was busy doing *The Bob Cummings Show* and I wasn't available, so the studio took my name off of the list of possible Dobies. I should mention that my agents at MCA never bothered to ask me if I would be interested in playing Dobie or the fact that Fox had inquired about my availability.

This was a perfect example of how an agent can kill a

performer's career. Many a wonderful actor has been offered a career-making role in a movie or television show, only to have his or her agent turn down the project without ever mentioning it to the client. When Ted Wick followed up by calling Fox about their interest in me, he was shocked to discover that MCA had pulled me out of the running. Thank goodness for Ted, who quickly made a few phone calls to the producers and assured them that I was very available and very interested in playing Dobie Gillis. A few days later I had a meeting with Martin Manulis, who was the head of television for Fox, and Max Shulman, who had created the character Dobie Gillis in a series of short stories: "The Many Loves of Dobie Gillis" and "I Was a Teenage Dwarf." In 1953 MGM turned out *The Affairs of Dobie Gillis*, starring Debbie Reynolds and Bobby Van (as Dobie). I had never seen the movie and I wasn't really familiar with the character.

Max's "Dobie" chronicled the life of a teenage boy shortly after World War II. He was a slice of Americana, a middle-class "everyman" that every teenager could relate to. He was idealistic and a hopeless romantic who neglected work and studies to pursue his one passion, his search for the perfect girl.

In Shulman's books and in the MGM movie, Dobie was a college student, but for the television series he would be in high school, making the character younger and giving the show broader teenage appeal.

Originally George Burns had acquired the rights to Dobie as a project for his son Ronnie, who had become a regular on *Burns and Allen*. Max was distressed because he didn't feel that Ronnie Burns was right for the part. As hard as George pushed, no one seemed interested in a show about a teenage boy and his quest for "one soft, round, creamy, dreamy girl to call his own," so the option on the show ran out and the property reverted back to Max Shulman. For the next two years he shopped his *Dobie Gillis* series around town and finally ended up with a deal at Fox.

When I met with Max, I knew that *Rally* was a sore point with him, so I soft-peddled the fact that I had just spent the summer playing his rewritten character, Grady Metcalfe. As I read a few monologues and a scene for Max, I didn't really feel nervous. Working on a successful series the past four years and having just completed a feature film, I was feeling very confident about my work. As much as I wanted to play Dobie Gillis, I wasn't uptight or pressed, and that's probably why my audition went so well.

Max seemed pleased, thanked me for coming in, and told me that they would talk to my manager, Ted Wick. Ted was more excited than I was, and said that every young actor in town wanted the part. Dobie Gillis was the most coveted role in Hollywood, and the producers were seeing all the hot young actors like Tab Hunter, Troy Donahue, and Michael Landon.

A few days later I was called back again to read for Max and the director, Rod Amateau. I had worked with Rod when he directed the first two seasons of *The Bob Cummings Show*, and we had always gotten along very well. He had left us to direct *Burns and Allen*, where he met and later married Sandy Burns, George and Gracie's daughter. Since Rod knew my work, I felt confident and comfortable when I auditioned for him. I didn't hear anything for several days, then my manager called me with the good news that they really liked me. The bad news was they wanted me to test for the part because they also like several other actors. That was not what I wanted to hear. I had never gotten a part that I had to test for. The testing process always made me nervous, as it does most actors, and I never felt that I did my best work under that kind of pressure.

Reluctantly I told Ted that I would agree to test but not to get his hopes up because I really wasn't comfortable with this kind of audition. The days dragged on, and no one called to set a time for the test. Finally I was called in to read again for Max, Rod, and Martin Manulis. Each time I had read for Max, his eyes seemed to light up and he laughed out loud, and as I read for him again, Max seemed to enjoy his material as much as he had on my first reading. Everyone acted like I had the part, but no one said anything to me, so I went home and tried to forget about the whole thing. Later that day Ted called to tell me that I had been cast as Dobie Gillis. He was ecstatic. In fact, I think he was even more thrilled than I was. He went on to explain that Max and Rod decided that I didn't need to test because they knew my work from *The Bob Cummings Show* and Max felt that I was the only one who sounded the way he had imagined Dobie Gillis would sound.

I had no idea that after that day my life would never be the same. I was thrilled to be doing another series and excited to have my own show, but that was all Dobie Gillis was, just another job. At the time I didn't know that Dobie would become a classic television series and that I would be identified with the character for the rest of my life.

Years later Michael Landon told me that he had wanted to be Dobie Gillis more than anything in the world. When he lost the role to me he was so upset that he was ready to quit the business. It was a good thing that he didn't, because only a few months later Michael was cast in the role of Little Joe on *Bonanza*. That show ran fourteen years and gave him the opportunity to write and direct. All things considered, I wish he had gotten Dobie and I'd been cast as Little Joe; I'd be a lot richer today!

Later in the week Ted Wick called me to say that Max and Fox Studios felt that I should be blond, so they wanted to bleach my hair. At first I was annoyed, then Ted went on to explain that Max's image of Dobie was the blond-haired, blue-eyed, all-American boy, so my dark brown hair would have to go. I sarcastically asked what they planned to do about my eyes because they were hazel, not all-American blue. Ted chuckled and said maybe they hadn't noticed, so don't bring it up. Fox Studios had a different reason for turning me into a blond, and it had nothing to do with all-American looks or artistic interpretation. Fox was concerned that I would be too identified with *The Bob Cummings Show*, whose sponsor was R. J. Reynolds Tobacco, and they might have trouble getting a sponsor for *Dobie*. To make sure there was no conflict of interest between one sponsor and another, Fox wanted me to look as different from my Chuck character as possible so they jumped on the "Dobie must be blond" bandwagon.

In those days the large companies that sponsored television shows had a lot of control because they were the only ones buying the advertising time on the show. There was the *Colgate Comedy Hour*, *Lux Video Theater*, *G.E. Theater*, and *Schlitz Playhouse of Stars*. Along with companies like Procter & Gamble, Philip Morris, and R. J. Reynolds, they had a lot to say about the television show they attached their name and products to. Today a show's content is entirely controlled by the network, and it makes all creative decisions. Now the sponsors stand in line to buy advertising time.

The *Bob Cummings Show* had been on hiatus during the time I had been auditioning for Dobie. When we returned to work and I announced that I had been cast as Dobie Gillis, everyone game me their enthusiastic good wishes. Although Bob had told me for years that I would have my own show, when it suddenly became a reality, his enthusiasm was restrained, to say the least. I think his mixed emotions came from his fear that the student might suddenly eclipse the teacher. When we finished filming that week's show, Paul Henning called me into his office and told me that Fox felt that if I continued on *The Bob Cummings Show* as Chuck, the sponsors would get upset, so they asked that I be written out of the show for the rest of the season. Paul said he hated to see me go, but he understood Fox's position. He also knew that I would be rehearsing and filming the *Dobie* pilot in a few weeks and I would be missing several shows anyway. He graciously let me out of my contract and told me how proud and happy he was for me. Two weeks later Paul and his wife, Ruth, gave me a fabulous going-away party at their Toluca Lake home. He invited all the cast and staff from *Cummings*, along with Max Shulman and Rod Amateau.

The *Bob Cummings Show* went off the air the next season, but Paul wasted no time in creating another hit series. *The Beverly Hillbillies* ran for nine very successful seasons, and two more hits, *Petticoat Junction* and *Green Acres*, made Paul Henning one of the most successful writer-producers in Hollywood. Paul treated everyone like his family, and we responded with respect and loyalty.

The role of Dobie Gillis was the only one that had been cast, so the producers had to find Dobie's buddy, beatnik Maynard

G. Krebs, and Dobie's parents, Herbert T. Gillis and his wife, Winifred. Rod and Max asked that I be available to read with the actors who were auditioning for these parts.

Maynard G. Krebs was a pivotal character in the show because he was Dobie's best friend and confidant. Maynard was a beatnik who played his bongo drums and listened by the hour to Thelonius Monk. He was totally devoted to Dobie, more interested in jazz than girls, and every time anyone mentioned the word *work* in his presence, he would recoil in shock and screech, "WORK?!!" While Dobie was searching for the perfect girl, Maynard's idea of a good time was going downtown to watch the "Old Endicott Building" being knocked down. He had a stuffed Armadillo named Herman, whom he confided in, and he claimed the "G" in his name stood for "Walter." When he and Dobie couldn't find anything better to do they would go to the Bijou Theater to watch the only movie that ever played there, *The Monster That Devoured Cleveland*. Always clad in a torn T-shirt and jeans or sweatshirt and pants, this goateed man-child would pop up at any moment and say, "You rang?" And if something touched Maynard and he became sentimental, he'd turn to Dobie and say, "Hey, Dobe...I'm getting, like, all misty." The actor playing Maynard had to have an innocence and gentle quality. Maynard was really like an "old dog"—true-blue, sometimes a nuisance, but always there when you needed him. There also had to be a natural chemistry between me and the actor who would play Maynard.

The casting director had been auditioning a lot of actors and had finally narrowed the field down to six or seven potential Maynards who would have to test on film for the part, opposite me playing Dobie. I was relieved that I had already been cast, but I still felt very nervous and sorry for the actors who had to go through that awful testing process. We had worked all day rehearsing and then filming the scene with every actor, none of whom were really right for Maynard. Exhausted and discouraged, the director, Rod Amateau, decided to call it a day. He told me and the camera crew to go home.

As I was getting ready to leave, Rod stopped me and said that casting was sending down one more guy and would I please stay. He told me that the actor was the casting director's secretary's brother. We rolled our eyes, figuring this was a favor and probably a big waste of time, but we should do it anyway. When I returned to the set, the camera crew was in place and Rod was talking to the casting director's secretary's brother. It had been a very long day and I just wanted to get this over with and go home, and from the annoyed looks on the camera crews' faces they weren't in any mood for this last-minute audition either.

Walking over to Rod, I got my first look at the actor; it was my friend from Loyola University, Bob Denver. We talked for a moment, and I tried my best to make him feel comfortable; then we rehearsed the scene. From the moment we started saying our dialogue I knew that he had something very special. All the actors we had tested had something missing. That "something" is hard to define, but once you find a performer who has it, you suddenly realize the difference between an actor who is just reading the words and one who is bringing a character to life. Bob was funny and loose, not at all nervous or uptight like I would have been. I had the feeling that he didn't really care if he got the job or not. It was the same attitude that Maynard would have had. I thought he was acting, but when I got to know him better I realized this was Bob's real personality; easy, laid back, and totally unfazed by anything. We shot the scene a couple of times, then Rod dismissed everyone and as we walked out of the stage he asked me what I thought about Denver. I told him that I felt he was the best person we had seen. Rod agreed and said he'd look at the film and see how it played.

Two days later when I was shopping in Beverly Hills I ran into Rod and asked him who they had finally cast in the role of Maynard. I was thrilled when he told me that it was Bob Denver. He went on to say that Bob and I looked so natural together and our timing was so perfect that it seemed like we had been working together for years. So, as it turned out, Bob's sister, the casting director's secretary, really was doing us the favor when she got Bob into the audition. Bob Denver was the perfect Maynard. He naturally possessed all the qualities of the character. It was that same offbeat, gentle innocence that also made Bob the perfect Gilligan. I always thought Gilligan was really Maynard stranded on an island without his beard and bongos!

The next role to be cast was Dobie's curmudgeonly father, Herbert T. Gillis. Max had written the first anti-father for television when he wrote this character. While Robert Young was hugging his daughters Princess and Kitten and warmly giving his son Bud advice, Dobie's father was calling him a bum because he wouldn't work in the family store, Gillis's Grocery. Vain, petulant and small-minded, Herbert would only admit to being forty-six years old and reminded everyone that he was a veteran of "The Big One, WW II." He was a lodge member, as many men were during the 1950s, but instead of being an Elk or a Moose, he was a member of the Benevolent Order of the Bison.

Herbert T. Gillis was a middle-class sourpuss who had married his sweetheart Winnie and believed that hard work was the American way. He looked at his son Dobie and his weird beatnik friend Maynard and shook his head in disgust. It never occurred to him that his son or the younger generation would have anything to say that was worth listening to. Herbert saw the world from his own perspective, which was probably the same as his father's. The idea of questioning authority, pursuing your dreams, or avoiding hard work could only be viewed as subversive. He ran Gillis's Grocery, located at 285 Norwood Street in Central City. His days were filled with stocking the shelves, "Crackers—2 boxes 59¢, Soup—2 for 19¢, or Ham—53¢ per pound," and keeping his lazy son's hand out of the cash register. An early prototype of Norman Lear's Archie Bunker, when pushed to the limit by Dobie, he would bellow, "I gotta kill that boy, I just gotta." No one had ever seen that kind of father portrayed on television.

When I was called into Max's office to read with the actor they had chosen to play my father, I saw Frank Faylen standing in the hallway. I had known Frank for many years because he and his family attended our church, Immaculate Heart of Mary. Frank had studied for the priesthood but decided to become an actor. My mother, Louise, knew him very well because he had appeared in two pictures with my brother, Darryl, *The Grapes of Wrath* and *Two Years Before the Mast*.

I was surprised to learn that he had been cast in the role of my father. I liked Frank but couldn't imagine him playing my father, because in films he almost always played a villain and in real life he was a grouch who complained about everything. I must say that Herbert T. Gillis wasn't a great stretch for Frank as an actor. Actually, Max and Rod knew exactly what they were doing: Frank *was* Herbert T. Gillis. We were so opposite in personality that it set up the perfect conflict between father and son, and that relationship made for some wonderful shows.

A few days later I met the actress they had cast as my mother. Frank Faylen had been reading with several actresses, but he told me that when veteran actress Florida Friebus read, everyone knew they had found Winifred Gillis. Florida had appeared in some films but was best known for her work in the theater, especially with the great Eva LeGallienne. Winnie Gillis was always in Dobie's corner. She would give Dobie money from the cash register for his dates and calm his father with a "Now, Herbert" when he overreacted. Totally devoted to both her grumpy, opinionated husband and her idealistic, girl-crazy son, Winifred Gillis usually found herself in the middle, trying to keep the men in her life away from one another. For all his loud, pig-headed ways, the perfect 1950s wife adored her Herbert. She would blush like a schoolgirl when he would recount that he fell in love with her while dancing the "Kangaroo Hop," at which point she and Herbert would hop around the store as an embarrassed Dobie watched his crazy parents. Herbert thought his Winnie was the most beautiful woman in the world. He proudly reminded Dobie that his mother had been in a beauty contest and finished twenty-seventh out of twenty-nine entrants. Winnie was just as crazy about her Herbert and was fiercely jealous of any woman that she felt had designs on him. Hard to believe that Herbert T.

Grandmother Mary Ellen Ostertag. When this woman tells you to play the trumpet... you play the trumpet.

Twenty-one-year-old Louise Ostertag moves to Los Angeles with her parents and becomes aspiring "moving picture star" Louise Lang, movie extra.

Photos not otherwise credited are from the authors' collection

At five years of age I'm standing
outside a studio office waiting
for my brother to audition.

My listing at the age of twelve
in *The Academy Players' Directory.*
Notice my billing!

DWAYNE HICKMAN
•

CAPTAIN EDDIE, 20th-Fox
HOODLUM SAINT, M-G-M
RETURN OF RUSTY, Columbia
Brother of Darryl Hickman
12 years old

Management
Lola D. Moore
Agency
CR-6-5401

THE PLAYERS DIRECTORY   *Page 645*

In the 1946 movie *The Secret Heart* I played Robert Sterling as a child.
Ann Lace played June Allison as a child with Elizabeth Patterson and
Claudette Colbert, who played my mother.

The first Christmas Show on *The Bob Cummings Show*. Ann B. Davis, me, Rosemary DeCamp, and Uncle Bob trim the tree.
—*Rosemary DeCamp Collection*

With Tuesday Weld in *Rally Round the Flag, Boys*. I was trying to be cool, but Tuesday said I reminded her of a farmer!

Covers of my rock and roll debut record "School Dance"
and my *Dobie* album.

First-year blond Dobie in the park
with Rodin's "Thinker," contempla-
ting "one soft, round, dreamy girl
to call my own."

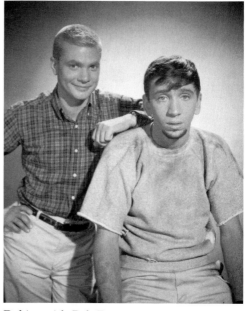

Dobie, with Bob Denver
as Maynard G. Krebs.
The "G" stands for "Walter"!

With Tuesday Weld
as my "tawny beast,"
Thalia Menninger.

Dobie tries to
discourage the
romantic overtures
of Zelda Gilroy
(Sheila James),
but she's not a girl
who gives up easily.

On the day of my wedding to Carol, March 7, 1963.

Leaving the hospital the same day as Jayne Mansfield with her baby girl. I couldn't understand why the woman with the biggest breasts in America was using formula!

My favorite film was the comedy-western *Cat Ballou*. Here's Cat (Jane Fonda) and her gang: me, Michael Callan, Jane, Lee Marvin, and Tom Nardini.

My favorite role, Jed, the outlaw in *Cat Ballou*.

Frankie Avalon and I made several AIP pictures in the 1960s. In *Ski Party* we are reading up on how to have fun without sex. That was the theme of every AIP picture! —*Aron Kincaid Collection*

Crashing the girls' slumber party, with me dressed in drag as Nora and Frankie Avalon as Jane. Patti Chandler doesn't feel very threatened by the "new girls" in *Ski Party.*—*Aron Kincaid Collection*

Gillis was the kind of guy women would fight over! Warm, loving, and devoted, Winnie Gillis did her best to please everyone. Yet she always seemed to have a strange logic about life and gave the impression that she marched to her own drummer.

Florida naturally had the same "out there" look in her eye as the character Winifred Gillis. I was never really sure that Florida understood half the things I told her. She always referred to herself as the character... "I think mother would stand here." Always prepared, very professional, and sweet natured, Florida was so convincing in her part that no one was really sure when she was playing Winifred or when she was herself.

With the main characters cast, we were ready to begin rehearsals. The pilot was called "Caper at the Bijou." Dobie meets the snooty flaxen-haired beauty, Thalia Menninger, who quickly informs him that she will not date a boy without money. Dobie and Maynard hatch a plot to rig the jackpot drawing at the local movie house. Overcome by a guilty conscience at the last minute, Dobie refuses to collect his prize money, only to find out that Maynard had arrived late at the theater and that he had legitimately won the money.

The role of Thalia Menninger was supposed to be a guest appearance, not a regular character on the show. When Tuesday Weld was cast, her career was already starting to take off.

Thalia Menninger was a gorgeous, money-hungry beauty who was sort of infatuated with Dobie, but never really felt that he would make anything of himself. She had no intention of wasting her perfect looks on a man who didn't have "oodles and oodles" of money. Then she quickly said that it was not for her but for her poor family; "A sixty-year-old father with a kidney condition, a mother who isn't getting any younger, a sister who married a loafer, and a brother who is becoming a public charge." Thalia knew she was the most desirable creature on the planet, and she was full of self-confidence and not really concerned what others thought about her. Tuesday and Thalia had a lot in common. Beautiful, luscious, Tuesday knew that she had it all. She was a naturally gifted actress and once she spoke Max's sharp, satirical dialogue she made Thalia's greedy, manipulative, and vain attributes almost desirable. She had an advantage over any other young actress who auditioned for the role because her personality embodied many of Thalia's traits. She was difficult, spoiled, petulant, and totally self-absorbed. It's no wonder that Tuesday was so wonderful in the role and that Max decided to make her a running character in the show.

It wasn't long before the press was hounding her day and night. Smart and sophisticated beyond her sixteen years, Tuesday was a publicist's dream, giving outrageous quotes, but the love affair with the press didn't last very long. Tiring of their constant presence, Tuesday soon refused to grant any more interviews. Louella Parsons, the powerful celebrity columnist, finally turned on her, branding Tuesday a "disgrace to Hollywood," and that, in the long run, short-circuited a very promising career.

Before we began rehearsals the producers wanted to take care of the first order of business; turning dark-haired Dwayne Hickman into blond all-American boy next door, Dobie Gillis. I reported to the hair and makeup department, where hairdresser Helene Parrish was given the job of dying my hair. My hair was brunette and very short, and the bleaching process had to be repeated several times. As I watched my hair change from dark drown, to orange, to strawberry blond and finally to a medium blond, I was already losing faith in this whole blond-hair business. In the pilot my hair looked sandy blond, but once the series was picked up, I had to have my hair dyed every week. Because I wore a crew cut, Helene couldn't just touch up the roots, so all my hair was bleached over and over until I became a very bizarre-looking platinum blond.

The cast of *Dobie Gillis* assembled on Stage B on the backlot of Twentieth Century-Fox, which is now Century City Shopping Center, and we began rehearsing the show. Looking around at my fellow performers I realized that we didn't seem like your everyday television sitcom cast. I was twenty-five, playing seventeen; Bob Denver was twenty-four, playing seventeen; Tuesday Weld was sixteen going on thirty; and I don't know how old Frank Faylen or Florida Friebus were, but he was a grouch and she was off in her own world. As we sat down to read Max's script, the cast and the studio executives heard the smart, sarcastic, and hilarious dialogue. We all knew that we had something very special. With its hip commentary on life, *The Many Loves of Dobie Gillis* was the first television show written from the teenagers' point of view.

The pilot opens with Dobie sitting on the park bench where he is striking the same pose as Rodin's *Thinker* statue, which looms behind him. He turns and laments to the camera, "My name is Dobie Gillis, and I love girls. I'm not a wolf, mind you. A wolf wants lots of girls. I just want one. One beautiful, gorgeous, soft, round, creamy girl for my very own. One lousy girl. But to get a girl you need money, and standing between me and money is a powerful obstacle." Then the camera does a quick cut to a close-up of Dobie's father, Herbert T. Gillis, with a sour look plastered across his face.

I was not the first actor to break the fourth wall and do a monologue to the viewing audience. George Burns had been doing it on *The Burns and Allen Show* for years. He would sit in his study watching a television that enabled him to eavesdrop on what all the other characters were doing, then he would turn to the camera and do a running commentary. Most producers and actors didn't want to take the chance of breaking that fourth wall and speaking to the camera because it destroyed any feeling of reality. *Dobie Gillis* was written, directed, and acted with little concern for reality, and that is one of the reasons the show was so special. The sets were not particularly real-looking, the dialogue was poetic and far-fetched, and the characters were fairly one-dimensional. With the camera sweeping, spinning, and quick-cutting as characters conveniently popped out of bushes or from behind buildings on cue, the show did little to convey any sense of reality. This was definitely not *Father Knows Best*.

We rehearsed Max Shulman's tight, funny script for several days. There was very little rewriting once rehearsal started, and Max was on the set every day supervising every area, from commenting on the look of the sets to making suggestions about the characters. He had cast the show so perfectly that all the actors really had to do was say the words and their characters came alive.

The decision was made to shoot *Dobie* with two cameras since Rod Amateau had years of experience directing *The Bob Cummings Show* and *Burns and Allen*. Much like Cummings, Rod was a stickler for rehearsing, which was fine with me since I was in nearly every scene. With all of our rehearsal the filming went very smoothly and by the end of the five days Max, Rod, and the executives at Fox felt that we had a hot, innovative, new show. The word around town was that Max Shulman's *Dobie Gillis* pilot was a sure thing. As usual, the "sure things" in Hollywood are never sure. When Max and the Fox executives went to New York to sell *Dobie Gillis* to the networks, they were met with an initially cold response from NBC. After viewing the pilot, one executive was appalled. He ranted and raved at Max, "How could you expect to put this filth on the air?" ... "Who is going to buy a show about a lazy, sex-hungry, girl-chasing teenager and his antisocial, derelict, beatnik friend, not to mention his cruel, unloving father." I don't think anyone had coined the phrase "dysfunctional family" at that time, but if they had I'm sure this gentleman would have thrown that in as well. Max and the studio were shocked. They had never thought of *Dobie* in those terms. Could they have made such a terrible miscalculation? Max didn't think so and took his film under his arm and headed right over to CBS, where, after viewing the pilot, the network made a deal that afternoon.

When Max returned from New York he called to tell me that CBS had picked up the show. It had been two years since he had started trying to sell *Dobie* as a series and finally, in January of 1959 its time had come.

Between January and May, when we started filming the series, Max worked on scripts and I took those months off. I had been working nonstop for five years, so I needed a little time. Dorothy Provine and I were still dating, but she was now under contract to Warners and very busy doing the series *The*

Roaring Twenties. The realization that I was going to be carrying a television series was starting to sink in. It was one thing to be a supporting player on *The Bob Cummings Show*, but it was quite another to be in every scene and be the title character.

It had been nearly a year since I bought my dream car, the black Mercedes 190SL. What had started out as a dream was slowly turning into a nightmare. As much as I had loved driving around town in my flashy car, I was starting to feel that it was taking over my life. I was obsessive about washing and waxing it every week, and each night I would lock it in the garage. I guess I thought some marauding gang was scouring the city in search of my car. Every time I had to park it I would circle the block countless times until I found the perfect parking spot, with the perfect amount of space on either side so that I would be assured my car wouldn't get a scratch. Every time I went through this meticulous routine I would return to my car and find that someone had bumped my door, cracked my grille, or dented my bumper.

During a lunch one day at the Brown Derby on Vine Street, the maitre d' came over to the table and asked me if I had parked in front of the restaurant. Apparently he had seen me do my parking routine when I arrived for lunch. Without answering him I jumped up from the table and ran out to the street. As I got to the car, my heart sank. Someone had backed into the front of my car, punching a big hole in the grille. I couldn't believe it. It was as if I carried a big sign that read "Please hit this car." That was the last straw. I drove over to Hollywood Mercedes-Benz, which had almost become my personal body shop, and left it there to be repaired. When I returned to the body shop and picked up my once again pristine Mercedes I had decided that enough was enough.

For the past year the car had owned me, and the love affair had soured, to say the least. I sold my beloved Mercedes 190SL and bought a Ford convertible. When Dorothy found out, she thought I was nuts. "What idiot sells a Mercedes and buys a Ford?" Maybe it seemed crazy, but for me it was like getting out of a bad marriage. I had also learned a great lesson. When all

you think about is "Don't hit my car.... Is my car all right?...
Somebody might steal my car..."etc. you are almost guaranteed that someone will back into it, run into it, or drive off with
it. The more I concentrated on the negative, the more I became
like a magnet for every reckless driver in the city. This not only
applied to my car, but to every other area of my life, and it's a
lesson that I have learned over and over. Think positive, and
good things happen; concentrate on the negative, and misery
will find you everywhere you go...even other people's misery
will seek you out.

We began shooting *The Many Loves of Dobie Gillis* in May of
1959. Instead of working on the lot at Twentieth Century-Fox,
where we had shot the pilot, we moved into Hollywood to
another Fox-owned lot called Fox Western Studio, located at
Sunset Boulevard and Western. It was sold and torn down
years ago and was replaced by a Ralph's Supermarket.

CBS had ordered a full season of *Dobie*, which, at the time,
meant thirty-nine shows with thirteen repeats, giving the
network fifty-two weeks of programs. Eventually it was
dropped to thirty-six shows per season and today the number
of episodes for a comedy series has dwindled to twenty-two.
Most sitcoms today shoot three shows, then take off a week,
giving the cast and crew a breather. We shot thirty-nine shows
of *Dobie* back to back, no hiatus or breaks except for Christmas.
For me the schedule was relentless. We rehearsed one or two
days then filmed the show with two cameras, as we had done
on the pilot. Once a week, after a long day of rehearsal, I would
report to the makeup department to have my hair bleached,
then I would go home, grab a quick bite, and study my lines
late into the night. Week after week I had the same hectic
schedule. On the few days we weren't rehearsing or filming I
was doing interviews and publicity for the show. *Dobie Gillis*
was consuming every waking hour of every day, and the
schedule was grueling.

The first show we filmed for the series was titled "Best
Dressed Man." Tuesday had been brought back to play the
delectable Thalia Menninger, who is impressed by the well-
dressed rich kid in school, Milton Armitage. Dobie tries to

compete by making a deal with a local tailor to borrow his clothes because he can't afford to buy them.

The tailor was played by the amazing Mel Blanc, who was called "The man of a thousand voices" because he was the voice for such cartoon characters as Bugs Bunny, Porky Pig, Elmer Fudd, and many, many more.

This episode introduced two characters who would recur in many shows; Leander Pomfritt and Milton Armitage. In the pilot, "Caper at the Bijou," the role of Mr. Pomfritt, the high school teacher, was played by Herbert Anderson, who went on to play the father of *Dennis the Menace*. For the run of the series the role would now be played by William Schallert, a terrific actor with a gentle, easy quality. Leander Pomfritt, world weary from trying to teach his "young barbarians," was a frustrated novelist. He wrote nine books and destroyed eight of them. When he looked out at the sea of blank faces in his classroom, he would lament that he should have gone into the aluminum siding business. As much as he tried not to become involved with his students, "Mr. P." had a soft spot in his heart for Dobie and Maynard. Bill Schallert went on to play Patty Duke's father in *The Patty Duke Show*, became president of the Screen Actors Guild, and has a very successful "voice-over" career.

The second character introduced in "Best Dressed Man" was wealthy Milton Armitage. Aloof, vain, and snobbish, Milton considered himself God's gift to women and far superior to the poor average humans that circumstance had forced him to come in contact with. And who better to play conceited Milton Armitage than the handsome and arrogant young actor Warren Beatty, who possessed all of Milton's endearing qualities. From the moment he walked on the set until his last show, he hardly spoke to me, and I don't believe he ever spoke to Bob Denver either. Although relatively unknown, Warren already acted like he was a big star. In fact, when he was around, I had to keep reminding myself that *Dobie* was my show, not his.

On Warren's first day on the set we were getting ready to shoot a scene. As the director called for quiet, Warren held up he turned, moved me to one side, took his comb from his pocket and began combing his hair in his reflection in the camera lens. We all stood by and watched in amazement.

On another occasion, Tuesday, Warren, and I were rehearsing a scene in Charlie Wong's Ice Cream Parlor. Suddenly, Warren announced that he couldn't do the scene the way it was staged, and that it would have to be reblocked. When I asked him why, he gave me a disdainful look and condescendingly explained that the way he was seated had put his bad side to the camera. So we reblocked the scene, and this time Tuesday had a problem because now she was at a bad angle. So we reblocked again. By the time we finished I ended up with my back to the camera. When you did a scene with those two, it was every man for himself!

Warren didn't exactly endear himself to the cast and crew. One day somebody thought it would be funny to lock him in his dressing room while he was changing his wardrobe. We all started to laugh as we heard him trying to open his door. After a few minutes we went back to shooting our scene, when suddenly Warren started singing as loudly as he could. The scene was ruined and had to be reshot. Not to be outdone, Warren had gotten the last laugh.

Warren hated working on the show. He had set his sights on a film career, and his stint on *Dobie Gillis* apparently seemed an embarrassing waste of his time and talent. Actually, he denies that he was ever on television, which takes a lot of guts considering the shows he appeared in still play in syndication.

I thumbed through his autobiography one day and noticed that his amnesia regarding *Dobie* was still affecting him. I am told that Dustin Hoffman frequently kids him about his *Dobie* appearances and Warren just laughs and shrugs, but never answers one way or the other. I never understood why it was such a big deal. After all, Clint Eastwood got his start on *Rawhide*; James Garner played *Maverick*; and Burt Reynolds was *Dan August*. It seems to me that if Warren Beatty were going to deny giving a performance it wouldn't be the one he gave in *Dobie Gillis*; it would be the one he gave in *Ishtar*.

When Warren went off to do *Splendor in the Grass* with

Natalie Wood, Max retired the character of Milton Armitage and replaced him with Chatsworth Osborne, Jr. A wonderfully funny actor, Steven Franken, was cast in the role. Max had spotted Steve in a play and called him in for the part of Chatsworth. It was a big break for Franken because he had never worked in television before.

The role of Milton Armitage's mother was played by Doris Packer. She was perfect as the rich matron, so when Warren left, taking Milton with him, Max decided to keep Doris Packer and simply changed her name to Clarissa Osborne.

Steve Franken played Chatsworth with terrific comic energy. As the quintessential spoiled rich kid, Max provided him with great material. His blood type was "R" for "Royal," and he was president of The Silver Spoon Club, which only snobs could join. The Chatsworth mansion had broken glass embedded in the surrounding wall to keep low-lifes like Maynard, whom Mrs. Osborne called "dregs," from invading the family's forty-seven-room mansion. Chatsworth lovingly referred to his mother as Mumsey, and she caustically referred to her only son as "You nasty boy."

Throughout the run of the show Osborne family members would come to visit. Lynn Loring, now an independent producer in Hollywood, played Edwina Kagel, Chatsworth's third cousin, twice removed; and Barbara Babcock, who is best known for her role on *St. Elsewhere*, played Chatsworth's cousin, Pamela Osborne. Franken made condescending, obnoxious Chatsworth almost charming, even when he referred to Dobie as "Dobie-do."

The early shows went very well because the director, Rod Amateau, had us so well rehearsed. I have always loved to rehearse because it makes me feel secure with the material. The more you work on a scene the more natural it becomes and you can add little touches that you wouldn't be able to add if you were always worried about remembering your lines or where you were supposed to move. Unfortunately, not all actors enjoy rehearsing, and Tuesday Weld was one of them. She would rather run a scene once, then disappear until we had to film.

Since she was still going to school on the set, she had a
built-in excuse not to rehearse. Once, after blocking a scene, I
asked her if she wanted to run the lines. She said that she
couldn't because she had to take a biology test. I asked her
what was more important, biology or the show. She gave me a
little smirk and said, "Biology, of course," turned on her heels
and walked away.

Over the years there has been a well-publicized story about
a feud between me and Tuesday Weld. And over the years my
response has been to deny that we had any differences, but
now I would like to set the record straight. The truth is that I
never really cared much for Tuesday and I know the feeling
was mutual. Our problems started on *Rally 'Round the Flag,
Boys!* and continued through *Dobie.* Tuesday was very young,
very spoiled, and even though she led a very adult lifestyle for
a sixteen-year-old, she was extremely immature and irrespons-
ible. Fame had come quickly and easily to Tuesday, and she
began burning the candle at both ends, so it was no surprise
that she didn't always know her lines, didn't like to spend time
rehearsing, and was sometimes late for work. I felt that she was
a petulant pain in the neck, and from her point of view she
probably felt that I was picky, demanding, and impatient... and she was right, I was all of those things. I was also
overworked and I had the enormous responsibility of carrying
a television series. I was older than Tuesday, had been working
since I was a child, and had just spent five years with a strict
taskmaster, in Bob Cummings.

In fairness, I probably took out a lot of my frustrations on
her because I didn't feel that she was serious about her work or
as committed to the show as I was. But to say we had a feud is
not really true. We certainly had our differences, but, with one
exception, the time I blew up at her in front of the cast and
crew, we got along fairly well for two people who had totally
different personalities. On this one occasion I told her that she
was unprepared and unprofessional and that she made my job
more difficult and since it was my show I wanted it to be good.
She fired back that it was her show too, and she wanted it to be
good just as much as I did. Things simmered down, and we

went back to work. That was the extent of our "big feud." The reality was that we were two very different kinds of people who were thrown together because of our work situation. I must say that for all her annoying habits, I have always recognized Tuesday's talent as an actress and I believe that she made an enormous contribution to the initial success of *Dobie Gillis*.

One of the reasons I was so overworked was that after all of the other actors had been sent home at the end of the day, I still had to film all of my monologues for that week's show. Most of the time we didn't get to them until eleven at night. I had to memorize every word because in the first season we didn't use cue cards or a TelePrompter. It was an enormous amount of work for me because I was in nearly every scene, plus I had several page-long monologues per show. By the end of the first year I got smart and told Max and Rod that I had to have a TelePrompter. It made it easier for me and saved production time because in the next season I could sit down and knock out half a dozen monologues in half an hour.

The second show of the first season was titled "Love Is a Science," and it introduced Zelda Gilroy. Once again, the character of Zelda was not supposed to be a regular on the show.

In this episode Thalia decides that Dobie should stop writing love poems and start thinking about the future. She tells him that he should be a doctor. Thalia says, "Dobie, doctors can make ten dollars an hour making house calls. If you schedule them fifteen minutes apart you can make forty dollars an hour and we'll be rich, rich, rich." When Dobie tells her he can't stop writing poems because he loves her, Thalia replies that "Love doesn't butter any parsnips," and she sends him off to take a science class. Zelda Gilroy sits next to Dobie and is his lab partner. Frustrated when he receives a hard time from the zoology teacher, played by the character actor Charles Lane, Dobie turns to Zelda and says, "You don't make things any easier, you know.... A whole month I've been sitting next to you and I haven't heard one word out of you...even a hello.... You sit there doing everything right, giving me the big freeze.... For Pete's sake, speak to me.... Say something.... Say anything...." to which she replies, "I love you!" Those were the first words Zelda Gilroy said to Dobie Gillis.

Plain, brainy, devoted Zelda Gilroy had her sights set on Dobie. No matter how hard he fought it, even he knew, deep down, that he and Zelda would end up together. Zelda told Dobie that it was "propinquity" that brought them together, "You're Gillis, I'm Gilroy.... Think about it, Dobie, we were meant to be together by accident, by biology, and by social necessity. We're a fact of verity.... Dobie, you and I are simply a thing that exists." She was smarter than anyone around her, and because of her love for Dobie, Zelda tolerated Maynard, even though he referred to her as "small girl." For all of Dobie's girl-chasing and unending devotion to Thalia, Zelda had a foolproof method of proving that Dobie really loved her. She would sneak up and wrinkle her nose and Dobie would uncontrollably wrinkle his nose back at her. Self-satisfied, she would smile and say, "See Dobie...you can't fight it," and Dobie would respond, "Now cut that out!"

I hadn't seen Sheila since I had guest-starred as her boyfriend on *The Stu Erwin Show* several years before. As I got to know her better I realized that she was even brighter than the character Zelda. Gifted with a photographic memory, Sheila could learn a script after one reading. During rehearsal one day, Bob Denver, Sheila, and I were doing a scene. I gave Bob his cue and he replied with a totally inappropriate response. Sheila said, "Bob, you've jumped from page nine to page eleven. Your cue is at the top of page ten." We looked at her in amazement. Then Bob said that his script didn't have a page ten. When we asked him why, he replied, "Because my baby ate it." Sheila and I just looked at him and shook our heads. Of course, with Sheila around, who needed a script anyway.

The last scene in the "Love Is a Science" episode has Dobie explain in a voice-over that Zelda found a new boyfriend, as we see Zelda looking through a microscope with her new, nerdy-looking lab partner. Had any other actress played the part of Zelda, the character would have only appeared in that one episode, but once Max saw Sheila James in the role, he recognized the wonderful possibilities the character of Zelda offered. Not the least of which was the great rapport and terrific timing Sheila and I had when we worked together. Sheila James and Zelda Gilroy were here to stay. In fact, the character of Zelda became so popular Max wanted to give Sheila her own series. A pilot was shot but the series was never sold.

Sheila and I have remained friends over the years. She left show business and became a successful law professor and attorney for women's rights. Not long ago, in an appearance on *Geraldo*, she announced that she was a lesbian. The producers of the show asked me for a comment, so I sent a letter of support, which Geraldo Rivera read to her on the show. Since she "came out," I've been asked if I knew when we were doing *Dobie* that Sheila was gay. To be honest, I never thought about it. You have to remember that we worked together in the late 1950s and early 1960s, and someone's sexual preference was not the topic of conversation that it is today. It's not that we didn't know about gay men or women, it was simply that people kept a lower profile in those days. I think that it is a much healthier atmosphere today. Certainly it must be less stressful for people who are gay to live a more honest and open life. I'm sure Sheila's courage in going public with her lifestyle will be very helpful to others who also want to take that first step.

The Many Loves of Dobie Gillis was off to a great start. Tuesday Weld and Sheila James had been added to our fabulous cast, and Max's scripts were sharp, witty, and wonderfully irreverent. Best of all, I had, in Bob Denver, the perfect partner to play Max's wonderful scenes. With all of this going for us, nothing could possibly go wrong... or could it?

• SEVEN •

THAT'S DOBIE WITH A "B"

WE HAD FINISHED ONLY THREE EPISODES of *Dobie* when Bob Denver announced that he had been drafted into the army. The thought of losing our Maynard G. Krebs sent Max, Rod, and me into a panic. The studio had made some calls to see if they could persuade Uncle Sam to do without one particular beatnik, but the U.S. Army could not be swayed. Max and Rod scrambled to rewrite the next week's show and look for a replacement for Bob. I was very upset because I was losing a terrific partner. In the few shows we had filmed, Bob and I had found a rhythm together. Our timing came naturally, and the scenes we played were fast-paced and very funny.

The episode, "Maynard's Farewell to the Troops," centered on a farewell dinner that Dobie arranged for Maynard at Charlie Wong's Ice Cream Parlor. The sign on the wall read LIKE, FAREWELL MAYNARD, and all the kids, parents and their teacher, Mr. Pomfritt, turn out to say good-bye. As I stood up to read Dobie's speech I was speaking as much from my heart as I was from Dobie's when I said, "I've never really been sore at Maynard.... He's been a good, true, loyal, and trustworthy friend.... I'm really gonna miss that kook.... Life won't be the same.... Well, I better quit cause I'm gonna get misty."

In our short time together I really felt close to Bob, and, like Dobie and Maynard, we had never had a harsh word. With the departure of Maynard there would be a big hole in the show. Max tried to fill that hole by bringing in Michael J. Pollard to play Jerome Krebs, Maynard's cousin. Jerome would live with Maynard's parents while he was away in the Army and, like his older cousin, Jerome was a member of the "beat generation." His wardrobe was the same as Maynard's, as was his love of jazz. The only thing Jerome didn't have was Maynard's sense of comedy!

Michael J. Pollard and I were rehearsing our first scene together, which takes place in Maynard's room. Dobie goes into the bedroom and tries to have a conversation with the spacey Jerome. As soon as I said my first lines to Pollard, I knew I was in trouble. Playing comedy with a partner should be like a great tennis game. You "serve" the joke and your partner "returns" it, and then you give your response and he returns that. There should be a rhythm. Unfortunately, Pollard and I must have been playing two totally different games. I "served" the joke and there was a beat...beat...beat...beat..., then Michael looked around, sighed a lot, then he "returned" some line that he made up, which had nothing to do with the script. Just like letting the tennis ball bounce six or seven times and then hitting it into the net....Not only does the ball die, but so does the joke. Michael may have been a great dramatic actor and a wonderful character actor, but when he worked on *Dobie* he was a Class A joke killer. We finished rehearsing the scene, and I walked over to Max and Rod and asked them if they had seen the rehearsal. They said that they had. When I asked them if they had any idea what Pollard was doing in that scene, which I pointed out to Max had dialogue that didn't remotely sound like his script, they looked at one another, very concerned. Max said, "I think we may have a problem here." Max and Rod said that they didn't know what to do because they'd had to replace Denver with so little notice and Pollard seemed to have that same childlike quality that Maynard had. I agree that Pollard was a great type, but he was making up his own script as he went along and he was killing the jokes.

Suddenly, in a scene that was so perfectly timed even Max couldn't have written it better, we heard from across the stage, "Hey guys." We turned and there was Bob Denver. It seemed too good to be true. As we pounced on him and bombarded him with questions like, "You're supposed to be at the draft board?"..."Did you take your physical?"..."What are you doing here?"...Bob told us that he had come up 4-F because he had broken his neck years ago in a car accident, and he came by the set to see if he could return to the show. We couldn't believe our good fortune. Denver may have been 4-F to the army, but we welcomed him back like a war hero. Then we all looked over at Michael J. Pollard. What would we do with him since he had just signed a contract to appear in thirty shows? As cost conscious as Max and Rod were about the show, they readily agreed to pay off Pollard's contract and send him to his next acting assignment. Everyone came out a winner. Pollard got paid for thirty shows that he never filmed, and I had my "ol' buddy" Maynard back.

Years later I saw Michael J. Pollard in *Bonnie and Clyde*, which starred Dobie Gillis's own Milton Armitage as Clyde Barrow. It launched the career of Faye Dunaway, won Estelle Parsons an Oscar, and gave Michael J. Pollard his big break. It also starred one of my favorite actors, the tremendously talented Gene Hackman. It was a terrific movie, skillfully directed by Arthur Penn, and it was a much better vehicle for the talents of Michael J. Pollard than playing the role of Jerome Krebs on *Dobie Gillis*.

The next week we filmed the episode, "Greater Love Hath No Man," which centered on Maynard's quick return from the army. The reason that was given for Maynard's discharge...he was allergic to khaki! Later in the series Max sent Dobie and Maynard back to the military for half the season. Apparently Maynard had been cured of his khaki allergy because it was never referred to again.

We had filmed several episodes when Max called me into his office to talk about a new character that he wanted to add to the show. He told me that Dobie Gillis was supposed to represent the "everyman" teenager and most teens were not "only children," so he decided to give Dobie a sibling, an older brother named Davey. And who did I think would be the perfect actor to play Dobie's college-age brother? I said that I had no idea. Max laughed and said, "Your brother Darryl, of course; it's perfect casting.... You even look like brothers!" Darryl and I hadn't worked together since we were kids. He had just been discharged from the army and I knew he was looking for acting work, so I thought it would be a great opportunity for him. On the next week's show Herbert made some reference to his son Davey, who was away at college. The following week we filmed the episode, "The Right Triangle," in which Davey returns home for a visit and gives Dobie some big-brother advice on how to get the latest girl of his dreams. Davey's advice backfires when everyone thinks Dobie is in love with his math teacher, a married woman. The role was played by Jean Byron. Jean came back on the show playing the history teacher, biology teacher, and any other teacher the script called for. She also came back with a new name—Imogene Burkhart. After *Dobie*, Jean Byron went on to play Patty Duke's mother opposite Dobie's Mr. Pomfritt, Bill Schallert, as the father on *The Patty Duke Show*.

The idea of giving Dobie an older brother never really worked. The main theme of the show dealt with the escapades of a nice, average all-American teenage kid who was searching for the perfect girl. Dobie had so many wonderful eccentric characters to play off that he really didn't need a straight, mature, college-aged brother, something Max realized after writing only a few scripts. The character of Davey Gillis appeared in only two more shows, "Deck the Halls," which was our first season's Christmas show and also featured the warm, funny, and versatile Jack Albertson, and "Where There's a Will," which deals with Herbert T. Gillis's refusing to sign his will because he's too vain to admit that he's getting old. That episode featured a little boy who was a wonderful child actor, Ronny Howard. Ronny was so cute that whenever the script called for a little boy, Max brought Ronny in to play the part. He appeared in four shows in the first two seasons. He was unavailable for our third season because he had been cast as

Opie Taylor on *The Andy Griffith Show*, where he grew up in Mayberry for the next eight seasons. Years later he starred as Richie Cunningham on *Happy Days*. (Its creator, Garry Marshall, has said it was his version of *Dobie Gillis*.)

I was sorry to see Darryl go, but as it turned out, the role was less than challenging, and the story lines didn't really lend themselves to dealing with an older sibling. I think Max and Rod also thought that it would be interesting to have real-life brothers playing brothers on the show, feeling that it would be very promotable and good for the series. In reality, it was awkward for Darryl and unfair to him, because it was really a show about Dobie Gillis, so he would never be more than a supporting character. I had never thought Dobie needed a brother, and I also thought the whole idea was very contrived, but, as usual, Max and Rod hadn't asked my opinion. Davey Gillis was mentioned in a few more scripts, then suddenly Dobie became an only child again. In true television fashion Davey just evaporated into the air, no explanations necessary!

Dobie Gillis was the perfect series for young actors and actresses to get their start. There were always a lot of small featured roles for pretty starlets or young leading men. In the episode "The Hunger Strike," Thalia falls for the new rich boy in town, Chatsworth Osborne, Jr. One of the young actresses who appeared in this episode was Margaret Thomas. She had never done television, although it seemed kind of strange that *Dobie* would be her first professional job when her father, Danny Thomas, was starring in his own show, *Make Room for Daddy*. Shortly after Margaret's appearance on *Dobie* I ran into Danny at a Hollywood function. We stood chatting and I asked him if he really wanted his daughter to go into show business. He looked at me like I either was making a bad joke or was a total idiot. After a moment he curtly said, "Of course she should go into show business." I felt like a fool. He didn't realize that I meant it as an honest question because, after years of being a child actor and knowing the hard work and disappointment an actor can experience, I wouldn't have thought that he would want his daughter to have such a hard life. Of course, at the time, I didn't realize that Danny had plans for his eldest daughter and that he would make sure that she would never know any hard times. Between the successful production company he owned and his many show business connections he opened every door for his daughter, who later transformed herself into the glamorous Marlo. Within a short time she went from bit player to the star of her own series, *That Girl*.

One of the young actors who appeared with Margaret Thomas in this episode was a good-looking blond kid named Ryan O'Neal, also making his television debut. It didn't take him long to land his first series. In 1962 he starred in the show *Empire*, along with Richard Egan and Terry Moore. It was a drama set on a big ranch in New Mexico. The movie *Giant*, with Rock Hudson and Elizabeth Taylor, had been such a big hit that television couldn't wait to bring all the modern Western drama to the small screen. *Empire* lasted only a few seasons, but Ryan went on to star in the very successful nighttime soap opera *Peyton Place*. The role of Rodney Harrington made Ryan a star.

Since we had started shooting the show in May, by the time *Dobie Gillis* premiered in September we had already completed sixteen episodes. The television schedule for Tuesday, September 29, 1959 at 8:30 premiered *Dobie Gillis* on CBS, *The Life and Legend of Wyatt Earp* on ABC, and *Fibber McGee and Molly* on NBC. Our lead-in was *The Dennis O'Keefe Show*, a short-lived comedy which starred Dennis O'Keefe as a widower with a young son. He was a syndicated columnist in Los Angeles, which introduced him to all the beautiful actresses in Hollywood. If the premise sounds familiar it's because *The Dennis O'Keefe Show* was a knock-off of *The Bob Cummings Show*.

Your lead-in show is important because if it is popular, chances are very good that the audience will stay glued to their seat and not switch channels. *Dobie Gillis* was designed to appeal to a large teen audience that had never had a show that represented their point of view. Unfortunately, veteran actor Dennis O'Keefe didn't have any teen appeal, so he couldn't deliver the teen audience that *Dobie* needed. Apparently all the teens were out on the range with *Bronco* on ABC and *Laramie* on

NBC. America's love for the Old West proved stronger than Dobie's appeal, because we didn't exactly knock 'em dead when we premiered. We were so stylized and totally different than any other comedy show on television that it took a few weeks to catch on and have our teen audience find us.

Word of mouth among the teens started to spread. Suddenly catch phrases like "That's Dobie with a 'B'..."Hi, Poopsie"..."You rang?"..."Work?!!"...and "Hey, good buddy" were becoming the hip talk on high school and college campuses. Teens everywhere could relate to Dobie, the nice guy with a stingy father who never had any money and hated to work, preferring to spend his time writing love poems to the girl of his dreams. The parents who watched the show related to poor Herbert and Winifred Gillis because they, too, were hard-working parents who were raising lazy, girl-chasing, or boy-hungry teenagers. *Dobie Gillis* signaled the end of that postwar era where the earlier rules and values which had never been questioned were suddenly being tossed out the window. *Dobie* was on the cutting edge, with Maynard G. Krebs beating out the new message of freedom from the old rules and regulations. *Dobie* also represented the end of innocence of the 1950s before the oncoming 1960s sexual revolution. Those days of malt shops, good-night kisses, proms, and just being a kid were coming to an end. Maybe that's what the teen audience sensed as they watched Dobie, Maynard, Zelda, Thalia, and the rest of the outrageous characters deal with their teenage problems as only a teenager could.

The critics gave Dobie and me a lukewarm reception. The reviews said that one of the major drawbacks of *Dobie Gillis* was the casting of Dwayne Hickman in the lead. One felt that I was pretty vapid in my portrayal of the title character. Another said that I had no idea who Dobie was and that it would be nice if I gave some indication of having what it takes to grow up to be a man. This critic went on to comment that Zelda had everything needed to be Superman! There was also a hue and cry over Herbert T. Gillis's famous line, "Someday I gotta kill that boy...I just gotta." The network and sponsors felt that Herbert was sending the wrong message; he should be a more traditional sitcom father, like Robert Young. Within the first season Herbert's favorite lament and every parents' ideal threat was forever banished from the show. Frank Faylen replaced his line with one of his exasperated looks and America knew exactly what he was thinking, "Someday I gotta kill that boy...I just gotta." One of the worst reviews said that finally the network had put on such a terrible show that it would boomerang back into the CBS eye. The closest I got to a good review was a left-handed compliment from a critic who said that Dwayne Hickman was so clean-cut he could slice roast beef!

Somehow the bad reviews didn't get me down. Actually, I was so used to bad reviews that I probably wouldn't have believed a good one.

Fox and CBS weren't as upset by the bad reviews as they were by a *TV Guide* article about *Dobie* with a picture of me sitting under the hair dryer with a caption about bleaching my hair to achieve my Dobie look. You would have thought *TV Guide* had just blown the lid off some high-level government secret. Calls were flying back and forth among CBS, sponsors, Fox, Max, me, and *TV Guide*. Somebody had to be responsible for this treasonous act, and since I was the one under the dryer, looking into the camera, everyone blamed me. I thought the whole situation was silly and would be forgotten the next week; as it turned out, I was right. It was no big deal; everyone knew I dyed my hair, and to the surprise of Fox, CBS, and the sponsors, nobody cared!

As usual, bad reviews or candid pictures don't mean a thing. The only thing that really matters is what your audience thinks. We may not have been wowing the critics, but the television viewers didn't seem to care, and each week our ratings were getting higher and we were beating our competition. *Dobie* knocked out *Fibber McGee and Molly* and after airing only thirteen shows, NBC sent the McGees packing, leaving *Wyatt Earp* on ABC and *Dobie* to battle it out.

One advantage that *Dobie* had going for it was the constant stream of pretty young starlets that appeared each week. One of my favorites was Yvonne Craig, a dark-haired beauty with a fabulous figure and great comedy timing. Max thought she was so terrific that Yvonne returned to the show five times during the run of *Dobie*. Her first appearance was in a funny episode called "The Flying Millicans," in which Dobie falls for the beautiful Aphrodite Millican, who performs in her family's acrobatic act. Aphrodite decides that *Dobie* should be groomed to join the family's act, so her bodybuilding father and brothers try to turn him into a pumped-up man of steel. The father was played by the famous silent movie star Francis X. Bushman, in his day one of the highest paid and biggest names in the movie business. In several of the scenes Mr. Bushman was dressed for his circus act wearing a toga over his tights and sandals. We were talking between scenes and he told me that the toga and the sandals he was wearing were the same ones he wore when he starred in the silent version of *Ben-Hur*. I must say that I was really impressed. The chariot race between Bushman and the equally famous Ramon Novarro was awesome, especially when you consider that it was filmed in 1925.

Later that same season Yvonne returned as Myrna Lomax, whose pompous father was a retired navy man who didn't care for Dobie until he thought that Dobie had enlisted in the navy. The father was played by Harry Von Zell, of *The Burns and Allen Show*. I was always smitten with Yvonne Craig, but we never dated because we never seemed to be available at the same time. Actually, I had very little time to date anybody, including Dorothy Provine, with whom I was still involved. Between *The Roaring Twenties*, which Dorothy was filming each week, and my show, we were seeing less and less of one another. I don't think either one of us really wanted to end our relationship. I know I didn't, but the pressure of our careers and the stress of our work was getting to both of us. Dorothy was very special to me, and I've thought many times over the years that I was sorry that our relationship hadn't worked out.

Shortly after we broke up, I met a young actress who appeared in the episode "The Prettiest Collateral in Town." Sherry Jackson had been working on *Make Room for Daddy*, playing Danny Thomas's older daughter, Terry, for five years. She left the show in 1958 and was now doing guest work on different series. On our show, Sherry played the role of

Mignonne McCurdy, the spoiled daughter of a banker. I thought that Sherry was adorable, so I asked her to be my date for a big dinner that was being given in honor of Jack Warner; Jack Benny was going to be the emcee, and everybody in town would be there. When we arrived at the hotel there were stars everywhere, including all the contract players from Warner Brothers as well as every big name in the business. As we pushed through the crowd, I looked around and said to Sherry, "See, I wasn't kidding when I told you that everybody in town would be here." I don't remember whether Sherry replied, because at that moment I looked up and I was standing right next to Dorothy Provine. I couldn't believe it, and neither could she. There must have been a crowd of three hundred people, and if I had tried to find her that night I wouldn't have had a chance, but suddenly here we all were, Dorothy and her date and Sherry and me. We all were very awkward and tried to get away as quickly as we could, but in a room where people were packed elbow to elbow, it wasn't easy. The rest of the night I kept looking over my shoulder but I didn't see her again. Sherry and I only dated a few more times, and although I still cared very much for Dorothy, after our awkward encounter at the party I decided it was better to leave well enough alone.

We had finally reached the end of the first season. *Dobie* had been in production from May 1959 through the end of January 1960 and we had filmed thirty-nine shows. With only a couple of weeks off during the entire season, I was exhausted. The show was becoming very popular, and we were picked up for a second season. I wish I had been able to savor the success, but I didn't have the time. The hiatus between our first and second season would only be thirteen weeks.

I was looking forward to relaxing, sleeping, and just hanging out with friends, but all of that went out the window when I got a call from my manager, Ted Wick. A representative from Capitol Records had contacted him about signing me to a recording contract, because they wanted me to cut a rock-and-roll album. When we heard that, Ted and I laughed. They couldn't be serious; hadn't they heard about that nightmare called "School Dance"? Apparently they *had* heard about my recording fiasco, but felt that I hadn't been handled properly. They assured me that they knew how to produce a great rock-and-roll album with hot songs and hip arrangements, and with my popularity as Dobie Gillis, they could sell a million. They also assured me that they were well aware of my musical limitations and they would work with me so that I would feel comfortable. There was nothing the record executives at Capitol could do to make me feel comfortable, but I must say they tried their best. They assigned Karl Engemann, to produce my album and hold my hand. Karl was an easy-going and very knowledgeable guy who had endless patience and did his best to make the entire experience as pleasurable for me as possible. He knew that I wasn't a musician or a singer, so he had the orchestra lay down the songs so that I could record the vocal tracks on another day.

Unlike my "School Dance" experience, this orchestra was smaller, with a more hip rock-and-roll beat. The songs were given great arrangements by Jimmy Haskell and had a hot young sound, more like Ricky Nelson than Frank Sinatra. I would sit in on the session with the orchestra and run through the songs with them a few times so they could get a feel for my phrasing and timing, which was usually too fast or too slow. Then I would sit down and let these wonderful musicians record the songs without me. I have always been in awe of the studio musicians. They amaze me with the way they can look at a piece of sheet music for the first time and play the song so perfectly that you would think they had rehearsed it a hundred times. The album had twelve songs, so the orchestra was scheduled for four days, cutting three songs per session. Recording the orchestra was the easiest part of Karl's job; his real work came when I returned to the studio to do the vocals. After twenty or thirty takes of one song Karl would say over the loudspeaker, "Great job, Dwayne. . . . I know we've got one." Then the engineer would splice together a line from this take and a line from another until they finally had one song. If we got lucky and I was really hot we could record a song in ten or fifteen takes and lay down two songs in one session! It was really grueling work, especially for poor Karl and the engineer.

Imagine all the long hours they put in listening to my pathetic singing. I was either flat or sharp, never on key and I was always a beat ahead or two beats behind. After weeks and weeks of recording, the album was finished and a few days later I sat for a photographer who shot the cover picture for my album, simply titled *Dobie*.

While I was still on hiatus, Ted Wick booked me on *The Dinah Shore Chevy Show*. He couldn't understand why I was less than enthusiastic about appearing on a variety show. I tried to explain that variety shows wanted you to sing or dance and these were not exactly my areas of expertise, and if that wasn't bad enough, this was a live show, something I swore I would never do again after my heart-stopping experience on *The Lux Video Theatre* several years before. But Ted didn't have much sympathy and told me that I would be fine and not to worry so much. So I reported to NBC Studios in Burbank for a week of rehearsal before we performed the show live on Sunday night. The other guest star on the show that week was my old friend George Burns. The producers went over George's segment of the show, which consisted of a skit with Dinah and a comedy monologue. When I realized they hadn't given "Ol' Sugar Throat" a song, I knew I was sunk. One of us would have to sing, and before I could make a break for the stage door, somebody handed me the music for my big number, the song, "I'm in Love With Miss Logan" from the musical *New Faces of 1952*. Dinah and I would play a comedy skit in which I was her adoring student, and she, of course, was my beautiful teacher, Miss Logan. I rehearsed and rehearsed the song, and each time I sang I was either off-key or trying to remember the lyrics. Dinah was so kind. She would listen to me massacre the song, then she would smile and say, "You know, this is a very difficult melody." Then she would sing it with me, but I was a hopeless case.

In the meantime, George was rehearsing his monologue and kept telling me that I shouldn't use the cue cards because you get so busy reading the cards it takes away from the jokes. I was reading the cards without a problem; in fact, my monologue and scene with Dinah were great. After pressing George about his cue card advice, I found out that he didn't use cards because he couldn't see them; it had nothing to do with delivering a good joke. Finally it was air time. Memories of *The Lux Video Theatre* with James Mason and Gig Young flashed through my mind. My head was pounding and the adrenaline was pumping as the red light went on and I launched into my comedy monologue. It went smoothly, as did the skit with Dinah, which led into my big musical number. Before I knew it, the orchestra was playing the first bars of my song and I jumped in, a little late I might add. I had never gotten the song right during rehearsal and I never got it right on the air. As I sang the last few lines of "I'm in Love With Miss Logan," all I wanted to do was get off the stage as soon as possible.

While I was standing in the wings recovering from my song, I watched George Burns do his monologue, and the more I watched George, the better I felt about my performance. Old George, the master performer who had stood on hundreds of stages in front of thousands of people, had told me not to use cue cards because they took away from the jokes. In reality, he was too vain to wear his glasses, so this veteran performer was screwing up his monologue so badly that he just mumbled what he couldn't remember and played with his cigar. When he walked off stage, our eyes met. I smiled and said, "Good job, George." He lied back, "Thanks, kid...Your song was fine too."

A few weeks later I was booked on *The Tennessee Ernie Ford Show*. His producers must have caught my performance on *Dinah* because they never asked me to sing; in fact, they didn't even play music when I was on stage. Instead they decided that Ernie Ford and I would do a comedy skit. He was a gentle comedian, and a very smart performer. Our skit took place in a malt shop where Ernie and I sat in a booth wearing muskrat coats and drinking malts. During rehearsal we realized that the malts were made of styrofoam and they could be lifted out of the glass by the straw. Neither of us made any comment about them, but Ernie just filed it away. As we performed the skit live, in the middle of the scene Ernie suddenly pulled the malt out of the glass by the straw, looked at me, and ad-libbed,

"Boy, they sure make these malts thick around here." The crew broke up and so did I. Ernie never missed a trick. I really enjoyed working on his show, especially since I didn't have to sing or dance.

I had spent my entire hiatus working with Dinah, "Tennessee" Ernie, and completing my *Dobie* album, and now I had to report back to work. The bad news was I didn't have any time off between the first and second season; the good news was that because I had to start filming the show, I couldn't go on a record tour to promote the album. I was so relieved that I wouldn't have to humiliate myself by making singing appearances that I didn't really care that I hadn't had a vacation.

Capitol Records decided that the best way to promote the album was to have Dobie sing one of the songs on the show. Max thought that it would be a great way to open the second season, so he wrote the episode "Who Needs Elvis?" In it Zelda helps Dobie win a jazz contest at school. Unfortunately she makes him irresistible to a pretty girl who wasn't interested in him until she heard him sing. I introduced the first song on the album, "I'm a Lover Not a Fighter." It should have been titled "I'm an Actor Not a Singer."

The album didn't exactly top the *Billboard* charts. In fact, it was a big flop. With all the studio time and engineers' fees, the album must have cost Capitol a fortune, one they never got back. The costs of making a record are charged against an artist's royalties and, in my case, there were no royalties. I used to say that my album either sold sixty-three copies in 1962 or sixty-two copies in 1963. Either way, I never got a dime.

My singing career may have been a big flop but the show was becoming a big hit. The second season got off to a strong start and we were consistently beating our competition. NBC had replaced *Fibber McGee and Molly* with *Alfred Hitchcock Presents*, while ABC hung in with *Wyatt Earp* for another season.

The second season also brought about some major changes on the show. I was having severe problems with my hair because I needed to have it bleached once a week. It was so damaged that it started falling out in clumps and my scalp was full of sores. I decided that my days as a blond were over. When I announced that I would be going back to my natural dark brown hair, everyone had a fit. A meeting was called with Max, Rod, and the sponsors, and they told me that the audience wouldn't accept a dark-haired Dobie and I had no choice but to stay blond. I tried to explain that the audience would have an easier time accepting a dark-haired Dobie than a bald Dobie, which is what would happen if I kept dying my hair. They still seemed unmoved. Finally, I gathered up my things and headed out of my dressing room. Rod asked, "Where are you going?" I turned and faced the group. "Guys, you want a blond Dobie, then get yourself another actor, because I'm through." As I walked across the soundstage, Rod followed after me and said, "Hey kid, we've talked it over and we think you're right... You don't have to be a blond anymore. In fact, I never did think it was a good idea." Some years later I found out that the whole blond thing was Max's idea. I think Max always wanted to be a blond; in fact, I think Max always wanted to be Dobie Gillis. He used to kid that he created me and when he went to sleep at night I disappeared!

While I was fighting the blond-hair battle, Bob Denver had his own problems. With the success of the show and the popularity of the Maynard character, Bob felt that he deserved a raise. I certainly thought that he should be making more money, but Max Shulman didn't quite see it that way. Bob went into Max's office to ask him for an increase, and after he presented his side, Max was silent for a few moments as he puffed on his cigar. Then he leaned back in his chair and said that the way he saw it, Bob was labor and he was capital...so the answer was no. When Bob started to object, Max told him that he would simply write Maynard out of the show. I don't know if Max really would have gone that far, especially after all he had been through when Bob was drafted into the army for five minutes, but Bob didn't want to take the chance, so he accepted his role of labor to Max's role of capital and went back to work.

One of the greatest challenges of our second season was dealing with the loss of Tuesday Weld, who was tired of doing the show. Her career was very hot and she was receiving a lot of offers to appear in films. Tuesday had been so terrific in the role that Max never even considered having another actress play the part, so Dobie's love interests were now going to take on many different shapes and sizes.

During the second season, while blond Dobie was gradually turning into dark-haired Dobie, the opening of the show was also taking on a new look. The famous *Dobie* theme and cartoon character peeping through the fence at cartoon cuties had been replaced by a cold opening and a jazz chorus skatting "Dobie." A cold opening means that the show opens with a scene already in progress. On our show, after thirty seconds or so, the scene ended on a joke, and the jazz chorus would sing "Dobie," and then the credits would appear on the screen. I always preferred the cold opening because I found the cartoon character tiresome and, to be honest, I thought the funny-looking cartoon Dobie appeared kind of malevolent and weird as he motioned for us to peer through the fence at the beautiful girls.

With a bright new look for our new season, Max decided the direction of the show would change as well. Not to say that he ignored the "Dobie wants a girl" story lines, but Max started writing shows that focused more on the trials and tribulations of a teenager trying to grow up.

At the time, one of the real life challenges facing every teenage boy who reached eighteen was the possibility of being drafted. Since Dobie represented the "everyman" all-American teenager, what could be more all-American than joining the army. So halfway through the second season Max once again widened the horizon for his Dobie and sent him off to serve his country, along with his ol' buddy Maynard.

The army shows featured two performers who were old friends of mine, Jack Mullaney, an actor I had met in New York, who had co-starred in the series *My Living Doll* with Bob Cummings, and Julie Newmar, and my friend from Loyola, Richard Clair, who had appeared with Bob Denver in the Del Rey Players acting troupe. Dick Clair appeared on the show as Lieutenant Snavely in "The Battle of Maynard's Beard" episode, and returned to take over the role of Lieutenant Merriweather. Dick was a terrific comedian but he discovered his true talents were in writing. He later created *Mama's Family* from a skit that he and his writing partner, Jenna McMahon, wrote while on staff for *The Carol Burnett Show*. They also created the enormously successful series *The Facts of Life*.

The role of Lt. Spunky Merriweather was originally played by Burt Metcalfe. Burt landed his own series the next season: *Father of the Bride*, based on the movie with Spencer Tracy and Elizabeth Taylor. Burt played Buckley Dunston, the young man engaged to the bride. After *Father of the Bride* was cancelled, Burt continued acting, then turned his talent to casting shows. Years later he was one of the producers of *M*A*S*H*.

With the popularity of the show someone came up with the idea to merchandise a line of clothes. I had supplied my own shirts the first season, but with this new marketing scheme I was now wearing "Dobie Gillis" shirts. I never knew who designed the shirts, but judging from the corny patterns, strange sleeve length, weird collars, and zipper front, they were not in touch with the teen market. I hated the look and cringed every time I had to wear one. I was assured that they were selling well, which just goes to show that the public will buy anything, no matter how awful it looks, if it has a celebrity name attached to it.

I wasn't the only one on the show who was encouraged to supply his own wardrobe. Everyone was expected to pitch in because that was another way to cut costs on the show. Frank Faylen had, without a doubt, some of the strangest suits and sport coats imaginable. In the episode "Here Comes the Groom," Dobie and Zelda almost get married. We started to film the wedding scene with Zelda and Dobie's parents dressed up for the special occasion. When Frank walked on the set he was wearing the worst-looking pin-strip suit I had ever seen. It was so out of style, with its zoot suit pants, huge shoulder pads, and wide gangster stripes, that it looked like a costume left over from an old movie...and I do mean old. One of the cameramen yelled, "Hey, Frank, where'd you get that suit?" Everyone snickered, but Frank didn't think the guy was very funny. He launched into a long diatribe, Herbert T. Gillis style, about how expensive the suit was and how they didn't make them like that anymore. None of us could argue that point. From that time forward we never commented on Frank's taste in clothes; we rolled our eyes a lot, but we never said another word.

Max and Rod were always looking for ways to save money on the show. Fox had produced the 1955 hit film *Love Is a Many Splendored Thing* which starred Jennifer Jones and William Holden. They also owned the title song, which became an even bigger hit than the film, and every time we needed any background music for a scene in *Dobie* the song was always the same, "Love Is a Many Splendored Thing." Fox thus saved on paying royalties to another song-publishing company. The song popped up in episodes like "Taken to the Cleaners," "Love is a Fallacy," "Chicken From Outer Space," and "Put Your Feet in Our Hands," to name a few.

By the time the second season ended, *Dobie* was at the height of its popularity. It had been a much easier season than the first. Not only had we all settled into a groove but I was now using a TelePrompter for my many monologues and this helped to cut my work load considerably. Looking back, I realized that I had been working nonstop in television for seven years. Between my five years on *The Bob Cummings Show* and two on *Dobie*, I had filmed nearly 150 episodes of network television. It's no wonder that I felt worn out. I remembered Cummings telling me that the first year of doing a series was plain murder; the second year was nerve-wracking; then along comes the third year and you settle down and enjoy it. Once again "Uncle Bob" was right. We had been assured of a pickup for the third season, so when we took off on our hiatus we all had the security of knowing that in a few months we would be working again.

I decided that I needed a well-deserved vacation, so I booked myself on the ocean liner *Matsonia* and sailed to Hawaii. I was staying at the Royal Hawaiian Hotel in Waikiki, and as I went down to the terrace to have lunch, I ran into Jimmy Stewart, his wife, Gloria, and their children. He insisted that I join them for lunch, which I did and had a wonderful afternoon. They were heading back to Los Angeles the next day, so I was on my own for the rest of the week. Apparently *Dobie* was a big hit in the islands because everywhere I went I was given the star treatment. I met a Hawaiian businessman and his family who showed me the island of Oahu as only a local can. My week was over too soon, but I was hooked on Hawaii and have returned many, many times over the years. I flew home and immediately started doing publicity layouts and interviews for our third season.

When *Dobie* returned to CBS, the competition on NBC was, once again, *Alfred Hitchcock*. *Wyatt Earp*, however, had hung up his spurs and ABC had replaced him with *Calvin and the Colonel* starring Freeman Gosden and Charles Correll. They were the noted white actors who had created *Amos 'n' Andy* on radio. This was an animated show about a bunch of animals in the Deep South, and the plot lines and characters were a thinly disguised version of *Amos 'n' Andy*. ABC figured the use of cartoon animals would avoid any racial overtones, but this was not the case. It was now 1961 and times had changed. The animals may have looked innocent enough, but they all sounded like stereotypical black characters. This politically incorrect show lasted only one season.

As we prepared to begin our third season, Dobie would find himself falling in and out of love with some of Hollywood's prettiest starlets, attending college, rekindling his romance with his old flame Thalia Menninger, and meeting the future Mrs. Dwayne Hickman.

EIGHT

DOBIE...GONE BUT NOT FORGOTTEN

WHEN WE BEGAN OUR THIRD SEASON, Max Schulman decided that Dobie, Maynard, and Chatsworth had served their country long enough. It was time to bring his troops back to Central City and more fertile story areas. By enrolling Dobie and his pals in the local junior college, Max could keep Herbert and Winnie Gillis involved in the action, as well as Zelda, Mr. Pomfritt, and Chatsworth's mother, Mrs. Osborne.

Since we had ended the second season in the army, for continuity, we opened the third with a show that had Dobie and Maynard trying to reenlist but Uncle Sam wouldn't take them back, so they decided to go to school under the G.I. Bill. Max used this episode as Dobie and Maynard's transition into civilian life. They enrolled in S. Peter Pryor Junior College (named after Max's accountant) and discovered that their old high school teacher Mr. Pomfritt was now a professor there.

A new character, Dean McGruder, would be played by the versatile character actor Raymond Bailey. Ray went on from

Dobie to play Milburn Drysdale in Paul Henning's nine-year hit, *The Beverly Hillbillies.*

The look of the show had also changed. The monologues during the army shows were done in what is called a "limbo set." This is where Dobie would stand in front of *The Thinker* statue with only a blank background behind him since he couldn't very well stand in Central City's park when he was on the army base. It was decided that Dobie would still do his monologues in a limbo set, but he would add pictures of the characters he was talking about suspended in the air or propped up on an easel.

This limbo set was a welcomed change as far as I was concerned. Instead of sitting on a park bench and baring my soul about finding the perfect girl, I now had the opportunity to do more of a stand-up routine, commenting on everything that was going on around me. Today, Jerry Seinfeld is doing basically the same thing I did thirty years ago.

With all the characters back home where they belonged, the story lines could once again deal with Dobie's quest for the perfect girl, getting money, and growing up.

Because we preferred being far away from "Fox Hills"—as the main studio, Twentieth Century-Fox on Pico and Motor Avenue, was called—the series was still being filmed at Fox Western Studios in Hollywood. Only a few shows had been shooting there: *Dobie; The Rifleman,* with Chuck Connors; *Wanted: Dead or Alive,* with Steve McQueen; and *Perry Mason,* starring Raymond Burr.

When our third season started, *Perry Mason* had moved to another lot, leaving Raymond Burr's enormous dressing room empty. Max and Rod thought that they would be good to me so when Ray moved out I moved in. Actually, it was more the size of a small house, with a living room, two bedrooms, bath, and full kitchen. Burr had to work such long hours on his show that many times he just spent the night there so he didn't have to get up at four A.M. and drive to the studio. He loved to cook and enjoyed preparing meals for friends during his few free hours. Unfortunately, I was either rehearsing or filming all day, so I never really had time to appreciate my luxurious quarters.

It was ironic that one of the first shows of the season was a spoof of Perry Mason. The episode, titled "Move Over, Perry Mason," had Maynard taking Dobie's dad to court after getting his hand caught in the grocery store's gumball machine. It was in this show that Maynard turns to Dobie and says, "Everybody tells me that I'm an accidental prune." And Dobie replies, "That's accident prone, Maynard." Maynard was always mixing his metaphors. "Dobie, I've been like a gallstone around your neck..." — "Maynard, that's millstone!" or, "Dobie, do you think I look like a Ragged Muffin?" — "Maynard, that's ragamuffin...and the answer's yes!"

It was during this time that Steve McQueen and I became friends. He was starring in the role of Old West bounty hunter Josh Randall, a guy of few words and little emotion. He carried his famous weapon, a cross between a handgun and a rifle which he called his "Mare's Leg." Steve was a real gun enthusiast. Between scenes he'd go behind the soundstage and shoot a variety of different guns and rifles which he collected. When I had a few free moments I'd join him, and he'd explain to me the particular characteristics of each gun, then he and I would shoot off several rounds of blanks. Steve was a very quiet guy, but he and I got along very well. After his show ended in 1961, I didn't see him for many years. One day in the mid-1970s I was shopping in Beverly Hills and ran into him at a men's clothing store. We chatted and then he introduced me to his new wife, Ali MacGraw.

Dobie Gillis continued to provide an opportunity for a lot of actors to get their first professional jobs. In the episode "The Gigolo," a handsome young actor was hired to play a boyfriend of actress Diane Jurgens, my friend from *The Bob Cummings Show*. Diane had already made several appearances on *Dobie* and had recently married the young actor Peter Brown (Deputy Johnny McKay on *The Lawman*).

But in this episode, Diane's love interest would be played by Bill Bixby. While I was in the production offices I happened to see Bill's picture and resumé. His credits included Shakespeare, movies, and television; I was very impressed and felt that he had a lot more experience than I. Years later, while working at CBS in programming, one of the shows that I supervised was Bill's *The Incredible Hulk*. We were reminiscing about the *Dobie* days and I told him how intimidated I was by all his credits. He gave me a sheepish grin and confessed that his resumé was a phony. He had made up the credits in order to get his first acting job, which was *Dobie Gillis*.

Another young performer who made her television debut on *Dobie* was the pretty brunette actress Michele Lee. Years later I was sitting next to her at the People's Choice Awards and Michele told me that *Dobie* had been her first acting job and that she had been scared to death. She was a natural and went on to star on the stage and in movies as well as the long-running series *Knotts Landing*.

One week my love interest on the show was the wife of Ricky Nelson. Kristin Nelson was a delightful blonde, who also appeared on *The Adventures of Ozzie and Harriet* playing herself. Kris was in "The Sweet Success of Smell," along with Yvonne Craig, who played Elspeth Hummaker, a money-hungry beauty. Sound like a familiar theme? Max was fixated by beautiful money-hungry women, and it didn't matter if their names were Elspeth Hummaker, Giselle Hurlbut, or Poppy Jordan, these women were really Thalia Menninger. They were interested in only one thing, money and finding a wealthy husband. Dobie Gillis was always a sweet distraction, but his poetic notions and romantic ideals didn't translate into cold, hard cash.

Max even turned Cheryl Holdridge, a former Mousketeer, into a money-hungry heartbreaker when she played Daphne Winsett in "The Big Blunder and Egg Man." I was really taken with Cheryl and we went out several times, but I wasn't in her league. She was interested in Lance Reventlow, the wealthy son of Barbara Hutton, the heiress to the Woolworth fortune and former wife of Cary Grant. Lance had just divorced Jill St. John, and he and Cheryl had started dating, so I was no match for that kind of competition. Cheryl married Lance, but it lasted only a short time as he was killed in a plane crash.

The name "Dobie" was always a constant source of jokes: "That's Dobie...with a *B*." Whether he was called "Dopey" or

"Dobie" or "Dobe," or "Dobie Doo," no one had ever heard of anyone with such a silly name.

I was relieved when Max finally decided to do an episode explaining the origin of Dobie's ridiculous name. Every time I did an interview someone would always ask me about the name Dobie and I never really had a good explanation. Max loved to play with names and took great delight in coming up with the strangest combinations he could think of . Remember Comfort Goodpasture from *Rally 'Round the Flag, Boys!* as well as Zelda, Thalia, Chatsworth, etc., etc.? Max wrote the episode "Names My Mother Called Me," and in this show Dobie finds out that he was named after a famous Nobel Prize winner. Dobie is invited to New York to meet the retiring Dr. Dobie Kline. He discovers that the doctor is poetic, kind, and humble, and goes home with a newfound pride in his not-too-silly name. This episode finally put to rest all the questions about the origin of the name Dobie Gillis.

That particular show had a lot of heart, something I had been asking for over the years. I always felt that the warm, honest moments were some of the best in the series, but Max and Rod only sparingly gave into my requests for "a little heart" in the scripts. I always felt those special moments gave the characters added dimension rather than having them just play out bizarre situations. The real moments of warmth and friendship between Dobie and Maynard and the other characters always made the show more appealing. At least that was my opinion, but as I learned over the run of the series, my opinion was not necessarily asked for or appreciated. Max was capital...I was labor!

In fact, most of the time Max and Rod referred to me as "The Kid" and treated me more like the teenage character I was playing than a twenty-five-year-old man who had been on television nearly eight years. Max and Rod, Rod and Max— you rarely saw one without the other. They were like a vaudeville team. In his dry caustic style, Max would do a running commentary about almost everything, and Rod would throw in his comic asides in a delivery he had "borrowed" from George Burns.

Max was Max, but Rod Amateau had a personality that he had created over the years by taking a little from Bob Cummings, a little from George Burns, a little from Max, and throwing in some deliberate eccentric characteristics, to finally create the current version of himself.

Rod was a hot young director when we worked together on *The Bob Cummings Show*. He was smart, funny, and very talented. It was during his years with Cummings that he "borrowed" some of Bob's eccentricities, and, believe me, he had plenty to share. Rod, like Cummings, suddenly became a health food fanatic and vitamin specialist. I often wondered if Rod also shared Bob's love for a good massage and his youth serums! After Rod left Cummings and went over to *The Burns and Allen Show* I ran into him one day and was shocked to see that he had shaved his head. Overnight he was suddenly bald and the top of his head had been buffed to a high gloss. When I questioned him on his new look, he said that he realized that his head needed to breathe! I just looked at him and didn't say a word. Most of the time I had always found myself being his straight man when I'd question him about his latest strange new fashion. Not only did Rod want his head to breathe, but he felt his feet needed air as well. With great delight he would recount how he'd go to a network meeting wearing a suit and tie, and sandals on his bare feet. You can imagine how strange he looked, with his shiny bald head, suit, tie, and sandaled bare feet, sitting in a room full of stoic network executives. He also took great pride in the fact that he never wore underwear. Instead, he had flannel linings sewn into all his trousers. For years he tried to convince me that I should give up the constraints of wearing underwear and convert to his notion that "every part of you needs to breathe," but I assured him that my head, feet, and the rest of my body were fine just the way they were.

Rod's bizarre look was also enhanced by the fact that he was only about five-feet-five. He and Max were both about the same height and they would often say to me, "Well, it's easy for you tall guys." Tall guys!... I was only five-nine. Then they would tell me that if they were as tall as I was they could rule the world.

By the time we were working together on *Dobie* Rod had made his transformation into Max's artistic, comedic, and eccentric sidekick. I always felt that every move Rod made was for shock value. When he wasn't riding a bicycle around town, he was driving a big pickup truck. He told me that he loved to pull up in front of Chasen's Restaurant in Beverly Hills and toss the keys to the valet. After he tired of his pickup truck escapades, he turned it in and bought a very conservative four-door Chrysler. I made the foolish mistake of asking why he bought a four-door car and, in a typical George Burns delivery, he said that the car was a bargain because you got four doors for the price of two! Once again I was Rod's straight man. I was beginning to feel like Jack Benny.

Along with his bizarre look and odd behavior, Rod also had the habit of never letting the truth get in the way of a good story...or anything else for that matter. When you worked with Rod you had to stay on your toes. For all his eccentricities, Rod was tremendously talented and a born comedian, but with him you never knew what to expect from one day to the next. After years of this chameleon personality, all the parts he "borrowed" from one person and another eventually melted into one. He was exasperating, sarcastic, and sometimes condescending, and, like Cummings, he could drive me to the point that I was about to explode. And, just like Bob, he'd know when he'd gone too far and with a puckish grin he'd crack a joke, and in an instant all would be forgotten and forgiven. Rod definitely made the long days on the set interesting, to say the least.

When Max and Rod were together, they created such an energy they seemed to fill the room. Without question, with their expertise in writing, producing, and directing, they were the brains behind the success of *Dobie Gillis*. It's a good thing they weren't a few inches taller; who knows, maybe they were right...they could have ruled the world.

We were only a few episodes into the third season when I

got a call from Ted Wick that Disney wanted me to star in the movie *Bon Voyage*. I told him that I'd love to make the film but I was doing shows back to back without a break and I didn't think I could get the time off from *Dobie*. Ted suggested I meet the director and see when the studio's shooting schedule would start. So I went to Disney Studios and met with the casting director, who brought me in to meet James Neilson, the director of the film. Fred MacMurray and Jane Wyman had been cast as the parents who take their family on their first trip abroad and I would play the young male love interest. They wanted me as much as I wanted to do the film, but their work schedule conflicted with *Dobie* and there was no way that I could do both.

The casting director suggested we have lunch, so we went to the studio commissary. As we sat down I saw Walt Disney at his usual table with several executives. He got up, came over, and introduced himself, and proceeded to tell me how much he loved *Dobie Gillis*. I was very flattered and said, "Well, Mr. Disney, it's only a two-day show and it doesn't have the production values of your shows." He leaned over and said, "Dwayne, don't apologize for *Dobie*...It's a great show...And please call me Walt," then he excused himself and went back to his table. I felt very touched that he wanted me to be on a first-name basis, but I soon found out that I really wasn't so special. Apparently Mr. Disney told everyone to call him Walt. His employees always said that it was in lieu of a raise!

The hectic schedule of *Dobie* wouldn't allow enough time to make a movie, but Max and Rod gave me the time off to make a few commercials, like one of the first for the Polaroid Camera. The idea of taking a picture and a few moments later seeing the finished product was revolutionary. The company gave me a camera as a gift, but I always had trouble with it. My pictures were always curled up or I forgot to wipe the solution over the print, and the photos started to fade. I finally gave my new Polaroid away and went back to my Brownie Instamatic!

Halfway through the third season Max called me into his office and told me that he had great news, that Tuesday would be coming back to make a guest appearance on the show. I must admit I didn't exactly share Max's enthusiasm about Tuesday's return, but I knew that it would be good for the series. She had left *Dobie* after the first season to pursue her film career and had just finished an Elvis Presley movie, *Wild in the Country*." She was between films, so Max invited her back to do a show. In the episode "Birth of a Salesman," Max explains Thalia's absence by giving her a job as a traveling saleswoman. What better occupation for the conniving, money-hungry, Thalia? And, true to form, she is more "snake-oil salesman" than legitimate huckster.

When Max started the publicity that Thalia and Dobie would be together again, the press jumped at the prospect. The audience loved Dobie, but they especially loved him when he was being manipulated by his "Great Tawny Beast," Thalia Menninger. Despite our earlier problems, we got along very well and Tuesday's return to *Dobie Gillis* was a real ratings booster.

A few weeks later I was reporting to the makeup department on one of our filming days. When I entered the room I said hello to Chuck Connors, and as I took my place next to him in a makeup chair, I noticed a lovely young actress who was having her hair styled. I smiled and said hello and received a less than enthusiastic response. A glutton for punishment, I pressed her for some vital information and found out that her name was Carol Christensen. She was working on a circus picture, *The Big Show*, and had just returned from Germany where they had been shooting, and now they were going to do interior scenes on one of the soundstages. *The Big Show*, a story about a family of trapeze artists, starred Esther Williams, Cliff Robertson, Nehemiah Persoff, Robert Vaughn, and David Nelson.

It was during the filming of the show that David became interested in performing on the trapeze. He learned to fly and used a stunt double only for the more advanced and dangerous stunts. David became a very accomplished trapeze artist and performed in shows for many years.

It was very early in the morning and I wasn't feeling my best. For weeks, I had been fighting a low-grade viral infection which wasn't getting any better, and although I was trying to be as charming as possible with this pretty actress, I wasn't making any headway at all. In fact, the more I talked, the more sullen she became, and by the time I left makeup I had given up any ideas about asking Carol Christensen for a date.

The relentless work schedule on *Dobie* was finally catching up with me. I lost the fight with the virus and ended up in the hospital with pneumonia. With me sidelined, Max and Rod had to scramble with new scripts and story lines that didn't involve their title character. They could have closed down production, but it would have been too costly to carry a crew until I returned to work and from the way I looked, they didn't know when I would be back.

Max was faced with a real problem. His title character, around whom all the stories revolved, was out of the show, so the only thing he could do was to turn to his second lead, Maynard G. Krebs. In the episodes "The Truth Session" and "I Remember Muu Muu," I appeared only in the monologues, filmed after I returned and edited into the shows that featured Bob Denver.

After two weeks I was back at work, but I insisted that my workload be cut down so that I could fully recover. For the remainder of the season Maynard, Zelda, and Chatsworth carried many of the shows.

One of the first episodes we filmed on my return was "Back to Nature Boy," featuring the actress Lynn Loring as Chatsworth's cousin, Edwina Osborne. As the cast assembled to read the script I looked over and was surprised to see Carol Christensen, my pretty but sullen friend from makeup that I had tried to get to know a few months before. She had been cast in the show as one of Edwina's friends. As rehearsals progressed, I noticed that Carol's personality had greatly changed. To my surprise she was very pleasant. By the end of the show she and I were getting along very well, so I asked her out to lunch the following week. I discovered on our first date that she had broken up with a fellow that she had been seeing for quite a while and that was the reason she had been so unresponsive when we first met. We had a great lunch at a

Polynesian restaurant in Beverly Hills called The Luau and made another date for the following weekend. Before long, Carol Christensen and I were an item around town. Once again the movie magazines played out our romance in photo layouts and silly articles about *Dobie* fans crying themselves to sleep because I had fallen in love. I thought it was not only corny, but embarrassing, since I was almost twenty-seven years old.

We completed our third season and went on hiatus, and during that time Carol was working on a space movie with the Three Stooges called, what else, *The Three Stooges in Orbit.* I spent time on the set visiting her, and basically relaxed for the next two months.

When we started our fourth season, the show was retitled *Max Shulman's "Dobie Gillis."* The limbo sets we used for my monologues now had me standing in front of a black background with a shadowy silhouette of "The Thinker" behind me. Dobie was still going to college at S. Peter Pryor, but the show was taking on a very different look. That different look was me. I was starting to appear very mature and a little over the hill to play some of the silly girl-chasing, teenage scheming plots that had been the staple of the series for the past three seasons.

Max was aware of the problem and decided to bring in a younger character that Dobie could guide along in his footsteps. Max created Duncan Gillis, Dobie's teenage cousin, played by Bobby Diamond. The idea was to have the more mature Dobie orchestrating the escapades of Duncan, known as "Dunky," and his old pal Maynard, who never changed or matured in four seasons.

It was during this time that Sheila James filmed her *Zelda* pilot. It didn't sell, so she turned her attention to college and made only occasional appearances on the show during the fourth season.

CBS must have felt the show was grinding down because they moved us from our traditional Tuesday night at 8:30 to a death slot on Wednesday at 8:30 following a one-hour news show, *CBS Reports.*

NBC was blowing away the competition with the first

ninety-minute Western series, *The Virginian*, which starred Lee. J. Cobb, James Drury, and Doug McClure. Not only did *The Virginian* have a wonderful cast, but the show was one of the first big weekly productions to be filmed in "Living Color."

In 1962 most of the television shows and television sets were still black and white. ABC's *Wagon Train* formed a circle from 7:30 to 8:30, but it couldn't beat the megahit, color Western, *The Virginian*. For any of the viewing audience that was still awake after the erudite *CBS Reports*, they watched *Dobie Gillis*.

ABC thought Gene Kelly playing the Bing Crosby role of a priest in *Going My Way* would be strong competition for us, but no matter how hard Kelly tried, no one went his way.

It boiled down to *Dobie* vs. *The Virginian*. Our ratings started to drop but, surprisingly, not as much as we had expected. The teen audience still wanted to watch Dobie Gillis live out their own problems and fantasies no matter how mature he looked or how silly the situations.

Max was spending less and less time on the show. It seemed that he was flying off to his home in Westport, Connecticut, every few weeks, and each time he left he would stay away for longer periods of time. I could see that he was losing interest in the show, but I attempted to explain to him that we still had half the season left and we needed him desperately. Max tried his best to convince me that the show was in good hands, but we both knew that wasn't true. I told him that I understood that he might be getting tired of the show, but I still had nearly fifteen more episodes to do and I needed the kind of scripts only Max could write.

After one of these speeches Max would promise that he would give the show one hundred percent of his energy, but after a few weeks he'd sheepishly tell me that he had to fly to Westport, but only for a few days, then he would promise me that he would get the show back on track.

Once again he turned to the Dobie formula that always worked. When in trouble, call in Thalia. In "What's a Little Murder Between Friends," Dobie proposes to Thalia, but she points out that his net worth is his G.I. insurance policy, which is only good if he's dead. Dobie starts to have near-fatal accidents and thinks Thalia is trying to murder him. This episode seemed to be symptomatic of what was going on with the series. Thalia's return provided a ratings boost, and once again the show seemed to have more life.

The best shows that final season featured stories involving the original cast members. No matter what new twist the writers tried, the real magic happened when Dobie, Maynard, Zelda, and Chatsworth were getting into mischief. As hard as they tried to make Cousin Dunky Gillis into another Dobie, it just didn't work. The last few shows in the fourth season went back to the original premise that had been the foundation for Dobie's success—Dobie's relentless search for the perfect girl.

Unlike Dobie, in my personal life I had found the perfect girl in Carol Christensen. We had been dating throughout the fourth season and we were crazy about each other. I had found in Carol a warm, caring, and lovely woman. We enjoyed wonderful times together and it wasn't long before we both knew that we loved one another and wanted to spend the rest of our lives together. Shortly before the end of the fourth season I asked Carol to marry me. She was thrilled, and we planned our wedding during the show's hiatus.

As the season drew to a close, I started asking Max and Rod if we had a renewal for the next year, but neither of them had been able to get a network commitment. As we filmed the last show, I had a gut feeling that it would be the last time Dobie and Maynard would be together. On one hand I was "like getting misty" and on the other I felt kind of relieved. In four years we had filmed 147 shows, and if we had been on the air today that would have translated into a six-year run. I had been on network television for ten years, and *Dobie* had been especially difficult for me, so I was ready for a break. With the exception of my time in the hospital and a few lighter shows after my return, I was in nearly every scene of every show we filmed, not to mention having to do several monologues in each episode. I also felt that I had explored every facet of

Dobie's character, and as an actor I wanted to go on to other roles. I never thought for a moment that Dobie Gillis would haunt me for the rest of my life.

During the four years Dobie was on the network we had been fairly successful, but none of us had any idea that we were making a show that would become a classic. I always felt that our smart performances and Max's witty, satirical scripts made our series a cut above the rest. I played Dobie Gillis as a real person, not the television cartoon image of a teenager who would talk in a squeaky, hormone-popping voice. Despite the most outrageous situations, all of the cast played their characters with total believability. *Dobie* was the first teenage comedy that treated teens like normal people. We dealt with their problems and dilemmas from their point of view and that's why America's teenagers tuned in each week. We respected our audience, and in return they became our loyal fans for the next thirty years.

After the last show of our fourth season we all went home and waited to hear if we had a pick-up for the next year. Word came from CBS that *Dobie* would not be renewed. Max called and gave me the news, and even though I had been expecting our cancellation, it still came as a bit of a disappointment. I wished Max good luck and he wished me the same. Unfortunately, after four years of working together, our cast and crew never had an opportunity to say goodbye to one another. As strange as that may seem, it is more the norm than the exception in our business.

I didn't have much time to lament about *Dobie* because Carol and I were busy making wedding plans. We had planned to be married by Monsignor John O'Donnell at Immaculate Heart of Mary, the church my family and I had attended for many years. Having lived my entire life in Los Angeles and having spent the last ten years on television, I had a guest list that was growing by leaps and bounds. We couldn't invite one couple and not invite another, and what about the studio and network people? And, of course, the press considered the wedding of Dobie Gillis to be of great interest to America's teens, so they wanted to make the whole thing a big media event.

We set the date for the big day: March 16, 1963. The custom at the time was to send telegrams instead of formal invitations if the guest list was fifty or less. Our list was nearing the two hundred mark, with no end in sight. I was watching our wedding grow into the size of a royal coronation, so Carol and I decided to get married the next week and invite only our immediate families. The church had already been booked for a wedding on the following Saturday so it was unavailable. By the time we coordinated everyone's schedule, the only day that we could be married was on Thursday, March 7, so on that day our families assembled before Monsignor O'Donnell and Carol and I exchanged our vows.

Our wedding reception was a luncheon held at the Brown Derby on Vine Street in Hollywood. After the reception Carol went to the hairdresser's to have her hair combed out, something that has never made any sense to me, and I went to Beverly Hills for the final fitting of my wedding suit, which seemed anticlimactic at that point.

Our quick decision to get married ten days earlier than originally planned caused major wardrobe problems. Carroll and Company hadn't finished my suit, and I. Magnin's hadn't finished alterations on Carol's wedding gown, so I ended up wearing a three-year-old, dark gray suit and Carol wore a turquoise silk suit which she had bought at the last minute.

During the wedding luncheon I called my manager, Ted Wick, and told him that Carol and I had gotten married that morning with only our immediate families present. Then I invited him over to join us in our celebration. Ted was upset that we had passed up a great publicity opportunity, but he understood that we had wanted an intimate wedding, not a media circus.

As Carol and I drove to Palm Springs for a ten-day honeymoon, we left Ted to deal with the press and the marriage of Dobie Gillis.

When we returned to Los Angeles, we moved into Carol's

rented house in Hollywood and began looking for a home of our own. We were thrilled when we found out in early June that Carol was pregnant. The baby would be due in January and we still hadn't found a house. Carol had morning, afternoon, and evening sickness, so she would send me over to my parents for dinner. Just looking at a picture of food made her nauseous, and one whiff of anything cooking sent her flying out of the room. By early fall we bought a beautiful new place on the top of Mulholland Drive with a panoramic view of the San Fernando Valley.

As we celebrated Christmas and welcomed the New Year, I thought about the enormous changes that had taken place in the past twelve months. For the first time in ten years I wasn't starring in a television show, which also meant I didn't have a job to report to every week, and I had gotten married, bought my first home, and was about to become a father at any moment.

Closing the chapter on one part of my life, I looked forward with great anticipation to what lay ahead. If I had thought my career had been interesting up until this point, I soon discovered that I was heading for the biggest roller coaster ride of my life.

· NINE ·

SPURS, SKIS, AND BIKINIS

"JOHN FRANCIS HAS ARRIVED," said the nun as she stuck her head into the waiting room of St. John's Hospital in Santa Monica. It was the morning of January 20, 1964, and I had been anxiously pacing, smoking, and watching television for several hours waiting to hear those words.

A Caesarean section had been planned because my son had decided to try to enter this world bottom first. Carol had checked into the hospital the night before to be prepared for surgery. I barely had time to kiss her good-bye before she was whisked away to that no-man's land called "the maternity ward." And I do mean "no-man's land," because in those days men were not involved in the process of giving birth. We may have been a necessary element at the beginning, but for the next nine months, culminating in the birth of the baby, a man's only participation was to drive the car to the hospital, sit in the waiting room, and then pay the bill the day the new mother and child were released!

That morning I took my place alongside the other anxious fathers-to-be and their various relatives. Each time a nun appeared at the door we all jumped up in anticipation that she would announce the arrival of our new offspring. The waiting room was so thick with cigarette smoke that you could hardly see across the room.

Those were the days when everyone smoked...even if you didn't really enjoy it, because it was the social thing to do. I got started when I was doing *The Bob Cummings Show* because R. J. Reynolds was our sponsor, and every week they provided me with a complimentary carton of Winstons. On *Dobie*, Philip Morris sponsored the show, so they provided me with all the cartons of Marlboros that I could possibly consume. It wasn't until 1977 that I kicked the habit. But in 1964 I was nervously puffing away, along with the other expectant fathers.

The first time I saw my new son, John, was through the glass wall of the nursery. The tiny blue bundle was sleeping soundly. As I looked at him I was so overwhelmed that I could hardly speak. I went down the hall to visit Carol, who was also sleeping peacefully. She awakened long enough to ask about John and I reported that he was beautiful, then she fell back to sleep.

Five days later Carol and John were released, so I drove to the hospital to pick them up. I followed behind as a nurse pushed mother and son in a wheelchair out the front doors of the hospital. I was carrying a six-pack of baby formula they had given us as a going-away present.

As we waited out in front of the hospital, the doors opened and we were joined by Jayne Mansfield, her husband Mickey Hargitay, and their two older children. Jayne had just given birth to a little girl. A photographer appeared out of nowhere, probably arranged by Jayne's publicist, and took a picture of Jayne and her family alongside Carol, John, and me. As the pictures were being taken I looked over and noticed that Jayne's husband, Mickey, was also carrying a six-pack of baby formula. It struck me as very strange that Jayne Mansfield, the woman with the largest breasts in America, needed baby formula! I stifled a laugh and helped Carol and John into the car. When we arrived home we were greeted by Mrs. Frye, the baby nurse, who immediately took over and whipped us into shape.

John was nearly six months old when I was offered a TV pilot titled *Hey Teacher*. It was a cute premise about a young guy, fresh out of college, reporting to his first teaching job. He's green and his class of first-graders take full advantage of his lack of experience. The veteran character actress Reta Shaw played the crusty school principal. The show was being produced by Lucille Ball and Desi Arnaz's production company. Desilu's offices were located in Culver City on the old Selznick Studio lot where *Gone With the Wind* was filmed; in fact, "Tara" housed all the executive offices and didn't look much different than it did when Scarlet O'Hara owned the place.

A few days before rehearsal started, I got a call from Lucille Ball's secretary asking me if I would please come to Lucy's office the next day for a meeting. As I walked into her office, any notion I might have had that she would be the scatterbrained redhead from television was quickly dispelled; I was meeting Lucy the businesswoman and producer. Smart, gritty, and tough, Lucy knew as much about the production side of comedy as she knew about jokes and timing. We discussed the show and were in complete agreement about the way I would approach my character; neither of us wanted this to be "Dobie Gillis Teaches School." Looking at her, all I could think of was the time she set fire to her nose in the scene with William Holden, but that was not the Lucy I was dealing with. I got the distinct impression that the show would be done exactly the way she wanted . . . end of discussion.

The first day of rehearsal I met Bob Sweeney, who had been directing *The Andy Griffith Show* for several years. Bob quickly let me know that he had hated *Dobie Gillis*. He felt that Dobie was an obnoxious, smart-aleck kid, and he never understood how the show stayed on television for four seasons. As I stood listening to him, it suddenly dawned on me who he was. Bob Sweeney had been the actor who played Fibber McGee on TV, and it was his series, *Fibber McGee and Molly*, that aired on NBC opposite *Dobie Gillis* our first season. *Dobie* had sunk his show in less than thirteen weeks. After *Fibber* was cancelled, Bob Sweeney gave up his acting career and became a director. He had found great success directing, but apparently still had a chip on his shoulder toward *Dobie*. Bob's attitude about *Dobie Gillis* seemed to influence his attitude toward me, which didn't help our actor-director relationship.

Hey Teacher was based on a book of short stories by an elementary school teacher. In one of the scenes a student brings his pet snake to school and I have to get rid of it. I had never handled a snake before, and this was something I wasn't looking forward to. All I had to do was pick it up and hand it to the janitor and he would take it outside. We rehearsed the scene several times, and each time I picked up the cold, clammy reptile my skin crawled. Wallace Ford played the janitor, and he wasn't any happier about handling the snake than I was. When we got ready to shoot the scene, Bob Sweeney yelled "Action!" and I picked up the snake and proceeded to hand it to Ford. I could see he was nervous as he reached for it. The snake started to squirm, and he squeezed it tighter so it wouldn't get away. Suddenly, Wally let out a scream and dropped the snake, and as Sweeney yelled "Cut!" the snake handler rushed in to grab the slithering reptile as it headed across the floor. I looked at Wally's hand and was horrified to see two fangs sticking out of his skin. The snake had bit him and left its teeth embedded in his hand. Filming stopped and Wally was rushed to the emergency room for a tetanus shot. Several hours later he returned, only to have to reshoot the snake scene. Lucky for all of us we got it in one take.

Wallace Ford was a tough character actor who had been in the John Ford movie *The Informer*. He had recently starred, with Henry Fonda, in *The Deputy*, Fonda's first television series. He may have been a tough guy on the screen, but he was no match for a first-grader's pet snake.

The rest of the show was filmed without any further accidents or incidents. When I saw a screening of the pilot, I was disappointed. What should have been a funny, sweet show about a first-time teacher and his young students was flat and totally lacked any sense of fun. I wasn't surprised when the pilot was not picked up by the network.

It was late fall and Carol had decided that living on Mulholland Drive was too dangerous for John, who was almost a year old, and too inconvenient for shopping, which was at the bottom of the hill. We had been in the house a little over a year, but she wanted to move, so we put the place on the market. We sold our house with the panoramic view of the Valley and moved to our new ranch-style home in the flats of Sherman Oaks with a large pool, which we quickly baby-proofed with a six-foot-high fence.

While we were waiting to move into our new house, I got a call from my manager, Ted Wick, that Elliot Silverstein was directing a comedy Western called *Cat Ballou*. The screenplay was written by Walter Newman and Frank Pierson. Frank later went on to write *Dog Day Afternoon*. They had requested a meeting so I went to their offices at Columbia Pictures to talk about the role of Jed, the drunken preacher cowboy. By the end of the day they made me an offer, and I was cast in the movie. I had always loved Westerns and had yearned to play those Gary Cooper and John Wayne parts, and although I was never exactly the tall, rugged cowboy type, I was perfect for a comedy Western. Not only would I be able to dress in Western clothes, ride horses, and shoot guns, but I would also be working with a cast that included Jane Fonda, Lee Marvin, Michael Callan, Nat Cole, and Stubby Kaye. It was also exciting because part of the movie would be filmed on location in Canyon City, Colorado. We had only a few weeks before we would leave for location, and that was barely enough time for me to brush up on my horseback riding. I had ridden a little when I was a kid, but I was very insecure around horses; I felt the same way about them as I did about snakes. I took riding lessons every day for several weeks, and by the end of the third week I may have looked a lot more confident, but I still had very little affection for horses. I was also so sore from my crash course in riding that I could hardly sit in the saddle or anyplace else.

The rest of the cast had been set, so director Silverstein asked us to meet at the Beverly Hilton Hotel for a read-through of the script. We took our places around a large table and Jane

Fonda noticed me wincing in pain as I sat down and asked if I was all right. I embarrassingly explained that I was sore from my riding lessons, then she laughed and told me to use it and make it part of my character. That was great acting advice but hardly necessary because the pain was so bad I had no other choice but to incorporate it into my part. As we began to read the funny and very offbeat script I realized how exciting this movie was going to be. Imagine watching Lee Marvin reading his part as he rolled his eyes, took long dramatic pauses, and generally took over every scene he was in. Lee raised overacting to an art form. He would do bits that no other actor would have the nerve to do, and somehow, with his horse face and bigger-than-life character, he could make it work. Everyone was so well cast and so special that by the end of our first read-through the movie was starting to take shape.

For the next week we met every day at Columbia to rehearse the key scenes from the movie. On a large empty stage Elliot taped off areas and we ran the scenes over and over. It was a great way to work because each actor had a chance to become familiar with the dialogue and get comfortable with his or her character. We also learned the rhythm of the other actors, so by the end of the week it was as if we had been working together for years. This type of rehearsal is done in the theater, but rarely for a film, because there is never enough time to rehearse. By the time we boarded our chartered plane for Colorado Springs, each one of us felt secure with our role.

After we landed, we drove to Canyon City, a small town at the foot of the Rocky Mountains. The cast moved in and took over a small ten-room motel, complete with diner and bar. It was mid-September, and we needed to stay on a tight schedule because once the snow started to fall we would be unable to work.

On our first day of shooting I was thankful that I had very little to do. The first day is always the hardest, and if a director can schedule easy scenes for his actors it gives everyone a chance to settle in and get comfortable.

Unfortunately for Lee Marvin, the first scene of the first day was one of his hardest. It's the first time in the movie we see Kid Shelleen, who is so drunk he can hardly stand up. It was a five-page scene in which Shelleen had to try to pull himself together and shoot some targets to prove to "Cat" (Jane Fonda) that he could do the job she hired him for. It was a very physical scene and very demanding for Lee. He rehearsed several times and then went behind the barn and took a shot of vodka to steel himself. I ran into him in front of his dressing room where he had just gotten sick. When I asked if he was all right, he said, in typical Lee Marvin fashion, "Tension, baby...just a little tension."

He had every reason to be tense. Not only was this first scene a killer, he also knew that he was not the studio's first choice for the part of Kid Shelleen. He wasn't even the second choice. The part was first offered to Kirk Douglas, who turned it down, and then the part was offered to José Ferrer, who, after negotiating for several weeks, also turned it down. All the other roles had been cast and the movie had to begin filming in Colorado, so, at the last moment, Lee was cast in the role. He had just completed *Ship of Fools* and took a salary cut to work on *Cat Ballou*. Lee felt his career needed a boost and maybe the role of the drunken has-been gunslinger would bring him the attention he was looking for. It turned out to be the smartest move of his career, because he won an Oscar for his performance.

But thoughts of Oscars or career moves were the farthest thing from his mind as he steeled himself for his first scene. We shot about ten takes and I thought Lee was terrific. He and I quickly became buddies. I would egg him on to tell stories, some of which I know were not true, but he told them so colorfully nobody cared.

Jane Fonda and I had never met prior to *Cat Ballou*, but I found her very professional, even though she was less than enthusiastic about the movie. She wanted to do more serious work and playing straight man to a bunch of crazy characters wasn't her idea of great filmmaking. Fueling her disdain was her lover, Roger Vadim, the French director who was most famous for discovering Brigitte Bardot and giving the world its first bona fide movie sex kitten. Roger showed up on the set and Lee greeted him with "So you're the XXŒ*%& French-man." Nothing like an insult to get a relationship off to a good start! That set the tone for Jane and Lee for the rest of the movie.

Unlike my friend Lee, I got along well with Jane. I thought she was a very talented actress who was serious about her work...but then Jane was serious about everything. I couldn't resist kidding her about her liberal causes, and the more annoyed she got, the more fun it was to give her a hard time.

After Vadim arrived, Jane decided that she and Roger would drive to the location together in his rental car. Until then she had piled into the company station wagon and ridden to the location with the rest of the cast. When the teamsters realized that Jane was riding to the location with Vadim, they said that she was cutting one of their members out of his job as a driver and they demanded that she ride in the company car. Jane fired back that she had no intention of riding with anyone except Roger. The teamsters responded that Jane's decision was fine with them. If she had no intention of riding in a teamster-driven car, they had no intention of driving anyone else or moving any equipment; in other words, they were going to shut down the movie.

The next day a sullen and angry Jane was back in the company station wagon with the rest of us. As I jumped in, I leaned forward and said, "I'm disappointed in you, Jane, I always thought you supported our fellow union mem-bers....Who would have thought that you were really a union buster!" Boy, if looks could kill, I would have been a dead man.

Working with Lee Marvin was an unbelievable experience. Never have I met such an outrageous personality. Lee loved to drink, and the more he drank, the more outrageous he became. He had a story about everything and everybody. He also had very definite theories on acting and a style that was all his own. Lee figured if a little bit was good, a lot would be so much better. As a result, each take of a scene was bigger than the last.

During one scene in the outlaws' hideout called "Hole in the Wall," Lee and I were looking out of a window as Jane rode away on her horse. I couldn't help but notice Lee's eyes were darting all over the place as his tongue hung out and his head moved from side to side. After the scene I said, "Lee, what were you supposed to be doing?" Sarcastically, he said, "Who the hell knows? The audience will probably think I had gas!" I laughed, but he was the one who won an Oscar for *Cat Ballou*, not me.

One night, Lee, Michael Callan—everyone called him Mickey—and I were having dinner together. After having a few drinks, Mickey started telling us about his marital problems. Lee started giving him advice and I threw in my two cents. We finished dinner and moved into the bar to continue Mickey's marriage counseling. Several hours passed and the bar closed. Lee insisted we go back to his room and settle Mickey's marital problems once and for all. Given a little more time and a lot more vodka, Lee was convinced we could talk him out of getting a divorce. So we talked and drank and drank and talked trying to convince Mickey not to throw away his marriage. As Lee was giving an impassioned speech on the sanctity of matrimony, I looked down at Mickey, who was passed out cold, stretched across the bed. I stopped Lee in the middle of his monologue and pointed to our unconscious friend. Lee looked at him and wasn't the least bit fazed that his words were falling deaf ears. Without missing a beat, Lee continued his long speech defending marriage and the love of a good woman. Somehow I slipped out and made my way back to my motel room.

The next day Mickey and I were so sick we could hardly make it through the day. Lee invited us back to his room for a few drinks, but I quickly declined. He was way out of my league.

As it turned out, we all should have listened to our own marital advice. Not only did Mickey end up getting his divorce, but both Lee and I eventually got divorced as well.

Tom Nardini, who played Jackson, the Indian, was a favorite of Lee's. He had taken the young actor under his wing and constantly kidded him about "being in show business all of ten minutes." Tom had a terrific sense of humor and we both took great delight in Lee's antics.

John Marley, who played Cat's father, Frankie Ballou, looked at Lee and his rowdy followers like we were all undisciplined children. In addition to being an intense actor, he was a very serious person who always seemed to be in turmoil over the world's latest political injustice. As he railed on about politics, Mickey, Tom, and I would disappear as quickly as we could and look for Lee. John must have thought we were silly and very shallow, but we didn't care; Lee was a lot more fun.

Everyone had stunt doubles on the movie. Each of us had a double for horseback riding as well as fighting or jumping from buildings or trains. My riding ability had improved, but not enough for me to do what I considered a dangerous stunt.

In the scene following the shooting of Frankie Ballou, Jane as Cat jumps on her horse and speeds off after his killer, the silver-nosed outlaw, Tim Strawn, also played by Lee. When Jane rides off, Tom, Mickey, and I are supposed to jump on our horses and, at a fast gallop, take a sharp left turn at a barbed wire fence, and follow after her. There was no way I was going to do the stunt, because I felt that it was too dangerous. Elliot Silverstein had already set up the shot, but I told him that I was afraid that I'd fall off the horse and land on the barbed wire, so my double would have to do the scene. He was very upset because he had to reblock his camera moves, but I didn't care what he had to do, I wasn't going to take the chance of falling off the horse at a full gallop. Tom and Mickey said they weren't afraid, and they would shoot their part of the scene as Elliot had staged it. Tom was a very good rider and Mickey claimed to be, but we all knew better. Everyone gave me a disdainful look as my double took my place in the scene. Elliot yelled "Action" and Tom, Mickey and my double jumped on their horses. The speeding horses made the sharp left turn at the barbed wire fence and my foolhardy friend Mickey nearly fell out of the saddle, and was hanging onto the side of the horse as he made the turn. Elliot did only one take, so Mickey's daredevil stunt remains in the movie. After the scene I just gave him a look, like, "I told you so." He held up his hand and said, "I know...you were right."

We wrapped filming on our Canyon City location and prepared to head back to Los Angeles to shoot the remaining scenes on the backlot and sound stages at Columbia Studios in Burbank. The company station wagons were scheduled to leave for the airport at six A.M. It was cold and dark as the bleary-eyed cast piled into the cars. As we looked around we realized that Lee was missing.

As the minutes clicked away and we all sat shivering in the cars, two drivers finally went to his motel room and knocked on the door. When there was no answer they got a pass-key and found Lee stretched out on the bed, sound asleep, still wearing his costume from the day before.

A few moments later a very hung-over Lee emerged from his motel room and headed toward the car. Over his clothes he wore a bathrobe with a bottle of vodka in one pocket and a bottle of tonic in the other. He was wearing dark glasses and a woman's hairnet on his head. The drivers hurriedly threw his belongings into his suitcase and loaded it into the car. Lee got into the seat in front of me. As we were heading down the highway, I was staring at the back of his hairnet when he turned around and asked if I wanted a drink. I said, "No, thanks...it's a little early for me." Lee said, "Suit yourself, baby...," then he proceeded to pour some tonic into his bottle of vodka, shake it up and take a long swig. The hair of the dog was obviously bringing him back. He reached into his bag, pulled out a .45 automatic pistol. Checking the clip, he turned to me and said to roll down the window. Who was I to argue with a guy drinking vodka and tonic, wearing a bathrobe, a woman's hairnet, and dark glasses, with a loaded .45. Lee reached across me and started firing out the window. Four shots went wild, the fifth hit a sign that read 65 MPH and the sixth shot hit a poor cow standing in a pasture. The cow dropped like a stone. Lee gave out a loud "Yee-haw" and turned to us proudly, "Hot damn, I got me a cow." Scared to death, we all stared straight ahead. No one said a word.

We arrived at the airport, boarded the chartered jet, and headed back to Los Angeles. About an hour into the flight I decided to go to the back of the plane to check to see how my gun-slinging friend was doing. Walking down the aisle, I saw Lee and couldn't believe it. There he was, still wearing his bathrobe and hairnet, swigging vodka, and playing poker with the crew.

The game continued until we landed, and by this point Lee was so drunk he could hardly stand up. Someone decided to have a car drive onto the field to pick us up. I guess they thought Lee might turn a few heads if he sauntered through the terminal in his strange getup, not to mention his inebriated state, at eleven in the morning. What Lee didn't realize was that he was scheduled to work that afternoon, so the car took him directly to the studio, where he went into makeup.

The scene Elliot wanted to shoot was in the upstairs of the brothel. Kid Shelleen is dressed up and sober as he walks down the hall, opening each door, looking for the outlaw Tim Strawn. The scene didn't require any dialogue, but it did require a sober Kid Shelleen to walk a straight line down the hall.

The next day I asked Lee how his shooting went. He said the plane trip from location had been really hard on him, but he knocked out the scene in nothing flat. I learned later that after twenty takes Elliot decided to call it a day and he sent Lee home. They wound up shooting the scene as a retake several weeks later.

Two days had been set aside to rehearse and shoot the big barn dance scene. Elliot had decided that he wanted to shoot the entire dance in one continuous master shot, then he would shoot different angles to cover all the action. I danced about as well as I sang, so you know I was in big trouble. We were supposed to be dancing a version of the Virginia reel as we carried on our dialogue. Suddenly, in the middle of the dance a fight breaks out as the bad guys make a nasty remark to Jackson, the Indian, and he takes a punch at one of the men. Everyone gets into the act as chairs break, bottles crash, and people go flying through the air.

Tom Nardini as Jackson was really in the thick of it. I have always hated fight scenes because a lot of the extras and stunt people go crazy. They get caught up in the moment and someone can, and usually does, get hurt.

When it finally came time to film the dance sequence, I was a nervous wreck. I was trying my best to remember all the do-si-dos, turns, and dips, as well as my lines. Unfortunately, I didn't have a dance double or I would have requested that he do the scene. Mickey Callan looked terrific because he was a trained dancer; he even looked graceful when he did the fight scenes.

Once Elliot started shooting this long master shot, with its complicated camera moves, any mistake would blow the take and we would have to start again. "Action!" was called and the scene started. One of the cameramen missed a shot, Elliot called "Cut!" and we reset and started over. "Action!" "Cut!" "Action!" "Cut!" We started and stopped all morning long. Finally we were getting a good take. As the action progressed, we were approaching my part of the scene where I was suppose to swing Jane to and fro as I said my dialogue. I was so nervous that I'd be responsible for blowing the only good take we had all day that I forgot half of my lines. Fortunately for me, Elliot didn't notice my mistake, so he kept on filming. With the dance behind me, my next problem would be getting through the fight scene without getting injured. My character, Jed, was supposed to be somewhat of a coward, so I decided this would be my perfect defense. As the chairs started breaking and the fists started flying, I did my best to protect myself and stay out of the fray. It worked. Both the character Jed and I came through the fight scene unscathed.

Unfortunately that was not the case in the fight scene between Kid Shelleen and Mickey's character, Clay. It is one of my favorite scenes from the movie. Shelleen is jealous of Clay's interest in Cat, so he challenged him to a fight. Shelleen grabs up a chair and says to Clay, "Bottles, fists, clubs, knives, guns. . . . They're all the same to me. . . . All the same to you?" At that point, Lee throws the breakaway chair toward Mickey and me. It broke apart and a splinter flew up and hit me in the eye. I flinched, but kept on going. When Elliot called "Cut!" I was checked out by the studio nurse. The wood had nicked the corner of my eye, but I was fine...and very lucky.

The big final scene, in which I am disguised again as a preacher and walk Cat Ballou to the gallows, was shot on the Western street where Gary Cooper had filmed *High Noon*. Elliot had a tricky shot where a camera on a crane would shoot through the hangman's noose as Jane and I walked up the street toward the gallows. The first take, the cameraman called "Cut!" because the camera moved off its mark. The next take, Jane called "Cut!" because she could see from the ground that once again the camera was out of position. The next take, I yelled "Cut!" Jane turned to me, very annoyed, and said, "Why did you yell 'Cut!'?" I said, "For the same reason you did, the shot was off." Elliot had heard enough. His children were getting out of hand. He called for quiet and insisted that no one except the cameraman and himself would be allowed to stop the scene. The announcement was supposed to be for everyone, but it was Jane and me that he was glaring at.

When the movie wrapped, Jane asked what I was doing next and I told her that I had no idea. She said that she felt sorry for actors who had a family to support. "My brother, Peter, is an actor and he has two children...an actor's life isn't easy."

Shortly after completing *Cat Ballou* I was offered one of the starring roles in the movie *Ski Party* for American International Pictures. Jim Nicholson and Sam Arkoff, the owners of AIP, had been film exhibitors and they decided to start making "date movies," the kind that would run in drive-ins and appeal to the vast teenage audience. All their movies had basically the same theme: pretty girls in bikinis being chased by clean-cut, love-hungry guys. It may have seemed like a strange career move to go from a classic comedy Western like *Cat Ballou* to an AIP date picture like *Ski Party*, but at the time *Cat* was really just a "B" movie for Columbia. When we were making it, no one had any idea that it would become a classic or that Lee Marvin would win an Oscar, and I was paid the same salary for *Ski Party* as I had been for *Cat Ballou*. I also believed, and still do, that it's better to be a working actor than an unemployed one, especially when you have a family to support.

In *Ski Party*, I was set to play Craig Gamble, and the role of my buddy Todd Armstrong would be played by Frankie Avalon. When Frankie and I met at the wardrobe fitting, I reminded him of our first meeting on *American Bandstand* when I made my pitiful singing debut. Unfortunately, he remembered the show almost as well as I did, and we shared a lot of laughs... at my expense! Frankie and I hit it off immediately. We talked about the script and decided that we should play the characters like Hope and Crosby. Frankie would be the Crosby-type character, smart, in-charge and slick, while I would play the Hope role and be the bumbler. We added a lot of funny physical business which helped a not very imaginative script.

I went over to Frankie's house to work on the project and he introduced me to his wife, Kay. I had heard that my old heartthrob, Kay Diebel, had married Frankie Avalon. When she saw me, Kay laughed and asked, "Been on any roller coasters lately?" I then explained to Frankie that Kay and I had dated, years before, and on our last date I had unceremoniously lost my dinner on Sunset Boulevard after she and I had been riding a roller coaster. It suddenly dawned on me that both Frankie and Kay Avalon had witnessed two of the most embarrassing moments of my life. What better way to cement a friendship?

Ski Party was really AIP's attempt to take the beach party concept and move it from the sand to the snow. Our beach-bunny girlfriends, or in this case, snow bunnies, were played by Deborah Walley and, from *Dobie*, Yvonne Craig.

We all flew to Sun Valley, Idaho, where most of the movie was filmed. The ski lodge looked like something out of the Swiss Alps. With its hardwood floors, huge stone fireplace, and rustic European decor, it had something for everyone. There was a huge ice rink out back and a beautiful heated pool. If you wanted fine dining, there was a gourmet dining room, and if you were looking for night life, a disco featured rock-and-roll music into the wee hours. After a day of skiing the guests would return to the lodge and head to the bar, where they'd have a cup of "Glug" in front of a roaring fire. This was they'd have a cup of "Glug" in front of a roaring fire. This was my idea of making a movie! The night before our first day of shooting, Frankie and I went to the local movie theater to see *Becket*, starring Richard Burton and Peter O'Toole. Somehow we weren't really in the mood for twelfth-century England, Thomas Becket, or King Henry II. Like two bad kids, we got hysterical at every line in the film. Finally the manager came over and said that we were disturbing the other patrons. That made us laugh even harder, so we left.

The next morning our call was for six o'clock. We would be filming an elaborate ski sequence, and in order to get to location, Frankie and I had to take three different lifts to get to the very top of the mountain. Dawn was just breaking over the mountains and the wind blew our chair back and forth as we made our way to the top. I have never been colder in my whole life. With the wind chill it felt like fifty below, and since the chair lifts move slowly, Frankie and I nearly froze. As we made our way up the mountain I looked down and nearly passed out. We were so far up, we could barely see the ground.

In the movie Frankie and I are having trouble getting girls. Aron Kincaid played Freddie, the resident hunk, who, with his chiseled good looks, had voluptuous beauties hanging all over him. Throughout the movie Frankie and I would watch him getting all the action and lament, "What does Freddie have that we haven't got?" To try to learn more about girls and the way they trap a man, Frankie and I dressed up as women so that we could infiltrate the girls' quarters. Half of the movie Frankie and I were in drag. It was our version of *Some Like It Hot*.

On this first day of shooting we were all decked out in our wigs and false eyelashes. As the lift slowly made its way up the mountain, imagine Frankie and me dressed in drag, hanging on to each other for dear life. Finally, we reached the top. Nearly frozen, we were helped out of the chair lift only to discover that it was too cold to film. The cameras were frozen, so we had to turn around and go back down the hill. We were both scared to death to get back on the lift, but it was either take the lift or ski down, and the latter was out of the question because neither of us could ski. So Frankie and I braced

Years before *Beethoven*, Mary Ann Mobley and I starred in the Disney
TV movie *My Dog the Thief.* —© *The Walt Disney Company*

*Photos not otherwise
credited are from
the authors' collection*

I was giving my best Cary Grant imitation on *How to Stuff a Wild Bikini* as I tried to impress Annette Funicello. The pelican watching over us was supposed to be Frankie Avalon. I never understood the bit!
—*Aron Kincaid Collection*

In *Dr. Goldfoot and the Bikini Machine* Vincent Price gets ready to zap me with his laser lipstick as Jack Mullaney looks on. It took twenty-seven takes before we could get through the scene without breaking up.

Working on script notes in my office at CBS. The Star sign behind me was a gift from a coworker. They never let me forget!

Joan and I, on our wedding day, April 16, 1983.

I joined former series stars
David Nelson, Bob Denver,
Angela Cartwright, Elinor
Donahue, and Dawn Wells
in *High School U.S.A.*

Dawn Wells and I attend
the Senior Prom in
High School U.S.A.

Once again I'm Dobie to Bob Denver's Maynard G. Krebs and Sheila James's Zelda Gilroy on the set of *Bring Me the Head of Dobie Gillis*—and nearly thirty years earlier in the series *Dobie Gillis*.

Striking my classic poses in the park with Rodin's "Thinker" statue on the series and in the 1988 movie *Bring Me the Head of Dobie Gillis*. Some things never change!

Directing Jean Smart in an episode of *Designing Women*.

On Thanksgiving Day
I brought Joan and our new
son, Albert Thomas, born
November 23, 1992,
home from the hospital.

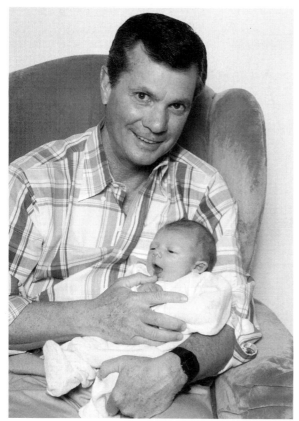

Homecoming Day,
Thanksgiving 1992.

Celebrating Halloween with John in 1968, and with Albert on his first Halloween in 1993.

Playing with Albert.—*Gabe Bandy*

moving down the mountain, bumping and swinging back and forth; then suddenly the lift stopped midway down. There we were, dangling over a ravine that looked deeper than the Grand Canyon. We felt like we were frozen in time...literally. Finally, after what seemed an eternity, we made it down the mountain.

For anyone who skis, you know the most humiliating thing for a skier is to take the lift *down* the mountain. Frankie and I certainly looked like great skiers in our expensive ski wear, but we felt like two fools as we finally hit the ground and were greeted by nearly twenty real skiers on their way up the mountain. I told Frankie that no one would recognize us dressed like women, so he made his way toward the lodge as I followed close behind. A tall, gorgeous blonde passed me and, as our eyes met, she stopped and said, "I know you, you're Dwayne Hickman. Look, everybody, it's Dobie Gillis." I felt like a fool, standing there in drag, signing autographs.

Several days later, in one particularly painful scene, Frankie, Deborah Walley, Yvonne Craig, and I were going on a sleigh ride. I say it was painful because we all were singing "Painting the Town." Lip-synching was never one of my strong points, but I tried my best to keep up. Frankie, of course, was as smooth and confident as ever. By the end of the scene he had the girls doubled over with laughter as he recounted my *American Bandstand* debut. Every time I opened my mouth to chime in on "Painting the Town," Yvonne and Debbie broke up laughing.

After three weeks in Sun Valley, we returned to Los Angeles for a few remaining scenes, one of which took place at the beach. After all, this was an AIP picture and that meant bikinis on the sand as well as bikinis in the snow.

In one particular scene Frankie and I are once again in drag and riding in the back seat of a car. As we pulled off our wigs and turned to say our lines, we took one look at each other and became hysterical. We looked ridiculous with our hair flattened down by the wigs, eye shadow, false eyelashes, and ruby red lips. We tried to start the scene again, but it was no use. We kept breaking up. Unfortunately, Alan Rafkin, the director, kept breaking up. Unfortunately, Alan Rafkin, the director, was not amused. Ten takes later and a lot of lip biting, we finally got through the scene.

We were still filming *Ski Party* when Columbia Pictures premiered *Cat Ballou* in Colorado. I was released for one day to fly up for the movie's premiere. The entire week had been filled with publicity events, but I couldn't get away.

When I boarded the plane, I saw Jane Fonda, who was working on a film and could also only be away for the day. I sat down next to her and asked her what she had been doing. She said that she was working on a movie called *The Chase*, with Marlon Brando and Robert Redford. It was a very dramatic piece written by Lillian Hellman and directed by Arthur Penn. As I listened to her tell about this intense and well-crafted film and the extraordinary performances of Brando and Redford, I hoped that she wouldn't ask me what I was doing. Before I could move to another seat, Jane said, "Well, tell me, what are you working on?" I mumbled, *Ski Party*. She said, "*Ski Party*.... Who's in it?" I told her Frankie Avalon, and she gave me a blank look. I said, "Frankie Avalon, the rock-'n'-roll singer." Jane smiled and said, lying through her teeth, "Oh, that sounds interesting." After a long, awkward silence Jane took out a script and began reading. I didn't have any script so I started reading the airplane safety instruction card, then I pretended to sleep for the rest of the flight.

Ski Party may not have been a dramatic masterpiece, but it was a totally enjoyable experience. Apparently AIP was happy with the film because a few days after it was finished they offered me another picture, *How to Stuff a Wild Bikini*, opposite Annette Funicello. It was to be directed by Bill Asher, who was married to Elizabeth Montgomery, who was tweaking her nose and casting spells as Samantha Stevens on TV's *Bewitched*. Asher had directed a string of "Beach" pictures starting with *Beach Party*, *Bikini Beach*, *Beach Blanket Bingo*, and now *How to Stuff a Wild Bikini*.

Frankie made a cameo appearance as a pelican who watches over Annette to keep her faithful while he's away. I got to do my version of Cary Grant and tried to sweep the unsweepable Annette off her feet.

I had met Annette over the years but didn't know her well until the movie. She was sweet, shy, quiet, and very ladylike. Annette had one of the best figures of any of the girls in the movie, but she always wore her one-piece bathing suit even though bikinis were the hot new look. Girls may have been wearing tinier versions on the beach, but in a film the bottom couldn't be any lower than three finger widths below a girl's navel. The rest of the cast included Beverly Adams, who later married and divorced the hair mogul Vidal Sassoon; Harvey Lembeck; John Ashley, who was married to Deborah Walley from *Ski Party*; Buster Keaton; and Mickey Rooney.

Once again, I was called upon to sing, and this time it was a duet with Annette. AIP got smart and dubbed my voice with another singer. Most of her love duets in the other beach pictures had been with Frankie. It must have been quite a comedown singing with my lip-synching to the voice of someone else, but Annette was gracious and acted like we were doing a great job.

With the bevy of bikinied bunnies prancing around Malibu Beach, Mickey Rooney must have thought he was in heaven. Annette was quiet and kept to herself, but Mickey was always "on," telling stories and entertaining the crew. He also felt compelled to tell everyone how to play their part and then he'd direct every scene he was in. After two days of Mickey telling me how to read my lines and where to move, I had finally had enough. I turned to Bill Asher, the director, and said, "Who's directing this movie, you or Rooney?" After that, Rooney never directed me again. In fact, he never spoke to me for the rest of the film.

After *How to Stuff a Wild Bikini* was finished, I started work on still another AIP picture, *Dr. Goldfoot and the Bikini Machine*. Frankie Avalon and I were teamed again, and this time I played Todd Armstrong, one of the richest men in the world, and Frankie played a secret agent. He was on the trail of the evil Dr. Goldfoot, who was plotting to take over the world by creating beautiful bikinied robots that he would send out to marry the world's richest men. What a plot!

Dr. Goldfoot was AIP's attempt to combine horror, bikini babes, and secret agents and take advantage of the popularity of the James Bond pictures. The studio had also made *I Was a Teenage Werewolf*, starring Michael Landon, and *I Was a Teenage Frankenstein*. AIP had its own formula for success. Put "Teenage," "Bikini," or "Beach" in the title and the kids would come by the thousands to see the picture. *Dr. Goldfoot* was a steal from *Goldfinger*, and the bikini machine was the built-in excuse to have bikini-clad cuties running around.

The mad scientist Dr. Goldfoot was played by the fabulous Vincent Price. Vincent had made a career of playing evil men and mad scientists in many horror movies, but nothing could be farther from his own personality. He was soft-spoken, gentle, and had a wonderful sense of humor. Vincent had a gift for making you feel that you had known him for years.

Dr. Goldfoot and the Bikini Machine was a truly terrible picture, but Frankie, Vincent, and I had such a great time that it somehow made it all worthwhile. Vincent was campy and charming, never taking himself seriously, and was always the first person to laugh at his own performance.

In one scene I was chained to the wall in the basement of his castle and Dr. Goldfoot was threatening to "zap" me with a "laser lipstick." Every time Vincent pulled out that lipstick and pointed it at me he would burst out laughing. It took twenty-seven takes before either of us could get through the scene.

Norman Taurog, who was Jackie Cooper's uncle, was the director. He had been very successful directing *Men of Boys Town*, with Spencer Tracy, and other hits in the 1930s and 1940s, but now he was older, very cranky, and difficult to work with. He acted like Cecil B. DeMille, but this movie wasn't an epic; it was a campy, silly, teen picture.

He directed me in the worst, overdone drunk scene I've ever played. Even now I shudder when I think of how bad I was, though I really shouldn't worry too much about it because hardly anyone saw this awful movie. In fact, it was so bad even

AIP waited to release the picture and the studio had never been known for its great taste in films.

Dr. Goldfoot was the last movie that I made for AIP, and judging from the way that it turned out, I wasn't getting away from them a moment too soon. I was happy, however, that I had been working nonstop, having done the three movies for AIP back-to-back.

After I completed *Dr. Goldfoot*, Carol and I decided to go to Las Vegas for a long weekend. I was especially looking forward to the trip because Nat Cole, my friend from *Cat Ballou*, was headlining at the Sands. I had been a fan of Nat's long before we worked together and enjoyed getting to know him. He kept a very busy schedule playing Vegas, Tahoe, and various club dates around the country. He had complained of not feeling well when we were doing the movie but had not slowed down. The night Carol and I saw him perform he was terrific. I had sent a note to him backstage telling him that we would be at the show that night. Our seats were down front, and during his act he would throw asides to me. The audience loved it, and so did Carol and I. At the end of his act he asked me if I had any requests. When I told him that I loved his hit "Ramblin' Rose," he laughed and said, "Dwayne...You're such a cornball." The audience laughed and exploded into applause. He never did sing "Ramblin' Rose," and later told me backstage that he hated the song. Most of the time, he said, the audience wouldn't let him off the stage unless he sang it. I also found out that he wasn't crazy about "Mona Lisa" either. That was the last time I saw him before his death. Whenever I hear "Ramblin' Rose," I always hear him saying to me, "Dwayne...You're such a cornball."

A few months later I filmed a TV pilot called *We'll Take Manhattan* for Hanna-Barbera. They wanted to get into the half-hour comedy business, so they decided to try to combine live action with cartoons. Unfortunately, network television wasn't ready for Joe Barbera's visionary genius, so they passed on the pilot. Years later Disney came up with the same idea and made a fortune with the hugely successful *Who Framed Roger Rabbit?*

In the spring of 1966 I was cast in the MGM movie *Doctor, You've Got to Be Kidding*. I played one of Sandra Dee's boy-friends, along with George Hamilton and Bill Bixby. Bill had just finished filming the last season of his series *My Favorite Martian*. He had come a long way since his first acting job on *Dobie*.

The movie was about a beautiful young woman, Sandra Dee, and her mother, played by Celeste Holm, who wanted to get her daughter into show business. Sandra falls in love with her handsome boss, played, of course, by George Hamilton. Bixby was her childhood boyfriend and I was an aspiring actor who worked in a shoe store. My specialty was dying, so I was dropping dead all over the place. When Sandra finds out that she is pregnant, both Bill and I offer to marry her, but she's in love with George, who finally ties the knot after she has the baby. Nobody can play a cad like George Hamilton.

He was dating Lynda Byrd Johnson, the president's oldest daughter, at the time. He'd drive to work in his Rolls Royce and make jokes about his mortgaged mansions and leased cars. He was always very charming about the whole thing and you got the feeling that it was all a big put-on. The interesting thing is that, years later, George really became the character that he was pretending to be.

We had a birthday party for Sandra on the set, and her husband, Bobby Darin, stopped by. Dressed in a silk suit and puffing on a big cigar, he turned to me and said, "Hold this for me," and started to hand me his cigar. I looked at him like he was nuts and told him to hold his own cigar, then I walked off. Bobby had quite an opinion of himself. He and Sandra were the golden couple around town. They seemed happy on the set, but a short time later they were divorced. Maybe he asked her to hold his cigar one too many times!

We were all pleasant to one another, but each cast member was very different. Sandra was reclusive and stayed in her dressing room, George was "Mr. Jet Setter," Bill had become "Mr. Hollywood," and Celeste Holm, the old pro, just took it all in and rolled her eyes.

In the two years since *Dobie* had gone off the air I had

filmed five movies and starred in two TV pilots. Carol and I had bought our second home, and I was enjoying fatherhood with my two-year-old son John.

I remembered Jane Fonda's comment about her brother Peter and how difficult it was being an actor with a family to support. I felt grateful and relieved that I didn't have to worry about my career. I was sure that sooner or later I would do another pilot, it would sell, then I'd be back on television for another long run. I would soon find out that an actor's life is anything but secure. The times were changing, and so was the direction of my life.

• TEN •

MR. HUGHES AND THE VEGAS BLUES

IN 1968 AMERICA WAS IN THE THROES of a revolution. The teens had grown out their crew cuts, burned their loafers, white shirts, and neckties, and taken to the streets in protest.

Suddenly I was looked on as an out-of-style throwback to the 1950s and my clean-cut image as Dobie Gillis was no longer what Hollywood was casting. Leads in movies and television shows were now angry and dark, and the hairy antihero was replacing the wholesome leading man of the past.

I had been cast in an episode of (Raymond Burr's) *Ironside* where I played a sleazy drug dealer. Thinking back, I realize how ridiculous I must have looked with my three days' growth of beard and the fake sideburns that were glued to my face. No matter how hard the makeup or wardrobe departments tried to transform me from the fifties "all-American kid" to the sixties "angry young man," it never really worked. Even in an episode of *The Flying Nun* I had to wear a fake mustache. Somehow everyone figured if they just kept gluing hair on my face, I would suddenly be transformed into Al Pacino or Jack Nicholson.

Aside from the fact that I felt foolish with this strip of hair glued under my nose, I really had a wonderful time working on the show with Sally Field. Sally and I shared the same style of playing comedy, but unfortunately for her, she was no more ethnic or gritty than I was, so after *The Flying Nun* her squeaky clean image was also out of style. Following a long dry spell Sally finally got a break when cast in the TV movie *Sybil* playing a woman with multiple personalities.

I was struggling to fit into the new, angry, hairy, antihero trend, and for the first time in ten years I was beginning to have trouble finding work.

That winter I was offered a play called *Drink to Me Only* at the Pheasant Run Playhouse in St. Charles, Illinois, a suburb of Chicago. Tom Poston had a successful run on Broadway in the lead role of Miles Pringle, a young lawyer defending a man who is accused of drinking two bottles of whiskey and biting a woman on her thigh. He sets out to prove that he can drink two bottles of whiskey in twenty-four hours and not get drunk. It was a wonderfully funny role because during the play Miles Pringle becomes progressively more drunk as he pleads his case.

While I was doing the play, Carol and John stayed with her family in Detroit, and during the run she flew to Chicago to see the show on several occasions. Chicago was hit by a blizzard after our first week, and the snow was banked so high along the streets that parked cars were completely covered. I couldn't believe that anyone would venture out in subzero weather and snow that was thigh high, but Chicago residents are hardy folks and every night was sold out. Working at night in a play in a strange city can be very lonely, and the days seem endless when you're trying to kill time prior to going to the theater.

The Playhouse had rented a Lincoln Continental for me to use during the run of the show, and when the streets were finally cleared of snow, I decided to tool around Chicago and see the city. Driving along, I'd turn down any street that looked interesting, and before long I realized that I had gotten off the beaten path. I stopped the car and took out my city map, but I was so turned around that the only thing I could figure out was that I was in the heart of the south side of Chicago, and I had no idea how to get out. Not only was I nervous about the area but it was also after four o'clock and I needed to get back to St. Charles or I'd be late for the show. It was getting dark and bitterly cold when I spotted a small market, so I decided that I'd better ask for directions. It was so cold that the glass on the front of the market was all fogged up from the heat inside so I couldn't see into the store. As I pushed the door open and stepped in, I looked up and my heart nearly stopped. The market was filled with nearly twenty of the toughest, meanest, and biggest guys I had ever seen. They also seemed startled to see a white man dressed in a black cashmere overcoat, hat, and kid gloves standing in their store. I didn't say a word and started to step back outside as gracefully as possible.

As I moved for the door, a voice behind me said, "Where you going?" I turned and discovered I was staring into the chest of a guy who looked like a fullback for the Chicago Bears. I tried not to let on that I was scared to death, but when I attempted to speak nothing came out. If it's true that people can smell fear, then I'm sure that I was permeating that little market. A smaller guy, only about six-feet-five came over and said, "Nice coat." I mumbled a thank-you and moved toward the door. When I turned, the guy put his hand on my shoulder, and I suddenly had sweat pouring from every pore of my body. He said, "Hey, man, don't I know you.... You don't live around here, do you?" I squeaked that I lived in California. Before I could finish my sentence another guy said, "Hey, man, I know you...you're Dobie." I wasn't sure if that would be good or bad, but I muttered that he was right, I was Dobie Gillis. Suddenly the entire atmosphere changed. Smiles broke out on their faces and I was being high-fived and hugged. For the few who didn't know who or what a Dobie Gillis was, they were told that he was this dude who couldn't get a chick and had no cash.

Then they asked me about Bob Denver; some knew him as Maynard, others as Gilligan, but they wanted to know all about him. I told them that he was a great guy and that he was expecting my call in a very short time, so I needed directions back to my hotel. Of course, that wasn't true, but Bob was being so well received that I figured I would throw that in as a little insurance that I would get out of there in one piece. They argued among themselves about who would escort me out of the area and back on the expressway while I signed autographs and made nervous small talk. I got back in my car and followed my new friends to the on-ramp, then I smiled, waved good-bye, and drove straight to the theater, where I arrived twenty minutes before the show. I was a wreck, but I can honestly say that never before or since have I been happier that I was Dobie Gillis.

The rest of the run was uneventful due to the fact that I didn't venture out of the Pheasant Run Complex, which housed the hotel, restaurant, and theater. After my experience on the south side I didn't want to push my luck. Once the show closed, I flew to Detroit, picked up Carol and John, and headed for home.

A few months later I did a terrible movie called *Don't Push, I'll Charge When I'm Ready*. Even the title was awful. It was about a prisoner-of-war camp, and I starred along with Sue ("Lolita") Lyon, Cesar Romero, and a hot young Italian actor, Enzo Cerusico. The movie was directed by a fellow named Nathaniel Lande, who was married to Bob Hope's daughter, Linda. She was a friend of the family, and this was Nat's first time directing a feature film. (His previous experience had been in documentaries.) Not only was the script terrible, but my performance as the stuttering soldier in charge of the POWs didn't do anything to help my career or the movie.

I made a few more guest appearances on TV shows like *Love, American Style* and *Mod Squad*. On *Love, American Style* I was dressed in the hippest clothes of the day: a polyester, burgundy bellbottom suit, flowered shirt, and a necktie that was wide enough to be a cummerbund. And, to complete the look, I had fake mutton-chop sideburns glued to my cheeks. Once again I was getting the distinct impression that I didn't fit into what Hollywood was looking for.

The last place in town that was still casting the clean-cut

all-American look was, of course, Walt Disney Studios. It had been several years since I had met Mr. Disney and had to turn down the movie *Bon Voyage* because of *Dobie's* shooting schedule. I was offered the starring role in a two-part TV movie, *My Dog the Thief*. My love interest was Mary Ann Mobley, the former Miss America, who was married to the actor Gary Collins. She had recently given birth to their daughter Clancy, and this was her return to work. The other star was comedian Joe Flynn, who was best known as the bumbling, bombastic captain in *McHale's Navy*, with Ernest Borgnine.

Mary Ann, Joe, and I hit it off the moment we met. Unfortunately, the director, Robert Stevenson, didn't seem to enjoy himself nearly as much as we did. In fact, Joe and I had the distinct feeling that Mr. Stevenson was not particularly impressed by either one of us. Stevenson was an older, very British gentleman who had directed such classics as *Jane Eyre* with Joan Fontaine and Orson Welles, as well as Disney's *Mary Poppins*, which won an Oscar for Julie Andrews. He was under contract to Disney, and we had the impression that he considered our television movie a bit of a comedown. I'm sure he would have been a lot happier if he'd been working with the two actors who had been his first choice for the movie, Dean Jones and Fred MacMurray. Instead, he got me in Dean's part, and Joe was trying to fill Fred MacMurray's shoes.

From the first day of filming Stevenson called me "Dean" and Joe "Fred." Instead of being upset it became a constant source of amusement to Joe and me. Joe pulled me aside one day and quipped, "If Dean Jones and Fred MacMurray show up, we'll know we're through!" Even the crew shook their heads and chuckled every time Stevenson called us by the wrong names. One day Joe was doing a funny scene that was very physical. He was concentrating on what he was doing, so when Stevenson gave him some direction and called him Fred, Joe didn't respond. Stevenson took this as an affront and yelled, "Fred, Fred, damnit, Fred, I'm speaking to you." Then, in unison, the crew yelled, "His name is Joe, not Fred." Stevenson looked confused. Joe snapped out of his deep thought, looked at him straight-faced and said, "Who the hell is Joe? My name's Fred." The crew fell apart as Stevenson gave them a self-satisfied look and said, "Of course, you're Fred, I knew that."

Dobie Gillis had been in reruns for several years and had become an even bigger hit than when we were originally on the air. When my agent put me up for roles, the feedback was that I was too identifiable as Dobie. On one commercial interview the client nearly leaped over the table to shake my hand and told me what a fan he was of the show. When he asked me for my autograph, I gladly signed the picture that I had brought in for the audition. As I signed, I figured that I was guaranteed this national commercial for his fast-food chain. National commercials can be extremely lucrative, and in typical actor fashion, I was cashing six-figure residual checks in my head as I handed the client my autograph. He shook my hand again and said that he couldn't wait to get home and put my picture on the wall in his den. Then he said that it was too bad that he couldn't hire me for the commercial, but it had been a thrill meeting me. This was obviously my cue to leave. I headed toward the door, but my curiosity got the better of me. I asked him why I wouldn't be perfect for his commercial. His exuberant attitude quickly chilled as he told me that he was paying big money to produce these commercials and if he used me, the public would only remember Dobie Gillis, not his restaurant chain. He thanked me again for the autograph and I left.

The next day Carol, John, and I were heading to Las Vegas to visit some friends for the weekend. During the long drive all I could think about was the experience on the commercial audition. I had enjoyed playing Dobie Gillis, but I could do other roles, yet no one really wanted me. I was either too clean-cut or too identified with Dobie. The whole business was grating on my nerves. For the first time in many years I was seriously considering getting out of show business.

I had been watching America go through some strange metamorphosis, from a country of traditional thinking to a war zone with angry mobs taking to the streets and demonstrating about everything from an unpopular war to free love. Although I wasn't "the older generation," I was almost thirty-six and a married man with a six-year-old son. My priorities were not the same as the angry protesters. I certainly understood the issues and agreed with the need for change in some areas, but what I couldn't understand was the need to burn flags, riot in the streets, or look like you hadn't changed your clothes or taken a bath in a week. I not only didn't relate to the hippie movement, I didn't even relate to the popular music of the period. Although I liked Janis Joplin, I never cared about the heavy metal bands or the Beatles, the Rolling Stones, or Jimi Hendrix. I was still enjoying Ray Charles, the Lettermen, and Elvis Presley, who was about to hit the same career stone wall that I was experiencing.

I guess I was really a product of the fifties, and in 1970 I seemed very out of step and very out of style. I didn't realize at the time that everything moves in cycles, and this, too, would pass.

During those angry years no one would have believed that by 1980 Ronald Reagan would sweep into the White House and that the American people would have tired of the chaos of the sixties and seventies. The baby boomers who had been marching in the streets would suddenly be hungry for the nostalgia of their youth. They would be looking for simpler times and more traditional values, and who better to share those precious memories than their old friend Dobie Gillis. But all of this was a long ten years away, and in 1970 I was seriously considering making some radical changes of my own.

By the time I arrived in Las Vegas, I was more and more annoyed by the whole situation. That weekend I talked at length with our friends about the frustrations of my career. I told them that I was thinking about getting away from acting and maybe moving my family out of Los Angeles. I had been acting all of my life and felt that I needed a change. Carol and I enjoyed Las Vegas with its desert climate, and we had often talked about moving there, but I didn't know what I would do with my time, because I wanted to be active and busy. The subject was dropped as I went off to play golf with our friends, but it stayed in the back of my mind.

Several weeks later, on another visit, I met some executives who worked for Howard Hughes. They were with the Hughes Nevada Operations, which ran his Las Vegas hotels. We were talking about the hotel business when one of the gentlemen asked me if I would ever consider moving to Las Vegas. I told him that I had thought about leaving Los Angeles and making some career changes. Then he told me that the Hughes Nevada Operations was looking for someone with a show business background to handle the entertainment and publicity for one of Hughes's newest hotels. Howard Hughes had just purchased the Landmark Hotel and, as the story goes, Hughes looked out of his penthouse window at the Desert Inn, which he also owned, saw the Landmark, and said, "Buy it," and twenty-three million dollars later they realized that they had a white elephant on their hands. This gentleman felt that I would be the perfect choice for the job in entertainment and publicity, so he gave me his card and asked me to call him. Carol and I discussed it and thought that working in a large Las Vegas hotel could be exciting and certainly different from anything that I had ever done. So we decided that I should sit down with the Hughes people; maybe this was just the opportunity that I had been looking for.

Several days later I met with Al Benedict who was in charge of all of Hughes's hotels in Las Vegas: the Sands, Silver Slipper, the Frontier, Desert Inn, and now the Landmark. He reported to Bob Maheu, who reported directly to Hughes. Bob headed up the Hughes Nevada Operations, while the rest of the mogul's company, Hughes Tool, was headquartered in Texas. Al Benedict was an Ivy League graduate, smart, refined, and totally in charge. As I sat across the desk and talked to him about the job at the Landmark, I looked into his piercing eyes and realized that this was not a guy to fool around with. Al sent me over to the Landmark to meet with the new general manager, Frank Modica. He and I talked, and I could see that he was about to offer me the job of director of entertainment and publicity, and if I wasn't serious about making this major change in my life, now was the time to get out. The moment came. Frank offered and I accepted. Before you could say "Ace

High Flush" we sold our house in Los Angeles, bought a new one in Las Vegas, and I was spending eighteen hours a day learning the hotel business.

From the moment I started I was entering a world that I knew absolutely nothing about. My experience with Vegas and casinos had been as a tourist. There was also the preconceived notion that the business was filled with guys named "Benny the Butcher," "Ice Pick Louie," and "Harry the Hammer." That notion was not entirely false. When any of these gentlemen of questionable character came around, they always made sure that I wasn't a part of any of their conversations. That was fine with me. I just tried to stay out of their way, be pleasant, and do my job.

Frank Modica, the new general manager of the Landmark and my boss, was a Vegas veteran. He had been the general manager of the Showboat, an older hotel that was a favorite of the locals. Frank set out to teach me everything he knew about hotels, casinos, gambling, and the politics of Las Vegas. When I arrived at the hotel in the morning until late at night, I became Frank Modica's shadow. If you saw Frank, you could be sure that I was no more than three feet away. I was used to working intensely on a movie and spending long hours on the set, but in the back of your mind you know that the shoot will be over in a few weeks. But unlike a movie my hotel job, with its long hours, was relentless, and there was no end in sight. I was also thrown into a totally foreign environment with personalities that were intense, to say the least.

A few weeks after I started work at the hotel, Frank told me that he was going to apply for a license to carry a gun. He felt that he needed protection because he got home late at night and he and his wife liked to walk their dog after midnight. I wondered who he might need protection from, but I wasn't about to press him for information, so I just smiled and told him that it sounded like a perfectly reasonable idea to me. A few days later I walked into his office and he was examining his new .38 revolver. I admired Frank's "piece," then left his office as quickly as possible. All I could think was "What have I gotten myself into?"

When I accepted the position at the Landmark, I was intrigued by the glamour and excitement of working in a resort hotel. With the twenty-four-hour gambling and hustle and bustle of Las Vegas, it appeared to be one continuous party. I think that I was under the impression that I would be working in the equivalent of an Aaron Spelling TV show; a combination *"Love Boat* Meets *Hotel."* What I soon discovered was a job that demanded that I spend nearly every waking hour at the hotel. For me, there would be very little glamour, fun, or excitement.

The Landmark required even more time than most hotels because business was slow, the entertainment was old-fashioned, and, worst of all, the casino wasn't making a profit. Frank quickly taught me that the key to a successful Vegas hotel is the casino. That's the element that drives the business—not the rooms, not the entertainment, restaurants, or conventions, only the gambling. Each morning we would go over the results of the prior night's business. We looked at "the handle," which is the amount of money that was gambled and "the hold," which is the profit the hotel made from the gambling. Unfortunately, our profits were down, and the entertainment, which is the draw to get crowds coming through the casino, wasn't doing the job. The Landmark had inherited some entertainment contracts from several of Hughes's other Vegas hotels, such as the Sands, Frontier, Desert Inn, and Silver Slipper. It wasn't that they thought the Landmark could benefit from the acts; they just wanted to push them off on another hotel and get some fresh entertainment into their showrooms. Singer Patti Page had a contract requiring that she be paid around $35,000 a week and the hotel would also pick up the expense of the orchestra, which ran an additional $15,000. Suddenly our entertainment was costing $50,000 a week, which would have been fine if Patti Page fans were big gamblers, but unfortunately they were not. Trini Lopez was also making nearly the same salary, and he was also drawing a nongambling family crowd.

Jimmy Dean, prior to his becoming the sausage king, drew a crowd that didn't mind leaving some cash at the casino. Jimmy was making a lot of money as a performer, so I was surprised when he told me one night that he was sick of show business and that he and his brother, Don, were going to start selling sausage. Sarcastically I quipped, "Oh, yeah, I've thought about getting out of the business and selling sausage too, but instead I went to work for Howard Hughes." Jimmy just looked at me, and I realized that he didn't think I was very funny. He said, "I'm serious. My brother and I are going to start a sausage business called 'Jimmy Dean Sausage' and I'm gonna promote it." Well, the rest is history. Not only was Jimmy Dean Sausage a huge success, but he later sold the company to the Sara Lee Corporation for millions of dollars.

The other entertainer who could draw a good crowd was Connie Francis. Connie was a very talented performer, but she was always plagued by colds, viruses, or "Vegas Throat." She told us that she couldn't sing if the air conditioner was running, so the moment she walked out on stage we had to turn off the air, which seemed like an unbelievable request, because Connie performed most of her show in a full-length mink coat. Under the hot lights it must have been nearly a hundred degrees on the stage, and unless she had the blood of a snake I could never figure out why she didn't keel over. Connie was also filling the house, which meant that hundreds of bodies were packed in the showroom like sardines. Within minutes the menus turned into fans, people were swabbing the sweat off their faces with the napkins, and some were having to leave the room for fear of heat exhaustion. If Connie felt hot, she had a signal, like putting her hand to her brow, which meant that a little air conditioning was okay. If she felt chilled, another signal, like a hand at her throat, meant "Cut the air." She made all of these subtle signals without so much as missing a lyric or note. The stage manager, on the other hand, kept his hand on the controls trying to make sure that he wasn't misinterpreting a dramatic singing gesture for an air-conditioning cue. Imagine watching Connie standing in a mink coat singing "Where the Boys Are" and clutching her throat or touching her brow as the air conditioner kicked on and off while her sweat-drenched audience rubbed ice cubes over their faces so they wouldn't pass out.

Frank Modica and I knew something had to be done to change the Landmark's entertainment policy. Because our entertainment was so expensive and wasn't drawing a gambling crowd, the hotel usually operated in the red. More than once we had to borrow money from the Hughes Tool Company so that we could make our payroll.

I had always been a fan of country music, but the only country performers in Las Vegas worked in the downtown hotels like the Golden Nugget, Binion's Horseshoe, the Four Queens, or the Showboat out on Boulder Highway. Country performers had never been booked into any of the major hotels on the Strip, and I felt that we had a wonderful opportunity to be the first to give the thousands of country-western fans a place to see their favorite stars and spend their money gambling. I also knew that many of the country acts traveled with their own bands, and many of the singers played their own instruments, so without having to hire a backup orchestra we would be saving the hotel around $15,000 per week.

There was a country music and comedy show called *Hee Haw* that was very popular and ran for years on television. The show featured some of country music's biggest stars and, of course, buxom "Daisy Mae" beauties. I felt that this kind of show would be the perfect way to bring country to the hotel, so I ran the idea by Frank and he agreed that we should give it a try. I contacted an agent in Nashville and booked some young country stars and surrounded them with older country performers like "Grandpa" Jones, Roy Acuff, Junior Samples, and others. We called the show, "The Landmark Presents the Grand Ol' Opry." Then I lined up bigger stars like Roy Clark, Buck Owens, Tammy Wynette, Waylon Jennings, Bobbie Gentry, and Jerry Lee Lewis to bring their shows to the hotel.

But before we could go forward with the plan, Frank and I had to get the okay from Moe Lewis, the head of entertainment for the Sands. Even though Frank was the general manager of the Landmark he still had to consult with Moe on all entertainment decisions. This practice did not please Frank at all, but as he had taught me, in Las Vegas when you deal with people you don't always know who they're connected to, so you have to try to get along with everybody. Frank and I met with Moe, and I tried to explain, with great excitement, about our plan to bring country music to the Landmark. Moe was not the easiest guy to deal with. He was a tall, bald man who always had a cigarette hanging from his mouth, and with his pasty white skin he looked as if he hadn't been outside of the casino for fifteen or twenty years. The expression on his face gave the impression that he had a perpetual case of indigestion. He even looked like a guy who should be called "Moe"! As I started to pitch my idea, I could see his eyes darting around the room, and I knew that he wasn't the least bit interested. I was hoping that once I told him about the big-name performers that I could book, he would see the whole picture and share in my excitement. That just shows you how naive and stupid I was.

I began reeling off names like Roy Clark, Tammy Wynette, and Jerry Lee Lewis, but Moe just continued to smoke and look around the room. I felt like an actor in a bad play as flop sweat started breaking out on my forehead. I had given him my biggest names, and the only thing I had left was to tell him about the Grand Ol' Opry. Smoke swirled around his face as he said, "Grand Ol' Opry...who's gonna be in that?" Now I figured if this guy wasn't impressed with Roy, Tammy, and Jerry Lee, he really wasn't gonna come to life when I told him about Roy Acuff, "Grandpa" Jones, and Junior Samples. I mustered up all the excitement I had left and said, "Do you remember Roy Acuff, who sang that great old song, 'The Wabash Cannonball'?" Moe said that he not only didn't re-member the song, he'd never heard of the guy. I told him that Roy Acuff owned Acuff Rose Publishing and the rights to nearly every big country song that was ever published. Then I added, "Moe, this guy is a multimillionaire." He eyed me with a "You're really getting on my nerves" look. Getting on Moe's nerves was definitely something I did not want to do. To Frank Modica's credit, he wasn't a country music fan, but he stood behind me and started telling Moe what he really wanted to hear, that we could put on a big show for $25,000 a week instead of $50,000, plus we'd be drawing crowds that were going downtown to see these country people. He told him that it was better to have them gambling at the Landmark than downtown at the Horseshoe. That made sense to Moe, so he gave his okay and Frank and I went into action.

I immediately began publicizing "The Landmark's Grand Ol' Opry." I went to one of the local radio stations, KVEG, and we set up a contest where the listeners could win albums and tickets to see their favorite country star perform at the hotel. From the moment we opened, the country format was a hit. The crowds came, the traffic in the casino picked up, and the patrons were, thankfully, leaving some of their money on the blackjack tables, at the roulette wheels, and in the slot machines.

Several days after the show opened, Moe came up to me and said that he had his people do some investigating and he couldn't believe how much money these country people made. Then he said, "And you wouldn't believe that ol' guy, Roy Acuff, he's worth millions, he owns some music company." I just smiled and acted surprised. Then he slapped me on the back and walked off. I can't begin to tell you how glad I was that Moe was happy. I was the new guy in town, and the last thing that I wanted to do was to come up with some idea that would blow up in my face, if you know what I mean.

After the Grand Ol' Opry show closed, the individual acts started to play the hotel. One of my favorite country stars was Roy Clark, who is an incredible talent. Roy was also a Dobie Gillis fan. When we first met, he thought I was one of the performers at the hotel. As we stood talking one day in the lobby, every few minutes our conversation was interrupted by fans coming up to shake my hand or simply passing by and yelling, "Hi, Dobie." Once they stopped to speak to me, they'd turn and discover Roy, and before long we were drawing a crowd. We decided to finish our conversation in my office. He watched in amusement as people came up to shake my hand or say hello as we made our way through the casino. When we finally got to my office, he said, "Hey, Dwayne, what are you doing, running for president?...I never saw so much hand shaking and carrying on." I think most of the fans were surprised to see me in the hotel. As many of them told me, they never expected Dobie Gillis to be working in Las Vegas.

Roy told me years later that I had revived his career by introducing country music to the Strip. Because of his success at the Landmark he was then booked into the other big Strip hotels.

Tammy Wynette followed Roy, then Waylon Jennings and Buck Owens. Each week the showroom was packed, and the casino was filled with country music fans happily losing their money. When the other major hotels realized how successful the Landmark was becoming, they decided to open their doors and welcome the country performers into their showrooms. Suddenly country music had moved "uptown," bringing throngs of loyal fans who loved to eat, drink, and, most important, gamble.

Frank was very pleased with the new business we were generating, but one day he pulled me aside and said that he wanted to give me some advice. He could see that I was friendly with the celebrities, but he felt that I should keep my distance from them. He said, "They'll get to know you, then start complaining and wanting you to do things for them." Everything had been going well for me, but I thanked him for his advice and went on my way. It wasn't long before I found out that, once again, Frank knew what he was talking about.

I had booked Bobbie Gentry, the sultry brunette singer and songwriter whose big hit, "Ode to Billy Joe" had made her a superstar. Many of the stars' contracts called for the hotel to rent a house for them while they were performing as well as provide them with anything from musical instruments to special foods, liquors, or massages, and we were only too happy to accommodate them. Most of the stars traveled with assistants, and Bobbie was no exception. Unfortunately, her "Girl Friday" was a very pushy young lady who demanded anything she could think of by simply saying, "Ms. Gentry would like..." and she'd fill in the order. After the first five phone calls from this gal, I started to see what Frank had been trying to tell me.

When I met Bobbie, she was cool but pleasant, so I figured we wouldn't have any problems. I had made sure the house was prepared and ready for her, and the only thing that I had requested was that she be available for some radio interviews to promote her show. She agreed, and I set up interviews with several radio stations for the next day. I had planned to pick her up at her rented house and drive her to the interviews, but before I left the hotel I called to tell her I was on my way. When Bobbie answered the phone, from the tone of her voice I knew I had a problem. She was cold and very short as she informed me that she couldn't make the interviews and then she hung up. I scrambled to cancel with the radio stations, still not understanding why she had a problem. Before long, Frank summoned me into his office and told me that he had received a call from our friend Moe Lewis. Bobbie had phoned him after she hung up on me, telling him that she was furious that I had been allowed to call her and disturb her concentration while she was writing a new song. She told Moe to keep me out of her sight and not to let anyone disturb her again. Frank looked at me with a "What did I tell you" look. I had been in show business and a celebrity for years, and I had never behaved in such an obnoxious manner. For the first time in my life I was seeing performers from a totally different perspective, and I didn't like what I was seeing.

One of my all-time favorite country performers was Jerry Lee Lewis, so you can imagine how thrilled I was when I booked him to play the Landmark. From the moment Jerry Lee arrived I knew it would be a week to remember. To say Jerry Lee was a handful is an understatement. He bounded onto the stage with incredible energy, bringing his audience to a fever pitch as he wailed out hit after hit. Playing the piano with a vengeance, he banged the keys with his fingers, feet, bottom, head, and anything else that could be used to hammer the piano. Amazingly, whatever he used produced that throbbing beat that he was famous for, and when he finished the act with "Great Balls of Fire" I thought the audience would go crazy. After the show his fired-up troops hit the casino and gambled into the night. Jerry Lee would take off after an exhausting performance and prowl the Strip, coming back drunk the next morning.

About three days into his engagement I got a call from security telling me they had a problem and asking me to come to Jerry Lee's room. His reputation as a wild, crazy man was legendary, so I didn't know what to expect. When Jerry Lee was sober, he acted fairly normal, but with the intake of a tremendous amount of alcohol he became a maniac. Even with all the stories I had heard, nothing in my wildest imagination could have prepared me for what I saw when I opened the door to his suite. It looked like a tornado had set down in the center of the room, sucked everything off the floor and walls, thrown it into the air, and let it land in a heap. Actually, a tornado had hit, and its name was Jerry Lee Lewis. Chairs were smashed, windows broken, the drapes were in shreds, and anything that wasn't nailed down or screwed into the floor was turned over. The security guard turned and said, "That must have been one hell of a party." I told him to keep an eye on our star performer for the rest of the week, then we moved him to another suite and cleared all the other rooms on the floor. I called maintenance to haul away the broken furniture and make repairs. Nothing was ever said to Jerry Lee, and that night he gave another incredible show and again he partied until dawn. Fortunately that was the only wild rampage we had during his stay. He only did minor damage the next few nights, like broken glasses and a few overturned pieces of furniture. Jerry Lee was definitely a guy you wouldn't want as a house guest. For the Landmark it was chalked up as the cost of doing business because Jerry Lee Lewis packed the house every night and filled the casino with gambling fans. No matter what he cost the hotel in damages, we would make the money back a hundred times over in the casino.

As the hotel was turning around, our Nevada bosses suddenly became embroiled in a power struggle with Hughes Tool Company of Houston. They were fighting for their jobs, so they were paying little attention to the fact that the Landmark was beginning to see more black ink than red. When Hughes asked Bob Maheu, an ex-FBI agent, to head up his Nevada business, it apparently led to a rivalry between the Las Vegas and Houston factions of his empire. One of the interesting things about working for Howard Hughes was that everything was cloaked in mystery. Everyone claimed to know him and talk to him, yet you couldn't get a straight answer from anyone about anything. Executives who had never laid eyes on the man would come up and say, "Mr. Hughes feels that the show could be better," or "Mr. Hughes wanted you to know he was pleased with the radio promotion." These statements were all said in a serious tone and given with a knowing look as if they had just imparted some special message from our mysterious leader. The truth was that only a few people ever saw Hughes during those years. I always believed everything I ever heard about Howard Hughes; but then again, I also believe in Santa Claus and the Easter Bunny!

The real power struggle between the Texas and Nevada factions took place shortly after I came to work at the hotel. The story, as I was told, was that several people from Hughes Tool in Houston came to the boss's penthouse at the Desert Inn and spirited him out of the hotel at night and into a railroad car where his final destination would be the Bahamas. Once he was physically out of Vegas, the fight for power between Bob Maheu's Hughes Nevada Operations and Hughes Tool in Texas really heated up. Eventually Bob was fired, and he later sued Hughes for slander. I knew Bob Maheu and found him a very entertaining and colorful character.

While all this drama was taking place over the next year and a half, I was dealing with my own problems at home. From the beginning I would go to work early, come home and grab a bite of dinner, then go back to the hotel until late at night. I never had any time to spend with my family, and it wasn't long before Carol and I started drifting apart. She was spending more time with friends to fill the empty hours while I worked late every night at the hotel. I knew my marriage was suffering and I had to take control of the situation.

A few months later I was introduced to a gentleman who was a partner in an advertising agency in Little Rock, Arkansas. He was in Las Vegas because the agency wanted to open a branch office and needed someone to head its new operation. He felt that with my experience with publicity and my high visibility through my work at the hotel I would be the person for the job. As much as I knew that I needed to get out the hotel business, I felt very torn about leaving the Landmark. There were many aspects of my job that I enjoyed, and I knew that Frank Modica had trained me with the idea that I would one day become general manager of a hotel and casino. I felt that I was letting him down, but my marriage was falling apart and the price of working the long hours the hotel business required was too high. When I told Carol about the offer from the advertising agency and that I would be heading the office and keeping normal hours, she begged me to take the job. After a lot of soul searching I realized that I had to resign from the hotel or my marriage would be over. I felt terrible as I gave Frank my notice. He had been a very decent man. He had worked very closely with me and taken great pride in my accomplishments, but he understood why I had to leave. Reluctantly he said good-bye and wished me luck.

It was wonderful to be able to spend time with John and Carol and keep normal business hours. I hustled around and tried to sign up accounts, but I soon discovered that Vegas was a very cliquish town. When I would call on different companies or make requests as a representative of the Landmark, I had the muscle of the Hughes Nevada Operations behind me. But now, calling as Dwayne Hickman, advertising executive, I received a cooler and tougher response.

The Bank of Nevada was looking for a new ad agency, and every advertising man in Las Vegas was after the account. I put together a campaign and went in to pitch my ideas. I was waiting to hear if I had been awarded the account when my partners from Little Rock flew in for a meeting. They were not happy with the progress we were making in the Las Vegas office, and I, on the other hand, was not happy with their sloppy bookkeeping and the way they conducted business. After a long, loud, and very unpleasant meeting, we decided to dissolve the partnership and close the Las Vegas office. I wanted to continue in the advertising business, so I was going to open my own agency. While I was in the process of closing the office, I got a call from the vice president of advertising at the Bank of Nevada, Cal Sheehy. He wanted to congratulate me on landing the Bank of Nevada account and to tell me how much they looked forward to working with me. I told him how pleased I was to be awarded the account, but my partners and I were closing the Las Vegas office. Cal was shocked and a little annoyed since this put him in an embarrassing position with the bank. He had personally fought to give the account to me rather than an older, more established agency because he was so impressed with my presentation. He asked me what I would be doing after I closed the office and I told him that I was going to open my own advertising agency and continue looking for accounts. Once again I apologized for the situation and we said good-bye. A few hours later Cal called me back and told me that if I thought I could handle their account, they would give me all of the Bank of Nevada's business. I told him that I could and graciously accepted his offer. I also said that I would appear in their radio and television commercials. We put together a very successful campaign featuring the bank's employees. Suddenly these local people were instant celebrities, and the ads were talked about all over town. Cal later told me that this had been one of the bank's most successful advertising campaigns, and was responsible for a substantial increase in its business. I will always be grateful to Cal Sheehy because he gave me a wonderful opportunity when I needed it. We have stayed in touch over the years, and he and his wife Florence have remained good friends of mine.

Unfortunately, the Las Vegas advertising market hadn't changed, and since you can't run a business with only one account, I was back to working long hours trying to keep the agency afloat.

This time our marriage couldn't take the strain. Sadly, Carol and I were divorced. She moved with John to Newport Beach, California, to be close to her family. I stayed with the business, and with the help of my ever faithful secretary, Linda Kelly, I tried to make a go of it for the remainder of the year, but my heart wasn't in it anymore. I missed my son, and I had been terribly hurt by Carol's decision to leave. After nine years of marriage, it was suddenly over in a quick Nevada divorce. After a lot of soul searching, I decided that I was an actor and that I wanted to return to Los Angeles and resume my career.

It was the spring of 1973, only two and a half years after I had moved to Las Vegas, and so much had happened in that short period of time it was overwhelming, but as I made the long drive back to Los Angeles, I felt relieved to be going home.

I rented an apartment and had hardly gotten settled when I got a call from my agent who told me that I had just been booked in Albuquerque to star in the stage production of *Butterflies Are Free*. The production was a huge success, and with the popularity of dinner theater, I soon found that I was in big demand around the country. Hollywood may not have been interested, but the American public loved Dobie and gave me a warm reception.

I was very successful on the dinner-theater circuit and met some fascinating people, including a future Oscar-winning actress and one of our hottest sex symbols. Single again, and on the road, I found my life taking a very interesting turn.

ELEVEN

WHILE TRODDING THE BOARDS...I DIED IN CHICAGO

WITH MY LAS VEGAS EXPERIENCE far behind me, I threw myself back into acting. I crisscrossed the country starring in plays like *Sunday in New York* in Lubbock, Texas, *6 Rms Riv Vu* in St. Louis, and *Star Spangled Girl* in Denver.

I had been married for nine years, and before that I had been so busy working on *Dobie* that my social life had not exactly been a bachelor's dream. Now things were considerably different. Each new show in each new city gave me the opportunity to meet some very interesting and beautiful women. But one of the most interesting and beautiful was a statuesque brunette that I had worked with in *Star Spangled Girl* at the Colorado Music Hall in Denver. Unfortunately, she was married, and her ever-present husband was also an actor in the show.

In all the shows that I had been doing around the country I was the star, and local actors would fill in the remaining roles. If local actors weren't available, then a casting call would go out to New York, Los Angeles, Chicago, or Minneapolis, where acting companies and regional theaters would supply the necessary actors.

Star Spangled Girl is a three-person play, and when I arrived at the Music Hall for the first day of rehearsal, the director informed me that the other two actors in the show had been cast out of Minneapolis. As if on cue the door opened and in walked a good-looking guy, followed by a breathtaking brunette wearing a scoop-necked top that revealed her ample and perfect figure. I stood up and the fellow shook my hand and introduced himself as Ross Bickell, then he turned to the stunning woman and said, "I'd like you to meet my wife, Loni Anderson. When I heard the word *wife*, any preconceived notions I may have enjoyed for a moment about the lady and myself suddenly disappeared. Little did I know that in a few short years this ravishing brunette would transform herself into the blond sex symbol Loni Anderson, who would become the staple of the supermarket tabloids.

We started to chat, and Loni told me that she had a young daughter from a previous marriage, named "Dee Dee," who had come with them from their home in Minneapolis. I soon discovered that the Music Hall had given them an apartment in the same complex where I was staying; in fact, they were two doors away.

By the end of the first day of rehearsal we were like old friends. Since I had a rental car that was provided by the theater, I offered to drive them around. In return, Loni and Ross would invite me to join them for dinner. Ross and I would go to the grocery store, and Loni would do the cooking. That was a big treat because when you're on the road you never get a home-cooked meal. We all got along very well and I really enjoyed their company.

Ross had a strong stage background, and Loni, although not classically trained, had a natural talent and was very professional. In fact, Loni took her work quite seriously and prided herself in being letter perfect with her dialogue. One night the audience was in a particularly good humor, laughing at nearly everything we said or did, so in one of my scenes with Loni I threw in an ad-libbed line that brought the house down.

After the show Loni came over to me with fire in her eyes and said that she was furious that I had ad-libbed with her on stage. I couldn't believe that she could really be seriously upset. Not only had the ad lib gotten a laugh but it hadn't thrown off her dialogue. From the look on her face, though, I knew she was not only serious but very angry. I tried to laugh it off, but she turned to me and said, "Don't you ever ad-lib with me again; just do the play as it was written." I was about to ask her who she thought the star of the show was, but I realized that she figured that she was, so what was the point. By the next day it had all blown over and we were back to being the happy threesome.

One evening at dinner we were talking about show business and Ross told me that they were considering moving to Los Angeles and did I think they could find work. I told them that I thought they could do very well; he was good-looking and very talented, and Loni with her gorgeous looks would be a big hit. Loni told me that she and Ross had toured with Pat O'Brien in a play and that he had told her the same thing. Everyone seemed to agree that Loni was perfect Hollywood material. As it turned out, we were one hundred percent correct.

After the show closed, I flew back to Los Angeles, and Loni, Ross, and Dee Dee headed back to Minneapolis. About three weeks later I got a call from Ross. He was coming to L.A. because he and Loni had made the decision to give it a go in Hollywood. By the end of the week I was driving Ross around town as we tried to find a suitable place for the three of them to live. He rented an apartment in Van Nuys in the San Fernando Valley, then he flew back to Minneapolis, fired up and ready for the big move.

In no time we were all sitting around the dinner table just like we had in Denver.

One evening we were talking about our careers, and I said that I hoped to do another series and more feature films and buy another home. Ross was interested in doing really important work in well-written films and plays, and Loni said that she wanted a big house with a swimming pool and tennis court in the hills with a view of the city. I told her that it was a great idea, but she might have to buy a regular house first and then work her way up. I took one look at her icy glare, and I knew that once again I had said the wrong thing. She said, "Don't tell me what I can and I can't have. I'm going to have the exact house that I want." I tried to explain that I wasn't trying to keep her big house, pool, and tennis court away from her; I simply meant that it seemed a huge leap to think that she could move out of a very modest apartment in Van Nuys to a Beverly Hills mansion. Well, I guess Loni had the last laugh, because she eventually got that glamorous home with the pool, tennis court, and view. But I wasn't entirely wrong; there were several smaller homes before she moved into her dream house. I learned another lesson that night. Never ad-lib with Loni, and even if you have the best of intentions, never suggest that she won't get what she wants.

Over the next few months I watched as Loni was transforming herself from a dark brunette beauty to a strawberry blond, ash blond, and finally, as she described herself, "baby chick blond." The stunning brunette I had met in Denver was long gone, and a blond bombshell had taken her place. None of us realized that this was a new beginning for Loni and the beginning of the end for Ross. Loni was on her way. In the next few years our paths would cross again in very different circumstances.

In the meantime I had been off the road for nearly six weeks, and I enjoyed the time at home because I could drive down to Newport Beach to visit my son, John. Many times I would take him for the weekend, but visiting his dad and grandparents wasn't quite as exciting for a nine-year-old boy as hanging out with friends and playing sports. I had always been an avid reader, so with great enthusiasm I tried to introduce John to the classics, books like *Treasure Island*, *Tom Sawyer*, *Ivanhoe*, and, my favorite, *The Adventures of Sherlock Holmes*. Unfortunately, my enthusiasm was dampened as he rolled his eyes and looked at me like I was the most uncool, unhip guy in the world. Divorced parents who have tried to entertain a child for the weekend know exactly what I'm talking about. Since your child no longer lives with you, every time he visits you feel the need to fill up every waking moment with some special fun activity. He is bored because he's out of his routine and you know that he would really rather be back home playing with his friends. He feels guilty, you feel guilty, and the whole situation is miserable.

To compensate, you find yourself trying to make him happy by going to some lousy fast-food restaurant that serves greasy burgers and fries and has a playground for the kids to run around in after they eat so they can throw up on the way home. Then you both suffer through the rest of the evening watching TV or trying to play some board game that you've never seen before. By the end of the night you know your child thinks you're a total idiot because you've never quite caught on to how to play his favorite game. Finally, the next morning you drive for an hour and a half to take him back to his mother's house. Then you spend the hour and a half return trip trying to come to grips with the fact that you're missing all the everyday moments in your child's life. Your heart breaks a little every time you go through your single parent routine.

Not all the weekends were that awful, but none of the time was really great because I always knew that my son would have to go home, and that home wasn't with me.

After one of my weekends with John I got a call from my agent regarding a play at the Pheasant Run Playhouse in Chicago's suburb of St. Charles, where I had had a successful run in *Drink to Me Only* a few years before. Don Murray was currently starring in a production at the Playhouse but needed to be out of the show for three nights. He was flying to Los Angeles to film a pilot for a new television show and they were looking for an actor to fill in while he was away. The gentleman who called me wasn't my theater agent; he usually booked film and television work and the world of theater was foreign to him. This should have been my first clue that he could be in over his head, but he seemed enthusiastic about the play, and apparently the director of the Playhouse, Carl Stohn, Jr., wanted me to fill in for Don. When I asked about the production, my agent told me that it was a dramatic piece by the young playwright Michael Shurtleff, titled *Call Me by My Rightful Name.* I figured that it would be a dramatic piece because Don Murray wasn't known for playing comedy. I suggested to my agent that since my talents lay in the field of comedy perhaps a dramatic actor would be a better choice. He came back in typical agent fashion, telling me that I could stretch myself as an actor and that it could open up a whole new career and best of all, they'd pay me Don's weekly salary for three days' work. As he worked on me, my actor's ego inflated. Maybe he was right; now was the time to stretch my talents and, best of all, while I was stretching I'd be making a good deal of money for only three days' work.

I agreed to do the part. Then I asked the magic question, "When do they want me to do the show?" My agent nonchalantly said, "Oh, you fly out tomorrow morning and you go on Tuesday night." I nearly choked. It was already late Thursday afternoon. He assured me that the role was "a piece of cake" and that he would send the script and airline tickets to my apartment that evening. When I asked him how he could already have airline tickets when he didn't know if I'd take the job he just gave me a laugh and said, "Dwayne, I'm your agent. Trust me, I know what's best for you."

I guess I was too busy running to the bank, the cleaner's, packing, and making the necessary arrangements to leave town on such short notice to see all the red flags popping up. You know, all those little indicators that the subconscious tries to throw out so we don't hurl ourself toward self-destruction like some crazed lemming. As I was trying to decide what to pack for my journey into the unknown, the messenger arrived with the play and my airline tickets. I threw the play into my briefcase without a glance, put the tickets in my coat pocket, and finished packing.

The next morning was heart-stopping. The cab arrived late, and as we sat on the freeway in bumper-to-bumper traffic, I looked at my watch and realized that my plane was going to leave in twenty minutes. At the rate we were going I'd never make it. When I told my driver that I was going to be late, he growled that he'd never made anybody miss a plane. Suddenly he made a sharp right-hand turn over the off-ramp divider and then took off down a side street, laying on his horn as we flew through red lights and around unsuspecting pedestrians. I closed my eyes and prayed that no one would get killed. As we squealed to a stop, I unglued my eyes and was surprised that we were in front of United Airlines. I was even more surprised that I was alive. When I paid the cab driver, he smiled smugly. "I told you you wouldn't miss your plane."

Fate had moved its dark hand over me and it seemed that nothing was going to prevent me from going to the Pheasant Run Playhouse.

For those of you who are squeamish, easily embarrassed, or overly sympathetic when you witness another person in a totally humiliating situation, I suggest that you skip the next few pages. What you are about to read is even more horrific that when George Bush threw up all over the prime minister of Japan and had to be carried away from the table. At least he only did it once; then he had the good sense to pass out. My humiliation would last through three days of rehearsal and three performances. Even as I write about it now, my palms are sweating and I can hardly swallow.

It all started falling apart the moment I got settled on the plane and decided to read through the play. I opened the script and saw that Robert Duval had played Don Murray's part in the original Broadway production. Both of these actors are intense and very dramatic and not at all like me. Then I casually started thumbing through the play to see how much my character, Doug, had to do and as I looked at each page I became more and more panicked. Doug was on every page in every scene of the play. He was never off the stage, and to make matters worse, the character had page-long speeches, one after another. The story is about a love triangle involving a white couple and a black man. The black man is described as "powerfully built and a man of stature." As the play progresses, Doug and this black man have several big fight scenes as they throw one another around the set. Suddenly I felt like I was suffocating. I was committed to the seventy-page, highly dramatic play and I was in every scene. I had only three days to memorize the dialogue and stage directions, then I would have to perform the show. And if that wasn't horrible enough, I was going to have to play fight scenes with "a powerfully built black man of great stature."

I knew that Don Murray was several inches taller than I, so I figured that this black man had to be at least as big as Don, if not bigger. As the plane carried me toward my date with disaster, I could almost hear the minutes ticking away. I wished the flight from Los Angeles to Chicago had been about two weeks long, but unfortunately, it was only three and a half hours. Carl Stohn, Jr., the theater director, picked me up and we drove out to the Playhouse in St. Charles. He must have wondered what was wrong with me because I could hardly carry on a conversation. I was so nervous I nearly jumped out of his speeding car as he glowingly told me about Don's superb performance and how happy he was that I could come on such short notice. Then he said, "You have no idea how many really good actors turned this opportunity down." When I foolishly asked why, he said, "They just felt it was too demanding a part to learn in such a short time. . . . We didn't know what we were going to do, then we thought of you. . . . You're a real trouper and we knew you wouldn't let us down." I just looked at him with this sickening smile plastered across my face. Now I knew the real reason they had called me. They had figured I was the only actor who was foolish enough to try to take on this impossible task. "You're a trouper" really translated to "You're a fool." As Carl chattered away, I looked out of the car window and seriously considered jumping out.

That night I went to the theater to see *Call Me by My Rightful Name*. I was very impressed by Don's dramatic performance and overwhelmed by the entire production. Ranting, raving, shouting, fighting, weeping—Don had run the gamut of every emotion. Not unlike what I had done when I checked into my room and was alone at last.

After the show I went backstage to meet Don and the two other actors, an attractive blond woman named Leigh Hamilton, who had come in from Los Angeles, and Frank Rice, a local black actor, who played her lover. Everyone was very pleasant and assured me that they would gladly rehearse the play until I felt comfortable, which, in my mind, would have been in about six weeks. As I stood talking to everyone, I realized that I was the smallest person in the room. Don Murray was at least six-two or six-three, Leigh was five-ten, and of course, Frank, my soon-to-be sparring partner towered over Don. I looked into the chest of this mountain of a man and wondered how I could ever do a fight scene with him. In one of the scenes I was supposed to beat him up. It was ridiculous. I could hardly reach his face. Maybe they planned to restage it and I'd just hurl myself into his chest and hope that my 155 lb. body would knock down this 250 lb. wall of steel.

I went back to my room and tried to study my lines until total exhaustion took over and I fell asleep with the book in my lap. When I awoke the next morning, for a moment I didn't know where I was. I had hoped that I had just been dreaming the actor's nightmare, but as I looked down on the bed and saw the play staring back at me, I knew I wasn't dreaming.

Don and the other two actors rehearsed with me all day on Saturday, and I watched the show again that night. I tried to write down all of Don's stage movements, but it was imposs- ible. To make matters worse, the actors had added additional dialogue to the play so I had to write down all their new speeches. The show was talky enough, so God only knows why they figured they needed *more* dialogue. In fact, the play ran nearly two hours. Two hours of intense drama that left the audience emotionally wrung out.

That night I went back to my room and, like the night before, tried to cram the dialogue into my head.

Sunday came and Don worked with me until the early afternoon, then he went off to pack for his trip, leaving me with the stage manager and the two actors: Leigh and my huge black friend, Frank. Now came the moment for me to start working with the two. We worked all day and I was even more panicked than when I started. Watching the play was one thing, but doing it was another, and trying to end up in the right place on the right line was impossible. The two actors couldn't have been nicer. They felt sorry for me and tried to help any way they could. I went back to the room, ordered room service, and studied into the night.

Monday arrived and Don was gone, leaving me alone to struggle with the ridiculous fight scenes and the even more embarrassing love scenes.

There is nothing more silly than seeing a man stand on his toes to reach the woman he is trying to kiss. I wasn't holding Leigh in my arms, I was clinging onto her so I wouldn't fall backward. The fight scenes were even worse. I moved around the stage flailing one arm at Frank Rice while I held the play script in my other hand and tried to read my lines. Then I'd lose my place and everything would stop. The situation was getting so unbearable that the actors had gone from feeling sorry for me to looking at me with great disdain. I was in a losing battle, and everybody knew it. That night I never closed my eyes.

The sun came up Tuesday morning and I was on a countdown to showtime. By the time the appointed hour arrived, I was so frightened I could barely move. I had long given up any hope that some miracle would save me. I decided that I would carry the script with me on stage. Actors in similar circumstances had done it; of course the idea is to refer to the script only if necessary, not to bury your nose in it and read every line.

As I got ready to go on stage, Frank came over and said, "We've got to do a good show tonight because 'the brothers' are out there." Absentmindedly I asked, "Your brothers are here?" He looked at me like I was incredibly stupid and said, "No, man...you know...the brothers..." I smiled like I understood, but we both knew I didn't get it.

The house lights went down, my heart began pounding, and I started to hyperventilate. I was so nervous all I could hear was the whoosh of the blood pulsing through my ears. Frank and I made our first entrance, coming into my apartment after a night of drinking. From the moment my foot hit the stage it was a disaster. I couldn't take my eyes off the script for fear I'd lose my place and I was desperately trying to read the messy stage directions that I had written in the margins so I'd know where to move. When we got to the first fight scene I tried to punch this huge man with one hand and then I started slapping him with the script that was in my other hand. Unbelievably, I was supposed to knock this guy across the stage, then he's suppose to fall down and say, "Why'd you have to hurt me?" It was ludicrous.

In another scene with Leigh we fight and I slap her, at which point Frank steps between us. He grabs me and we scuffle, then he throws me across the stage. He was so strong that I flew through the air and landed with a thud. He looked shocked and so did the audience. I lay stunned for a moment, then panicked when I realized that my script had flown out of my hand. I looked around, crawled over to it, and read my long dramatic speech sitting on the floor. At one point I'm supposed to beat my fists on the table like it's a drum, but I could only use one hand because the script was being tightly held in the other. During one of Frank's long speeches I glanced into the audience and, to my horror, they were shaking their heads in disgust and starting to walk out.

At intermission I prayed that something would fall on me and knock me unconscious, but no luck. In the second act the play called for me to come on stage with my head bandaged and one arm in a sling, so I had to hold the script in my other hand. In our final fight scene I pathetically slapped at Frank with the script as we sparred around the stage. He looked at me with such pity, trying not to hurt me as he knocked me around.

At the end of the play, at the big dramatic moment, I smash up the set, sob, and then turn to the audience and wail, "Phoenix...rise and tell me my rightful name." Then I pick up a guitar, which I don't know how to play, and try to strum a song, still holding the script. I looked out at what was left of the audience as a slow embarrassing smattering of applause died out before it got started. I came off stage and tried to leave the theater as quickly as possible. The two other actors never said a word to me as I left.

The next two nights were no better than the first. I was so far past total humiliation that I had moved into survival mode.

The only thing that kept me going was that I knew Thursday was my last show. Then I heard someone say that Don might be in Los Angeles for the rest of the week and I might have to do the show until he returned. I didn't say a word. After the disastrous show on Thursday night I packed my bags and waited until five A.M. when the first bus left the hotel for the airport. Without a word to anyone I slipped out of the hotel like an escaping prisoner, got on the bus, and took the first plane out to St. Louis, where I visited an old girlfriend. I couldn't go back to L.A. I needed some tender loving care...and a place to hide out in case they wanted me to come back to the theater. It's hard to imagine they'd want me back, but I didn't want to take the chance.

When I finally returned home a week later, my agent called and said, "What happened to you, they wanted you to do the show the rest of the week?" A flood of relief washed over me. I had successfully made my escape and saved myself any further humiliation. To this day I have not seen Don Murray, Frank Rice, or Leigh Hamilton again, and I hope I never run into them. In fact, I not only haven't been to Chicago since that horrific week, I won't even change planes at O'Hare.

I didn't know if I would ever go on stage again. In fact, I wasn't sure I'd leave my apartment again, but several weeks later I got an offer to do a silly farce called *Natalie Needs a Nightie*. I read the script and knew it wasn't great theater but it was fun and about as far away from the drama of *Call Me by My Rightful Name* as I could get. I jumped at the chance to get back on stage and do what I did best, comedy.

I was booked at the Alhambra Dinner Theatre in Jacksonville, Florida. Most of the shows ran for a month, so the first week was for rehearsal, then you performed for the remaining three weeks. It was August, and the theater was on the beach, so every day after rehearsal and then during the day before a performance, I'd go there to relax. It was exactly what I needed after my Pheasant Run Playhouse fiasco. *Natalie Needs a Nightie* is a play about mistaken identity; the girl who lives next door has a similar name to the character I play, then we pretend to be married to impress my boss. A gorgeous girl with a knockout body pops in and out wearing a nightie and the maid gets tipsy trying to cope with all the confusion. We're not talking Shakespeare; we're not even talking Neil Simon, but it was fast-paced fun and the audience loved it.

The gorgeous, scantily clad Natalie was played by *Playboy's* Playmate of the Year, Cindi Wood. Cindi was not a great actress, but since she ran around the stage with hardly anything on, no one seemed to notice or really care. The part of the tipsy maid was played by an actress from New York named Kathy Bates.

Kathy and I became friends and spent a lot of time together. She was quiet and very sensitive and had absolutely nothing in common with the extroverted, self-absorbed, sex-kitten, Cindi Wood. I, on the other hand, was able to overlook any flaws in Cindi's personality, as I watched her cavort around the stage in her sheer baby doll nightie. I was very interested in getting to know her more intimately; unfortunately, she had absolutely no interest in me. Kathy would roll her eyes in disbelief as I kept trying to make a play for this hot, sexy Playmate.

One evening Cindi must have had some free time on her hands because she decided to join Kathy and me for dinner. Cindi was dressed in a flashy, sexy outfit that might have been the norm on Hollywood's Sunset Strip, but in Jacksonville, Florida, it caused every head in the restaurant to nearly snap off as she walked by. A hush fell over the room as men and women alike watched Cindi undulate toward our table. Kathy and I felt like props as our glamour girl held court. Halfway through the evening we were exchanging looks as Cindi talked about her career as an actress and how she wanted to do really important dramatic work. Kathy, who had worked in New York and was very serious about her career, just looked at this cupcake in her low-cut outfit and shook her head. By the end of the evening I tried to convince Cindi that I had gained new respect for her depth and artistic sensitivity...but she still wouldn't go out with me.

For the rest of the run Kathy and I would hang out; she'd play the guitar and we'd exchange gossip about Cindi Wood and how plastic and shallow she was....I had been reduced to this because, by this time, I had given up hope of ever getting a date.

After the show closed, I went on to St. Petersburg, Florida, with a new supporting cast, and Kathy returned to New York. Years later I was thrilled when she broke through with her role in the film *Misery*, opposite James Caan, and won the Oscar for Best Actress. What must have seemed only an actor's dream back in Jacksonville became a reality for this talented woman.

It was during the next run of *Natalie* that I started doing an after-curtain speech. I'd come out and basically apologize to the audience because the play was so mindless and silly. Before long my speech was becoming a stand-up comedy routine that was getting even more laughs and more press than the play. I started writing monologues and tailored the comedy to the particular city we played in, and it was a big hit. The show moved on to New Orleans, where it and what was becoming my after-curtain stand-up act was playing to full houses. The Mardi Gras was taking over the city and I was enjoying every moment. The city was in the throes of celebrations and every night following the show I'd be invited to one party after another. I had never seen so many drunken people in one place in my life. The party never stopped, and I did my best to enjoy every minute.

All of the fun and excitement abruptly ended when I received word from home that my mother was seriously ill with cancer. I was numb as I played out the remaining days of the show, then I flew home to see what I could do. When a loved one is terminally ill, we think that somehow we can maybe fix the problem or have some control over a heartbreaking situation, but, in reality, the only thing we can control is how we deal with it. During the past several years, with the many changes that had occurred in my life, I had started studying metaphysics and the works of New Thought writers such as Mary Baker Eddy, Joel Goldsmith, and Ernest Holmes. This was quite a departure from my background in Catholicism, and, as a devout Catholic, I was even a little amazed at how comfortable and compatible I was with New Thought. I found in this less traditional approach to religion a peace that I had never found in the Catholic church.

With my mother's imminent death becoming more and more a reality, this new philosophy was helping me through this extremely difficult period. Unlike many who have left the Catholic religion, I have never been bitter about my years in the church. I will always have respect for the tradition and the sincerity of the people who follow its teachings. But, for me, I found a better way, and since that time I have become as devout in my study and practice of Religious Science as I was in my study of Catholicism.

By the time I returned from New Orleans my mother was beginning her downhill spiral as she went from rounds of chemotherapy to surgery. I was booked to play Houston in a few weeks, but after that engagement I decided to stay off the road and try to help my mother any way I could.

It was during this extremely difficult time that I was introduced to an attractive blond singer and actress named Joanne Papile, who told me that she had recently been divorced and was trying to pursue her career. While I was attempting to cope with my family situation, she became very supportive and caring during this difficult and sad period.

I had been touring around the country doing dinner theater for three years, and although I had been very successful, I was growing weary of being on the road and away from home. Maybe it was all the painful changes happening around me, but I felt a need for some kind of permanence.

I knew I didn't want to leave show business again, so I decided to pursue a job behind the cameras. My interest in production began when I was writing my material for my after-curtain speeches. I eventually hoped to create my own television series, but I felt that I needed to understand the way a studio and network functioned. This was an area of show business that I was not familiar with. I never doubted my ability to be a producer because I had been around series television for nearly twenty-five years. Even though I had been a performer, I was well aware of the elements that were necessary to produce a successful television show. The producer's side was familiar ground; it was the studio and network side of the business that seemed most foreign and challenging to me. So I decided to pursue a job with either a network or a studio, which would give me an education and insight into the "business" aspects of show business. Best of all, it would get me off the road so that I could stay in Los Angeles.

I contacted Bill Self, an old friend from my *Dobie* days at Twentieth Century-Fox Studios who had moved to CBS and was now in charge of West Coast Programming. We met at his office, and I told him that I wanted to be a producer and that I was looking for some behind the scenes experience at a network, so he set up a meeting with the vice president of current programs. Joanne helped me put together a buttoned-down résumé, and I went in to interview with Steve Mills, who was very supportive and encouraging. Unfortunately there were no openings at the network at that time.

In the meantime, I continued to turn down dinner theater appearances because my mother was getting progressively worse and I felt that I should stay in town. I was also staying in contact with CBS in the event that the situation changed and a job became available.

In January 1977 I finally got word that a position had opened in CBS's program department and that I could start work the next month.

A few weeks later, on February 1, my mother's long and painful fight was over. She had been deteriorating for months and had suffered terribly. Even though her death was inevitable, when I got the phone call telling me that she was gone I was totally devastated.

My mother had been the glue that had held my family together. Once she was gone, our family seemed to splinter off and go their separate ways. We had never been particularly close, and with Mother gone, all our differences seemed to greatly outweigh anything that we might have had in common. My father, who was busy running his insurance business and attending his many lodge meetings, had never spent a lot of time with us. Consequently, I had never been very close to him. Several years after my mother's death he remarried and now divides his time between Seattle and Palm Springs. My sister lives in the Midwest and my brother teaches acting in Los Angeles, and although I talk with my father and see him occasionally, I have had little contact with either my brother or my sister.

Shortly after my mother's funeral I got a call from Bill Self and Steve Mills at CBS, asking me to come in for a meeting. They told me that the network was developing a new *Dobie Gillis* project with James Komack, who had produced *Welcome Back, Kotter* and *Chico and the Man*, and they wanted me to star in their pilot. When I said that I would be glad to do the show, but I would rather have the job in programming, they looked at me in disbelief. Who would rather be a network executive when he can be the star of his own television series? They assured me that if the pilot didn't sell I could immediately begin my job with the network. I left the meeting feeling like I was in a win-win position. Driving home, I thought about the incredible changes that were taking place in my life, and I felt a little uneasy because I didn't know what would happen next.

During this intense and emotional period surrounding my mother's death, Joanne and I had become very close. Only a few weeks after the funeral, she and I decided to get married, so on March 3, 1977, in a judge's chambers in downtown Los Angeles, we unceremoniously exchanged I dos. Two weeks later I started rehearsals for the pilot, *Whatever Happened to Dobie Gillis?* Working with one-time comic actor-turned-producer Jimmy Komack was quite an experience. With his big curly hair and loud eccentric manner, he was a study in excess. He would be chauffeured around town in a limo and conduct meetings with his writers as he was being driven to the various run-throughs and tapings of his television shows. If that wasn't bizarre enough, this TV guru sported large garish rings on every finger which he claimed gave him special powers and insights.

Apparently, before I became involved in the project, Komack had hired Max Shulman to write the script. Unhappy with Max's work, which he felt wasn't hip enough for today's television audience, Komack engaged a young writer named Eric Cohn to work with him on the show.

After reading a second draft of the script, Jimmy called Max into his office for a meeting and proceeded to tell him that his big problem was that he, Max, didn't understand the character of Dobie Gillis. Can you imagine having the guts to tell Max Shulman, who created the character in several books, then turned the books into one of the most successful teen comedies in television history, that he didn't understand his Dobie? Actually, it didn't take guts, it took massive ego and gross stupidity! As if Jimmy hadn't said enough, he then took this insanity one step further by firing Max from the project. Then he brought in his staff of young urban writers from *Kotter* and *Chico and the Man*. Under his guidance, they started to reshape *Dobie Gillis*. That was the point where I came on the scene. On the first day of rehearsal we read the script that Max and Eric had written, and I thought that it was pretty good. The next day that script disappeared and we were given an entirely different one that was Jimmy Komack's version of Dobie Gillis. The story revolves around Dobie, who's now married to Zelda, has a son, and on his fortieth birthday is having a mid-life crisis. His old buddy Maynard arrives wearing long robes and sporting rings on every finger because he has become a traveling guru. At the end of the show, frustrated at the prospect of growing old and knowing that his dreams will never be fulfilled, Dobie goes to the park, takes a brick, and starts smashing his beloved *Thinker* statue.

When I read this, I was furious and confronted Komack. I told him that this was not Dobie Gillis, but a dark, sad, and very disturbing show for anyone who had been a fan of the earlier series. Trying to calm me, he sat me down and held up his hands like a surgeon and said, "Dwayne, see these rings... They give me great insight and power and I know that this is the perfect story." I couldn't believe this guy! And the scary part was that he was serious. When I complained about the casting of my son, he held up his hands again and pointed to a ring that was the head of a horse. "See this ring? This ring helps me know the perfect actor to cast in a role." His "casting ring" should have been the horse's ass, not the horse's head. Komack had hired a kid with a thick Brooklyn accent who looked like a refugee from *Welcome Back, Kotter*. He was a thinly disguised version of John Travolta's Vinnie Barbarino, not the offspring of Dobie Gillis. He had also decided to give my son a friend, not because he needed one in the script but because he thought one of the young actors who had auditioned was sexy. That's how the young Lorenzo Lamas got his start in television. The only thing Komack and his "casting ring" was right about was Lorenzo, who went on to appear in *Falcon Crest* and was indeed a heartthrob.

After I had aired all my objections and had listened to Komack's stories about the power of his rings, he walked me out and told me his most unbelievable bit of "wisdom." He said that I should trust him with *Dobie* and that he was the perfect guy for the show because he had never seen the original series so that gave him a special, fresh insight into the character. I was totally taken aback. This man had never seen *Dobie Gillis* and he felt that he understood the character. Before I could say a word, he held up his hands one more time and with a smile, flashed his rings in my face.

Walking back to the rehearsal hall, I knew that this project didn't have a chance. Not only did Komack not understand the concept of the series, but the erroneous version he had come up with kept changing. When I had done *The Bob Cummings Show* and *Dobie Gillis*, the script on the first day of rehearsal was the script that was rehearsed and filmed. If there were any changes they were very minimal.

In the two weeks we rehearsed Komack's *Dobie*, every day we got page after page of rewrites, so by the time we filmed the show we were underrehearsed and the script was flat and devoid of any humor. I realized that this was the new way to produce a television show. A large writing staff would sit around eating junk food, joking, and spit-balling lines back and forth until around four A.M., then new pages were typed and sent to the actors. They'd rehearse the new material, then do a run-through for the writers and producers, at which point everyone would act surprised that what seemed funny at four

A.M. made no sense at all. Then the whole process would start all over again until they ran out of time and finally had to shoot whatever script they had.

The days of writing and producing sharp, well-crafted scripts seemed to be a thing of the past. The Paul Hennings and Max Shulmans were being replaced by writing staffs of seven, eight, or maybe even ten writers. But quantity is not necessarily quality, as I painfully witnessed with Komack's *Dobie Gillis*.

Several weeks later I called Bill Self and asked if CBS was going to pick up the pilot. He almost sounded surprised when he said that they were very disappointed with the way the show had turned out. If anyone had asked me during the entire rehearsal process, I could have told them the show didn't have a chance. But I soon learned that my opinions concerning shows would not necessarily be asked for or appreciated.

Two weeks later, on a Monday in mid-May, dressed like a corporate executive, I headed off to CBS. I was determined to bury Dobie Gillis and any sense of being a celebrity and turn myself into what the artistic side of our business called..."a suit."

As it turned out, that wasn't as easy as I thought it would be.

• TWELVE •

IF YOU CAN'T BEAT 'EM...
JOIN 'EM

MY FIRST FEW WEEKS AT CBS were overwhelming and illuminating. After all the years I had spent as an actor, I had now crossed over to the other side and was faced with the enormous adjustment of becoming "one of the guys from the network."

Television networks have a strange mystique, an image of being all-knowing and all-powerful, not unlike the great and powerful "Wizard of Oz." But, just as Dorothy discovered that the "Great Oz" was really a guy behind a curtain working his smoke-and-mirrors act, I quickly learned that CBS, as well as the other networks, was not what it appeared to be.

All my years as an actor I was under the same impression, as most people are, that the network and those representing it were somehow endowed with greater insight and knowledge than the rest of us mere mortals. Once I had been hired, I felt that now I would be privy to all the inner workings of network television and exposed to that incredible brainpower that was housed at CBS Television City in Los Angeles. To my amazement I discovered that many of these so-called network geniuses didn't know any more than I did, and often not as much. It quickly became apparent that the network was like an exclusive club that was extremely reluctant to let anyone on the outside become aware of its inner workings. It was as if these honchos were afraid someone would discover that they were as fallible as the rest of us. Those who had finagled their way into "the club" wanted to protect themselves, so depending on his position in the pecking order, the average network executive tried his best not to have an opinion about anything, the theory being, if you don't have an opinion you can't antagonize your boss or vary from the company line, and therefore you won't jeopardize your membership in the hierarchy.

My first job was in the program department, where my title was program executive. I was supposed to supervise the production of the various TV shows that were assigned to me. That included reading scripts, giving notes to the producers, looking at the daily footage that was shot, and going to runthroughs and tapings of shows. Basically I was to be the liaison between the network and the producers. It all sounded very important. I'd read a script and make some notes regarding changes that I felt would improve the overall tone of the piece, then I would give general notes to improve the characters, dialogue, and story. When I sat in on note sessions with my contemporaries, they gave what seemed to be ludicrous notes, crazy comments, like "Why wouldn't the guy use a knife instead of a gun?" or "Why is the killer so unsympathetic?" I'd watch the poor producers and writers look at these network guys and try to politely accept their comments or explain their choices. What the producers and writers were really thinking was "What kind of a stupid comment is that?" But the executive represents the network that owns the rights to air the show, and therefore the producer, who has grown accustomed to living in Malibu, driving his Mercedes with the car phone, and pulling down a salary of close to a million dollars a year, not to mention residuals, isn't about to shoot off his mouth and in one brief moment destroy this grand lifestyle of the rich and famous. So he smiles politely and tries to please the "suits."

My usual notes were general and tended to deal with the

overall piece as opposed to small details that didn't matter. For example, if it was a comedy and a little flat, I'd tell the producer to try to make it funnier. If it was a drama, I'd suggest that he increase the jeopardy and the suspense. I respected the producers' talents and tried to give them encouragement rather than nitpick meaningless details. If a show really had problems, as a program executive you didn't have any power to exert pressure or play hardball with the producer, even if you were right. The last thing you wanted was some irate star like Carroll O'Connor or a "power producer" like Norman Lear calling your boss and complaining about how you are causing trouble on their show. For the most part my sympathies were with the producers. I totally understood the problems of producing and starring in a show, and when I would try to explain their dilemma to my network colleagues, they would look at one another like, "Who let this guy in here?" My peers at the network didn't think much of my approach.

No matter how hard I tried to be Dwayne Hickman, Network Executive, my co-workers never let me forget that I had been a celebrity. Nothing was more annoying than to have one of these guys come up and say, "Hi, Dobie" or "Look who's here, Dobie Gillis." If we all went out to lunch and someone came up and asked for my autograph, everyone seemed very uncomfortable, so it's no surprise that my happiest moments on the job were spent at the studio with the producers, writers, and actors.

The first two shows assigned to me were Norman Lear comedies that had been on the air several seasons, *Maude* and *Good Times*. *Maude*, which starred Bea Arthur, Rue Mc-Clanahan, Bill Macy, and Conrad Bain, had been on the schedule since 1972, so when I got the show, five years later, it was a polished, professional, and well-run program. Norman had based the character of Maude Findley on his former wife, Frances Lear. Maude was upper-middle class, liberal, and extremely outspoken, and the show was Norman's first spin-off from his enormously successful *All in the Family*. The actors were seasoned pros, and the writers provided well-constructed scripts, so working on the show was a pleasure.

My other assignment, however, was the exact opposite of *Maude*. *Good Times*, a spin-off of that hit, starred Esther Rolle, John Amos, and the comic Jimmie "Dy-No-Mite" Walker. John Amos was off the show when I arrived. To explain his departure the producers had his character killed in an automobile accident. I later heard that there had been some heated words and Amos started screaming like a wild man and chasing Norman Lear through the halls. If you remember John Amos in the miniseries *Roots*, you know he was quite an imposing figure. The idea of having him angrily chasing after you could be pretty frightening. Norman apparently got away, because he came out unscathed from their confrontation, but John Amos was not as fortunate, and the next season his character was only a memory. Years later, any resentments they may have had for one another were forgotten as Norman hired John Amos to star in his new rather short-lived series, *704 Hauser*, a black version of *All in the Family*, with John playing the Archie Bunker character and living in Archie's old house.

Good Times was not doing very well, so the husband-and-wife producing team, Rocky and Irma Kalish, decided to expand the story line and add a young adopted child to the show. They called me with great excitement to say that they had cast one of the Jacksons as the little girl. When I seemed unimpressed, they explained that the Jackson 5 was a hot black singing group, and the youngest daughter, Janet, would play the little girl. I couldn't see the logic in thinking by casting the nonsinging youngest child of the Jackson family there would suddenly be a big audience tune-in, but the network seemed thrilled, so I jumped on the company bandwagon. Janet Jackson was a shy little eight-year-old who was accompanied to the studio every day by her mother, Katherine. Janet was fine in the show, but apparently the Jackson magic the producers had counted on wasn't enough, and the show was canceled the next year.

Years later Janet reinvented herself to match the rest of the family, and although she is not as controversial as her brother, Michael, or older sister, La Toya, she has become one of the highest paid female singers in the business.

In my first year at CBS I had quickly learned that the program executive's job was a cushy berth a lucky few tried to settle into for life. Large expense accounts, invitations to lavish parties and awards shows, and the prestige of working for one of the three networks, not to mention the good salary and benefits, made it a coveted position. One would think this was a job created in heaven, but I later discovered that it was a velvet trap. In return for the salary and position, you must be devoid of any opinion, and you were under constant pressure to play company politics. This gentleman's club was really a hostile environment, and from the first day the clock was ticking on your job because you were expected to move up or move on.

The next season I covered *WKRP in Cincinnati* and *The Incredible Hulk*. These shows brought me together with two actors that I had worked with years before. I had starred with Bill Bixby in the movie *Doctor, You've Got to Be Kidding*, and now he was turning himself into a mean, green Lou Ferrigno each week on *The Incredible Hulk*. And on *WKRP* Loni Anderson, who had played my *Star Spangled Girl* when I starred in the play in Denver, had landed her breakthrough role of Jennifer Marlowe, the sexy, brainy, radio station receptionist.

My first day on the set of *Hulk* seemed as strange to Bixby as it did to me. The last time we had seen one another we were both in the same movie; now I had gone over to "the other side" and had become "one of them." At first Bill couldn't understand why I would work for a network, but before I could explain that it was giving me a wonderful insight into how shows got on the air and an insider's view on the way network and show business politics works, he was already launching into his complaints about the program. He told me that the series was ruining his life because he had to rewrite terrible scripts as well as work all day acting and sometimes directing. Even though Bill was doing well professionally, he was very unhappy, and every time I walked on the set he would corner me and give me his list of gripes. All I could think of was my friend Frank Modica at the Landmark in Las Vegas saying, "Stay away from the celebrities; all they'll do is complain and want you to do things you can't do." It was great advice, but unfortunately the CBS job demanded that I listen and at least appear to be concerned about the problems over which I had no control.

WKRP in Cincinnati was written and created by a very talented guy named Hugh Wilson who had been a successful advertising man and had taken Hollywood by storm. Southern, smart, and with a razor-sharp wit, Hugh took on the network and ignored the rules of the game. When Harvey Shephard, who was one of the programming chiefs, kept changing the show's time slot, Hugh would get extremely upset and call me and say, "Harvey hates me, I know he does....Why else would he try to kill this show?" I'd try to convince Hugh that schedule changes were not to be considered a personal attack, but after his show was switched ten times in four years you could see why a producer would get paranoid.

Loni was perfect for the role of the knockout receptionist, Jennifer Marlowe. Watching run-throughs of the show was never as entertaining as the clothes that Loni wore to rehearsal. Each day Loni appeared in special outfits with matching hats, boots, and the appropriate accessories. Loni had blossomed into a star; she knew it, and so did everyone else, and before long she became the centerpiece of this ensemble show. Following in Farrah Fawcett's footsteps, Loni came out with her own sexy poster wearing a bikini and a big smile. She sold millions and became a bona fide sex symbol. Her husband, Ross, had long ago been lost in the shuffle and had been replaced by *WKRP* costar, Gary Sandy. It was not long before Gary's run would be cut short and Loni would begin seeing Burt Reynolds. One day on the set Loni was wearing an expensive cowboy hat and a *Smokey and the Bandit* leather jacket. I couldn't resist asking her about her rumored romance with Burt. I said, "Well, tell me, Loni, are you in love?' She gave me a coy smile and said, "I'm in like..." Then she went on to explain that I had no idea how difficult it was for two sex symbols to be together. She was right about that...I had no idea. Apparently, even she didn't realize how difficult it could be. Eleven years later, after living together, getting married, and adopting a child, she and Burt called it quits, and the two battled out their highly publicized divorce in the supermarket tabloids.

All the elements of my job were falling into place, and it wasn't long before I realized that it consisted mostly of busy-work. On a typical day I would arrive at the office around ten, read some memos, and deal with the endless stream of reports. Then I would start the daily routine of "phone tag," the game where you place a call at a time you know the party won't be available, and you leave a message. Hours later, the party calls you back when he's sure *you* won't be available, then in about three days someone makes a call and "tags" the person who happens to be in the office. "Phone tag" can keep you busy for at least an hour.

Between 12:30 and 2:30 the town "does lunch" on company expense accounts at posh restaurants. This gives you a chance to gossip about the latest hirings and firings, who's sleeping with whom, and which powerbroker will be taking over which studio. If you're looking for a new job, then you use the lunch to "schmooze" and network with someone who can hire you or at least put in a good word for you. In most businesses, being fired from your job would carry the stigma that somehow you were an incompetent who couldn't hold down a job, but in show business no one bats an eye when someone gets fired; in fact, it's an accepted eventuality in some positions. It's like executive musical chairs, when the newly fired become the newly hired at the next studio or network. The rest of my day at CBS was filled with looking at dailies or rough cuts, which are the finished show prior to sound effects or music. Then I'd drive out to the studio and watch a run-through or taping of one of the comedy shows I covered.

When a network contracts for a series, the full order usually consists of twenty-two new episodes. To produce twenty-two hour-long dramas takes almost the entire year. Half-hour comedy shows, on the other hand, complete their production in less than nine months. If you happen to be a program executive who handles mostly half-hour comedies, you are left with three months in which you have no show to cover and virtually nothing to do.

After my first season on the job, I remember asking a colleague what we were supposed to do for the three months production was down. He gave me a very serious look and told me that we were to schedule the reruns of our shows and that would keep us very busy. In reality, it only takes about two days, and that's because you have to check your rerun schedule with the producer and you can't get him on the phone right away. Remember, everyone is playing "phone tag." My fellow program executives would walk the halls telling anyone within earshot how busy they were, then they would disappear into their office until the politically correct hour to leave. What many were really doing behind their closed doors was watching the evening news on the television in their office, then around 6:30 P.M. they'd try to time their departure to coincide with their boss's. If my work was finished, I'd leave around 5:00 or 5:30, and it never failed that someone would say, "Oh, working half a day?" It all seemed so silly to me, but I continued to try to play the game.

The next season I handled one of CBS's hottest new shows, *The Dukes of Hazzard.* It was the TV version of the popular good ol' boy movies like *Smokey and the Bandit.* In the show Luke and Bo Duke were down-home cousins who drove their souped-up Dodge Charger, "The General Lee," and played modern-day country versions of Robin Hood. Their nemesis was crafty Boss Hogg, who always had some scheme to catch the cousins and get them out of Hazzard County. Each week you could count on wild car chases and watching "The General Lee" fly over trees, rivers, houses, or anything else that got in the way. There were actually over three-hundred identical copies of "General Lee." Each time they filmed the car flying through the air and landing, the director would call "Cut," since the moment the car hit the ground the front end was destroyed. That mortally wounded "General Lee" would be towed away and a healthy replacement would be driven into the scene. Filming would resume, and Bo and Luke would drive off down the road as the unsuspecting audience cheered the amazing and indestructible "General Lee."

I sat in on the original casting of the show and must have seen every actor in Hollywood as hundreds of cowboy-clad would-be "Dukes" came in to read for the parts. We finally cast Tom Wopat and John Schneider as the country cousins and Catherine Bach as their sexy cousin, Daisy Duke.

The producers hired Waylon Jennings to sing the title song and narrate the show each week. The script would be sent to wherever Waylon was performing and he would record his narration and return it to Hollywood. These were Waylon's wilder days, when he was partying and hanging out with "all his rowdy friends," to quote his fast-living buddy, Hank Williams Jr. Waylon would do the narration in whatever condition he was in at the time and then back in the studio they'd edit out any mistakes, background noises, and, of course, Waylon's expletives as he'd blow the lines. The unedited version was much more colorful and more fun than the finished product.

At the same time I had the hit *Dukes of Hazzard* I also had a big flop called *Big Shamus, Little Shamus*, which starred Brian Dennehy. It lasted only two episodes. When you were assigned some clunker like this, you were looked on with great disdain, as if you were responsible for this fiasco and couldn't do your job.

All of the program executives had winners and losers; it was the luck of the draw. I was always amused when my cohorts who covered a big hit show would strut around referring to it as "their show"—as if they had something to do with the writing, producing, or acting. One of my colleagues who handled *Dallas* during the ratings-grabbing "Who Shot J.R.?" season-opener made a great show of locking the script in his desk every time he walked out of his office. Then at the end of the day he'd put the script in his attaché case and take it home. You would have thought he was carrying C.I.A. secrets. It all seemed so corny to me because *The Enquirer* ran the story line the week before the big episode aired.

If, in general, the ratings happened to be down, a feeling of gloom and depression would permeate the program department. Everyone would walk around shaking their heads, sighing, and speaking in hushed tones. I thought they were kidding. I told them that this morose attitude was silly because ratings would always fluctuate and in time we'd be on top again. They looked at me like I was a heretic, and even though I was proved right a few weeks later when CBS was back in the number-one spot, my coworkers felt that I wasn't playing on the company team.

I had been at the network two years when I was offered a job at NBC. I felt that the position and money were too good to pass up, so I went to see Bud Grant, who was the head of programming at CBS, to tell him that I planned to jump ship. Bud was a decent guy and I always found him very fair. To my surprise, he countered the offer and asked me to stay, promising to promote me to the position of director of comedy development. I accepted his offer, and within a few weeks I moved over to my new position.

Now my job would be to develop shows with writers who would come in to pitch their ideas. If we bought their idea for a series, a pilot would be made. Depending on how it turned out, the network would order additional episodes. If the pilot was a flop, since the network had invested a lot of money in it, they would "burn it off," that is, sneak it into the schedule some hot night in the middle of summer when no one was watching television.

In development I worked with an amazing guy named Kim Le Masters. Kim was a glib Machiavellian yuppie who spoke in shorthand and spit-balled ideas at the rate of a thousand a minute while shooting hoops through a mini-basketball net attached to his office door. I always thought that he was the perfect corporate executive because what he lacked in artistic creativity he more than made up in "schmooze," energy, and political savvy. In the process of developing the ideas with the writers, Kim had an insatiable desire to put his stamp on the material by reconstructing the entire story line. He would suggest moving the beginning to the middle, the middle to the end, and then put a completely different spin on the story.

Constructing a script is like building a house of cards, if you change one element the whole thing collapses. I would watch the writers' eyes glaze over as they listened to Kim dissect their script. They were totally confused, and I can't blame them, because most of the time Kim lost me as we all followed him down his winding, not always logical, road. The writers would take the suggestions because they wanted to make the network happy and sell their show. By the time we got the second draft, which incorporated all of our suggestions, the script was a mess. Once again the network had successfully killed the creative process.

Many times the writers who came in to pitch would direct their conversation to me because they had either worked with me as an actor or they were great Dobie Gillis fans. They would ask me about the show or Max Shulman or Paul Henning from my days on *The Bob Cummings Show*. This made a big hit with my colleagues as they sat, not so patiently, waiting for the "Dobie Fan Club" to finish a stroll down memory lane so that the development meeting could start.

I remember a meeting with the hot young writer, Anne Beatts, who created *Square Pegs* for CBS. *Square Pegs* was a teen show set in high school, and it was her version of a 1980s teen comedy. She was a huge fan of *Dobie Gillis,* which had been her inspiration for *Square Pegs.* Anne never missed an opportunity to talk *Dobie* trivia.

Another talented writer who was a *Dobie* fan was Linda Bloodworth-Thomason. Prior to her *Designing Women* days, Linda had *Filthy Rich,* which I toiled on when I was working in development. Linda would good-naturedly break into the *Dobie* theme song every time she saw me. I always found her charming, but my fellow executives' reaction was less than enthusiastic. As hard as I was trying to be Dwayne Hickman, Network Executive and corporate wizard, everyone else saw me as *Dobie Gillis* doing his imitation of a guy who worked for the network.

I don't know if it had anything to do with the attention I was getting, but frequently Kim Le Masters would schedule meetings that I was expected to attend and then he would somehow forget to tell me about them. When the appointed hour arrived and everyone was assembled in his office, he would buzz me and, on his speakerphone, announce that I was holding up the meeting and would I please come to his office. Not only did I look foolish but I was totally unprepared for a meeting I knew nothing about. Kim was making his ascent up the corporate ladder, and he didn't realize that I had no intention of standing in his way.

When the writers and producers would get me alone, they always asked the same question: why would I become part of the corporate world after spending my entire life on the creative side of show business? They didn't understand that I really wanted to get experience behind the cameras. It made perfect sense to me but no one else seemed to believe it.

One day word filtered back to me that Harvey Shephard, the gentleman whom Hugh Wilson had blamed for the demise of *WKRP*, had made the statement that he couldn't understand why I would want to be a network executive when I was already a celebrity. Maybe that accounts for the reason why I always felt that Harvey never took me seriously. In his typical way of cutting right to the heart of a situation he was only stating what everyone else was thinking. Everyone except me. I was doing my best to convince myself that I was where I belonged, working behind the scenes and learning the business side of show business. Harvey, who was one of the brightest men that I had ever worked with, could quote the ratings of television shows the way sports fanatics quote baseball scores. He had been brought out from New York by his friend and mentor, Bob Daly, who was president of CBS Television. Today, Daly is chairman and co-CEO of Warner Brothers and is considered one of the most powerful men in show business. Harvey was a brilliant executive. As hard as I tried I never really learned how to play the game or be as savvy as this corporate maven. On the other hand, I don't think Harvey would have been a particularly good performer, no matter how hard he'd try, so I guess we all have our own special talents. The important thing is to know what your talents are and to go with them. But at this point I was still trying to fit into a world that required me to deny who I was and everything that I had accomplished.

On the homefront my marriage to Joanne was in trouble. We had wed precipitously after my mother's death, with both of us marrying for the wrong reasons. Joanne had become bored with married life and wanted the excitement of pursuing her career as a single woman. After three and a half years, we parted amicably and filed for divorce.

I threw myself into the job as we worked long hours to get our pilots made for the 1981–82 season. Most of them that are filmed or taped never make it to series. One of our unsuccessful pilots that season was a comedy/mystery titled *Quick and Quiet*, starring William Windom. The show had a silly premise about a dead detective who comes back and helps his son solve crimes.

As I was sitting in the screening room watching dailies, I noticed a pretty brunette in a bathing suit getting out of a swimming pool. She was one of the guest stars in the show and I thought to myself that she must have been freezing because it was late January and the weather had been overcast and cold. When I got back to my office, I kept thinking about the actress in the bathing suit and how difficult it was to shoot scenes like that in the winter. I sympathized with her because I had spent many cold days at the beach in Malibu when I filmed the *Beach Party* pictures.

Several days later, Ed Self, one of the producers of the pilot, called and invited me to a wrap party on one of the soundstages at Goldwyn Studios. I wasn't really in the mood, but I figured that I'd make an appearance, then head back to my apartment where I was still trying to get settled. The party was in full swing when I arrived. I was talking to the producers, Ed Self and Bill Brademan, when I noticed the actress from the swimming pool scene. She was busy talking when I came up behind her and introduced myself. As she turned around, we locked eyes for a moment, then she smiled and told me her name was Joan Roberts. I made awkward small talk about shooting pool scenes in cold weather, and she asked me how I liked working for the network. An hour or so had passed, and before long we noticed that the party was over and the caterers were cleaning up. I accompanied her to the stage door where she said good-bye to Ed and Bill, the two producers, then I watched her walk off down the dark studio street. I turned and said, "She's really darling," at which point they told me that she was single, lived in Santa Monica, and that I should ask her to dinner. Before I could think of a good reason not to, they insisted that I go after her.

As I hurried down the dark street I noticed that Joan was coming back toward me. She said that she had gone the wrong way and that it was a dead end. I asked her if she planned to eat dinner, and she looked at me quizzically and said, "Well...yes." I realized that I sounded awkward and foolish. What I was trying to do was ask her to join me for dinner but suddenly I sounded like a kid asking a girl for his first date. To my amazement she accepted my invitation.

Driving her to her car, which was parked on the other side of the lot, I decided to tell her all about me in those few short blocks. I told her that I was getting a divorce, that I had a son from a previous marriage, that I had been an actor, and on and on. Then I pulled up next to her car, turned to her and asked, "Well, what do you think?" With a straight face she said, "On second thought, maybe I'll just have dinner by myself." Then she started to laugh. Joan had delivered the line with perfect comedy timing, and my interest was piqued.

We were in the heart of Hollywood so I suggested that we go to a favorite spot of mine, Musso & Frank's Restaurant on Hollywood Boulevard. Relaxing over dinner, I was amazed at all the things we had in common and how much we had to say to one another. It had been a long time since I'd had such a good time. Joan told me that she was from McLean, Virginia, a suburb of Washington, D.C., and that she had been in Los Angeles several years. Last season she had done a pilot at NBC and now she was going to test at CBS for the new series, *Private Benjamin*, which was based on the Goldie Hawn movie. It happened to be one of the pilots I was working on in development. Joan and I were chattering away and as I looked at her I thought how lucky I was that I had found the perfect date. She was smart, funny, very attractive, and exactly what I was looking for, and she was busy with her career, which was fine with me because I had no intention of getting seriously involved or ever marrying again. After a wonderful evening I walked her to her car and said good-bye. We both just stood there looking at one another. I wanted to kiss her but I didn't want to appear like I was coming on to her, so we just kept saying awkward good-byes. Then she got in her car and I told her to call me and let me know if she got home all right. I gave her my number, thinking that this was a good excuse to talk to her again and say good night.

Driving back to my apartment all I could think about was my wonderful evening with this terrific woman. A few minutes after I arrived home, Joan called. We talked for another hour. I didn't want to seem pushy, so I waited two days to ask her out Saturday night, even though I already had plans. It was late in the week, and I never dreamed that she wouldn't have a date, but to my surprise she said that she was free. Caught off-guard, I fumbled around and said, "Well, that's too bad because...I'm busy." Then she fired back, "What are you doing...taking a survey?" What a smark aleck, I thought, maybe I'd be better off to just hang up and forget it, but against my better judgment I asked her out for the next evening and she accepted.

On Sunday evening, stopping first to buy flowers, I drove in the pouring rain to Joan's apartment in Santa Monica. I had made dinner reservations at Madam Wu's Chinese Restaurant, which was only a few blocks away. It was raining so hard that I could barely see her building when I parked my car and headed up the walk looking for Apartment A. Not watching where I was going, I suddenly felt water pouring into my shoes and realized that I had just walked into a huge puddle. I found her front porch, poured the water out of my shoes, and rang the bell. As I handed Joan the bouquet and squished my way into her apartment, I felt like Peter Sellers's Inspector Clouseau as I stood in my soaked raincoat and soggy shoes.

Joan suggested that I dry off, and she handed me a towel and sent me into her bathroom. When I finished cleaning up, I tried to open the door, but I couldn't get out. I tugged, I pulled, and still I couldn't get the door open. The last thing I wanted to do was ask for help. Then Joan called from the hallway to see if I was all right. When I explained that I couldn't get out, she said not to worry, then with one turn of the knob she opened the door, informing me that it needed adjusting.

I wasn't smart enough to just leave the situation alone and let her fix her own bathroom door. Instead I decided to fix it for her, so out came a screwdriver and I started turning this and screwing that, giving it my best "Mr. Fix-It" act. With great fanfare I told her to try the doorknob. To my dismay, the moment she started to give it a turn the inside knob fell on the floor. Joan watched the knob as it rolled under the sink, then looked up and said, "Do you do a lot of home repairs?" I scrambled around and mumbled something about old doors and out-of-date doorknobs, then, ten minutes later, with Joan giving me directions, we repaired the door. This evening was getting off to a rocky start.

Once we got to Madame Wu's things improved. We were seated next to Pat O'Brien and his wife, who were friends of mine, and Joan happened to know the actor with whom they were dining. By the time dinner was over, I knew that she was different than anyone I'd ever met before. That night as I stood in her doorway and kissed her goodnight, Joan looked at me and said, "Boy, I'm in trouble now," which I thought was kind of an odd response; then she told me that the moment she had turned to speak to me at the wrap party she knew that she would marry me. She said that she never believed in love at first sight, but after we kissed she knew it was possible, which prompted the "Boy, I'm in trouble now" comment. To a guy in the middle of his second divorce this is the kind of news that would send him running in the opposite direction. Even though I nervously laughed it off, somehow I knew that she was probably right, so instead of heading for the door, I decided to stay and see what the future had in store.

Back at CBS I got word that the casting session for *Private Benjamin* would take place on February 19, which happened to be Joan's birthday. Her name was on the cast list for the role of the Southern girl from Mississippi, Barbara Ann Glass, which had been originally played in the movie by Mary Kay Place.

The morning of the casting session, Kim came to my office and told me that one of the other pilots was having problems and he wanted me to meet with the producers. I said that I'd go after the casting session, and he told me to forget it because the producers were expecting me in an hour. Joan had already left for the studio, so I couldn't let her know why I wouldn't be there. When I returned to the office, I asked for the cast list on *Private Benjamin,* and there, next to "Barbara Ann Glass," was the name Joan Roberts. I was thrilled because we would be working together.

CBS had ordered four episodes of *Private Benjamin,* to be produced by Don Reo and Judith Allison. Because the feature film had been such a success, the network had high hopes for the series. Despite some production problems the four episodes had very high ratings, and *Private Benjamin* was placed on the fall schedule.

I had spent the past year and a half developing shows, and I was getting very tired of the development process. Every day was filled with one meeting after another as I listened to an endless stream of writers pitching crazy series ideas. It was usually some ridiculous premise like two guys and a dog living over a funeral parlor, or a guy, a girl, and a talking car. One of the most frustrating parts of the job was that the majority of the shows we developed never got on the air. Hour after hour of this every day was making me feel claustrophobic. I was missing the opportunity to go to the studios and work with the producers, writers, and actors who were making shows that were actually on the air. Having had it with development, I met with Bud Grant, who was now president of CBS Television, and he let me move back into my old job.

As I resumed my duties in current programming, I was assigned *Private Benjamin,* the long-running series, *Alice,* starring Linda Lavin, and the superhit *M*A*S*H.*

Shortly after moving back to programming I got the news that Warners, the studio that produced *Private Benjamin,* was going to make drastic changes in the show. They decided to replace the producers and several of the actresses and recast the roles. Joan and a pretty black actress, Joyce Little, were among the casualties, because they wanted to cast performers who were funnier, character types. The show had been a huge success, with high ratings, and I thought these changes were ridiculous. Obviously the Warner executives had never heard the old saying, "If it ain't broke, don't fix it." They recast the series and brought in several sets of producers, but the show never had the chemistry of the old cast or the vision that Don Reo and Judith Allison had for the series. *Private Benjamin* limped along and was "dishonorably discharged" from the schedule the next season.

Alice was a well-run show that was produced by Madelyn Davis and Bob Carroll, Jr., the writing team that created *I Love Lucy*. When I took over the show, it had been on the air nearly seven years. To pump new blood Madelyn and Bob decided to give Alice (Linda Lavin) a boyfriend, and they were having a very difficult time casting the part. The boyfriend needed to be handsome, mid-forties, and good at playing comedy. As we threw around names, Madelyn said that all the actors in their mid-forties who were right for the part were either big movie stars, like Burt Reynolds, or out of the business. Then she turned to me and said, "What we need is a Dwayne Hickman. You'd be great." I laughed a little uncomfortably because I knew and they knew that I'd be perfect, but it would have been an awkward situation for CBS, so it was never pursued. Thinking about what Madelyn said, I had that little twinge in my stomach that I always got when I lost a part that I really wanted. I tried to shake it off by telling myself that I was no longer an actor, I was a network executive.

I had not yet been to the set of *M*A*S*H*, so I headed over to Twentieth Century-Fox to meet the cast. Driving onto the lot and parking outside of Stage 9, where *M*A*S*H* filmed, I was flooded with memories of *Dobie*. It was on this lot that we filmed the pilot, and it was also on this same lot where I learned to ride a motorcycle for the movie *Rally 'Round the Flag, Boys!* I walked onto the set and introduced myself to Alan Alda, who told me that he had enjoyed my work over the years.

He welcomed me to the show, and I realized that he thought I was there as an actor. When I told him I was representing CBS and that I was the program executive assigned to the show, he said, with a shocked and confused look, "You mean...you're one of them now....How can you work there?" Every actor and every producer I met kept asking me the same question and now I was starting to ask myself the same thing.

One of my favorite character actors is Harry Morgan. He has done so many television series and movies that I don't think he has ever been out of work. Now he was in his mid-seventies, and I was surprised to see how frail he looked as he slowly made his way into the set. I wondered how he would get through the scene. When the director called "Action!" Harry was suddenly transformed into Colonel Potter, with all the energy, stamina, and spunk of a thirty-year-old man. Then the director yelled "Cut!" and like someone letting the air out of a balloon, Colonel Potter shrank back to Harry as he slowly made his way back to his dressing room. Harry was a real trouper!

Burt Metcalfe, who had played Capt. Spunky Merriweather on several of the army episodes of *Dobie* had given up acting and turned to producing. After working his way up through the ranks he was now executive producer of *M*A*S*H*.

The final episode titled, "Good-bye, Farewell, and Amen," was one of the highest rated shows in television history. Burt went to CBS and asked for an unheard-of, two-and-one-half hours of prime time, and the network gave it to him. The final show was a national event as people held *M*A*S*H* parties and tearful get-togethers as they said good-bye to their favorite characters.

With the incredible popularity of the show and the astronomical ratings of the final episode, Burt tried to get lightning to strike twice when he produced the sequel *After M*A*S*H*, but the follow-up proved that the old adage was correct: you can't go home again.

Lacking so many of the key characters that had made *M*A*S*H* a hit, *After M*A*S*H* was a bit heavy-handed and never possessed the fun or humor of its predecessor. The show was in trouble from the beginning, and as usual the solution was to fire actors and recast their roles. Many times the problem is in the concept or execution of the show, but the writers are never the first ones to be axed.

One day I was sitting in on a casting session with Jean Guest, who was the head of casting; Harvey Shephard, who was now head of programming; and Kim Le Masters, my old boss from development. We were auditioning actors for a new character on *After M*A*S*H*. I thought several of the actors were pretty good, but for one reason or another my colleagues had been unimpressed. It was common knowledge that Jean held an affection for New York actors, so it was no surprise that the next one to audition had just appeared in a successful Off-Broadway production. The moment he started to read I cringed. This actor didn't seem to understand the material, and he was completely devoid of humor, so every joke fell flat. When he finished his audition and left the room, there was a moment of silence. Finally Kim asked me what I thought of him. We had read several good actors and not once did anyone ask my opinion; now they wanted me to comment on this "lox," who I knew was a big favorite. I wasn't about to say what I was thinking, so I decided to give the same safe, vague comment everyone else used at the network when they were put on the spot. I sighed and tried to look pensive and said, "I think...he's interesting." Before I had the sentence out of my mouth Harvey gave me one of those famous waves of his hand, like he was sweeping crumbs off a table or dismissing some imbecile, then he announced that he thought the actor was brilliant. Kim and Jean enthusiastically agreed, and the three of them headed back to their offices without giving me a backward glance.

Walking back to my office, I was very depressed as I thought about this actor we had just hired. Could I have been so wrong about his audition? I had spent my entire life in show business, and I always thought I could distinguish good acting from bad acting, especially in comedy. I called Joan and told her about the audition and my sudden crisis of faith. She told me that I shouldn't doubt myself and to wait until the actor shot his first episode. If I was right, the proof would be on film.

Several weeks later dailies started coming in, and as Joan had predicted the proof was on film. The actor was just as terrible in the show as he had been in his audition. This time his lackluster performance did not go unnoticed by Harvey, Jean, or Kim. Slowly they were coming to the realization of what I had known the first time I heard him read, that he was wrong for the part and a very mediocre actor. Within a few weeks they had turned on him, and after a few more episodes he was replaced. I'm never happy to see an actor lose his job, but at least I knew that I hadn't lost my touch.

Joan and I had been dating for a year, and everything about our relationship seemed to be right. She may have fallen in love at first sight, but I wasn't far behind her. We had talked about getting married, but I hadn't formally popped the question, so it became a running joke between us. If I'd say, "Hey...I gotta ask you something," she'd ask, "Is this it?" and I'd say, "No, I was just going to ask you about going to a movie" or if she had seen something on the news...anything but "Will you marry me?" I had planned to ask her on her birthday, but I had to go to a Friday night taping of *WKRP*. The next evening, at a romantic dinner, I said, "Joan, I want to ask you something." She stared at me. "This is it, isn't it?" I responded, "Yes," then I asked her to be my wife. After all the false alarms I'd figured she would jump across the table; instead she just stared at me, not saying a word. I couldn't believe it. I asked her if she had heard me, and she said that she had. Now I was getting annoyed. "Well, what are you doing?" She looked up and smiled, "I'm thinking about it." Then she took my hand and said, "Yes...I thought you'd never ask me."

If someone had told me that I would be married three times, I would have thought they were crazy, especially since I was a guy who is basically a homebody. But life has many twists and turns, and sometimes it takes a few false starts and mistakes before you find the right person.

This would be Joan's first marriage, and the idea of taking

that giant leap needed time to sink in. We were engaged for almost a year before we set a date.

It wasn't a problem for us, but for one of my CBS colleagues it became the topic of conversation. At the most inappropriate moments this guy would turn in a meeting and, out of the blue, humiliate me with, "Can you believe this guy Dwayne, not marrying that Joan Roberts?" He didn't just say it, he announced it in a loud voice like some radio personality; then everyone would look embarrassed and confused, and I would sit there with sweat breaking out all over me. This happened every time the guy was around me; at a moment's notice he'd give an update on our engagement.

One night I got on the elevator and was joined by Harvey Shephard, who hardly looked at me, and several other people. I glanced up and, to my horror, I could see this guy heading for the elevator. I frantically pushed the Door Close button, but it was too late; he jumped on as the doors were about to shut. We silently started our descent, and for a moment I thought he would maybe use good sense for a change and just keep quiet. No such luck! He boomed out in a voice so loud that everybody jumped, "Harvey, can you believe that Dwayne Hickman hasn't set a wedding date yet?" Harvey looked over at him like the guy was insane, and before he could look over at me I tried to shrink back into the crowd. No one said a word. The doors opened and everyone fled for their lives. Then my well-meaning but overzealous friend slapped me on the back and said good night. I stood watching this man drive away and wondered what in the hell I was doing in this crazy place.

• THIRTEEN •

"DOBIE GILLIS"...BOY EXECUTIVE

THE SUN WAS JUST COMING UP as I lay in bed, staring at the ceiling. I had been wide awake for the last six hours as I tossed and turned, trying to get a little sleep before the "big day." I gave up trying to relax and got up to check the weather. For the first time in three weeks the sun was out and the skies were clear.

It was Saturday, April 16, 1983, and Joan and I were going to march down the aisle in six short hours. For a guy who had been through this drill twice before, I was unbelievably nervous. Somehow, this time was different. Joan's parents, Tom and Margaret Roberts, and her grandparents, Albert and Naomi Doig, had flown in from McLean, Virginia, and my son John, now nineteen, had driven up from Newport Beach and would be my best man.

The more I thought about the wedding and the reception, the more nervous I became. And I had good reason to be nervous because the *National Enquirer* was going to cover the nuptuals. One of their reporters had called and asked if they could have an exclusive, and we had agreed. It wouldn't have done any good to say no, because they would have come anyway, either hovering over the church in a helicopter, disguising themselves as bridesmaids, or parachuting into the reception, so we decided to work with them and hope for the best.

As I started to think about the *Enquirer* and my coworkers from CBS and getting married again, I was getting more edgy by the moment. Even though this was my third marriage, I felt like it was really my first. But to the world and "enquiring minds," I was afraid I'd look like Mickey Rooney, who had taken as many trips to the altar as Zsa Zsa and Liz. The more I thought about this, the more I was sure that I'd keel over. I could see the headlines now: DOBIE FAINTS ON THIRD TRIP TO ALTAR. I had to do something. Then I got a brilliant idea. I would get some ammonia capsules and put them in my suit pocket; then if I fainted, at least someone could revive me so I wouldn't lay there like a dead mackerel.

I jumped into the car and drove to the drugstore. When I asked the pharmacist for ammonia capsules, he handed me a small box, then stood there looking at me in my navy blue pinstripe suit at nine o'clock on a Saturday morning and quickly figured out my dilemma. "Lemme guess...You're getting married." I said that he was right. Then he looked closer. "Hey, aren't you Dobie Gillis?" This was the last thing I needed to hear. I just wanted to get my capsules and quickly get back to my townhouse before my son arrived. I nodded yes. All of a sudden he calls to his assistant, who joins us, and he starts announcing that Dobie Gillis is getting married and he's so nervous he's afraid he'll faint. I was mortified as two more employees joined the group and started telling me stories about friends and relatives who had fainted at weddings, births, and surprise birthday parties. I pried myself away and headed out of the store, but not before the pharmacist yelled out, "Good luck, Dobie..."

I returned home and carefully placed two capsules inside my coat pocket, and when John arrived, we hurried off to the church.

One of the wonderful things that Joan and I had in common was our interest in metaphysics and the New Thought Movement. Having been brought up a Baptist, Joan felt much the same as I did, that something was missing in her religion. She had been studying metaphysics for several years and had been attending the Hollywood Church of Religious Science. I began going with her when we started dating, and now we were about to be married by our minister, Dr. Robert H. Bitzer, one of the leaders of the New Thought Movement. This brilliant man and his wife Marguerite have become close friends of mine over the years. Until his death at ninety-eight, he continued to speak every Sunday and was one of the oldest practicing ministers in the country.

As the appointed hour arrived, I took my place in front of friends, family, and CBS coworkers. The music started, and I watched the bridesmaids make their way down the aisle. Then everyone stood as Joan, in a beautiful white gown, on the arm of her father, started walking toward me. I suddenly realized, as my heart started to race and my palms began to sweat, that I had failed to tell anyone about my ammonia capsules. If I passed out, no one could revive me, but it was too late now. With my heart pounding I somehow got through the ceremony; at least that's what I've been told, because I don't remember anything between Joan walking up the aisle and us walking out together. For all I know it may never have happened.

The reception went without a hitch. But there's something about a reporter from the *Enquirer* with a tape recorder and your colleaques, friends, family, and a lot of champagne that can make for a volatile situation. As it turned out, we were lucky; the piece they ran was complimentary, and Joan and I came out unscathed. Two days later we left on our honeymoon to Hawaii.

In the late 1950s there was a TV comedy starring Joan Davis and Jim Backus titled *I Married Joan*. It was about a guy who was married to a funny girl who got them into crazy situations, much like *I Love Lucy*. There have been many times in our life together when I felt like I was living that show, and our honeymoon in Hawaii was one of them.

Our trip began in Waikiki where we spent three days relaxing and shopping. Then we flew to Maui, rented a car, and headed up the breathtaking coast to Kapalua, where I had rented a condo at a posh resort. From the moment we got there, it was an adventure.

As we headed north, the weather was getting progressively worse, and by the time we reached Kapalua it was pouring rain and very windy. Driving around the condo development, we couldn't find our unit, so when Joan spotted a woman standing on her porch, she decided to ask for directions. She introduced herself and started to tell the woman that we had rented a condo and were lost, but before she could finish, the woman started screaming, "Get out, get out while you can.... This place will make you crazy...Rain, rain, it's rained for days." Joan thanked the hysterical woman, who kept on raving, slowly backed away, and jumped into the car. We looked at one another, and Joan asked, "Do you think this is some kind of a sign?" I assured her that it wasn't, then we proceeded to drive around until we found our condo.

To be honest, I was starting to wonder if we had just stepped over the line into some kind of tropical "Twilight Zone," but when I opened the condo door and saw the lavishly furnished unit and the spectacular view, all my fears vanished.

We unpacked and went out for a relaxing and romantic dinner. It was late when we returned, and we were both exhausted from the trip and ready to collapse. I walked into the bedroom and Joan headed into the kitchen, when suddenly I heard a scream and ran in to see what had happened. I couldn't believe my eyes, the place was alive. Every corner, every cabinet, everywhere you looked was covered with bugs. It was as if every insect in Maui had decided to congregate in this one condo at the same time. Joan turned and said, "That's it...We're outta here." Then she proceeded to fly around the bedroom repacking our suitcases. I was as upset as she was, but I tried to explain that it was nearly midnight and it would be difficult to find another condo or hotel in the middle of the night. Determined that we were not going to spend the night with a million bugs, she started calling different hotels. I finally fell asleep around two A.M. and about an hour later, hassled from killing bugs and ready to kill her new husband, Joan phoned another resort on the other side of Maui, the Stouffer Wailea. When the woman on the reservation desk told her they would have a suite ready for us at seven, Joan burst into tears. She thanked the woman profusely and proceeded to tell her that she was on her honeymoon and this had been the worst night of her life. The woman was very sympathetic and said, "Don't worry, dear, just give it time. . . . Who knows, you might even enjoy it." Obviously she thought Joan's honeymoon problems were something other than a bug-infested condo. When Joan gave her new friend and confidant the reservation information the woman recognized my name. Now feeling protective of the hysterical bride, the woman said, "You mean your new husband is Dobie Gillis?" Joan said that he was. "Well," the woman snorted, "I'm very disappointed. . . I always thought that he'd be a perfect gentleman." Thankfully, Joan got off the phone before she could do any more damage to my reputation.

The next morning we checked into the new hotel. Sleep deprived and exhausted, Joan tearfully proceeded to tell the hotel manager, bellman, and every guest within earshot that she was on her honeymoon and last night had been the worst night of her life. Every eye in the lobby turned toward me with an icy stare. The hotel manager handed me the keys to our room and, in a no-nonsense tone, he glared at me and said, "Well, Mr. Hickman, I hope you and your wife won't be having any more problems." I smiled nervously and hustled Joan out of the lobby as quickly as possible.

Apparently the story of the arrival of the hysterical honeymooning Hickmans spread through the entire hotel staff. I was mortified as each time we passed the front desk, ran into a bellman, or spoke to a pool attendant, they would all give Joan a concerned look and ask, "How are things going, Mrs. Hickman?" and Joan would beam a big smile and say, "Oh, it's much better now."

The rest of the week we soaked up the sun, took romantic walks on the spectacular beach, and toasted the Maui sunsets.

Unfortunately, the time came to leave paradise and return to reality. Within a few days I was back to work at CBS and Joan had resumed her career as a free-lance actress, doing radio commercials and guest roles on various television series.

Over the years I had been asked many times to appear on a variety of talk shows or the morning news programs like *Good Morning America* and *Today*. I always turned them down because it made it very awkward for me at the network. I couldn't appear on the shows without their permission and if I asked the network it just pointed out, once again, that I wasn't "one of the guys." On the few occasions that someone would come to my office to do an interview for a book or magazine article my coworkers would keep walking by my office door or buzz me on the phone about some trivial business. I was getting more disenchanted with my job with each passing day.

It was 1983, and that fall I got a call from Rod Amateau, my eccentric friend who had produced and directed most of the *Dobie Gillis* episodes telling me that he was going to be doing an NBC movie titled *High School U.S.A.* It was a clever premise combining the hot teen stars of the day playing high school students, with former teen idols playing their teachers or parents.

The teen heartthrobs included Michael J. Fox from *Family Ties*; Anthony Edwards, of the film *Revenge of the Nerds*; Nancy McKeon from *The Facts of Life*; and Crystal Bernard, one of the stars of *It's a Living*. The former teen idols included David Nelson from *Ozzie and Harriet*; Angela Cartwright, Danny Thomas's youngest daughter on *Make Room for Daddy*; Dawn Wells, who played Mary Ann on *Gilligan's Island*; "my good buddy" Bob Denver, from *Dobie* and *Gilligan*; and Steve Franken, Dobie's Chatsworth Osborne, Jr. Rod wanted me to do the movie, playing Angela Cartwright's love interest, and when I read the script I thought the part not only was fun, but also gave me an opportunity to work again with Bob Denver and Steve Franken. The only problem was that I would have to ask permission from Kim Le Masters, who had now moved into Harvey Shephard's job as head of programming, to do a TV movie for our competition. To my surprise, Kim thought it was a great idea; maybe he hoped that I'd enjoy being in front of the camera so much that I'd just disappear from the executive ranks.

The movie would film for two weeks but the only hitch was that I would still have to cover my shows and do all my CBS work at the same time. So, half the day I was Dwayne Hickman, Actor, and the other half I was Dwayne Hickman, Network Executive. My coworkers were becoming even more awkward with me as they'd ask how filming on "my" movie was going. After the first few days I gave up trying to explain that I had a small part and it was anything but "my" movie. The show had a broad appeal because it had the current teen stars for the younger audience and the nostalgia element for their parents. When the movie aired it was a big success, as I knew it would be. It was too bad CBS hadn't aired it!

That season I had been given three shows to cover, *Charles in Charge,* starring Scott Baio; *T.J. Hooker* with William Shatner; and *Designing Woman,* which starred the brilliant writing of its creator, Linda Bloodworth-Thomason.

Charles in Charge was produced by Al Burton, who had the reputation for knowing exactly what the teen audiences wanted. For the young girls they had Scott Baio and Willie Aames to dream about, and the teenage boys could drool over a continuous parade of nubile young ladies.

T.J. Hooker had been a series on ABC, but when the network decided to drop the show from its schedule, CBS picked it up and put it on after the eleven o'clock news as an alternative to Johnny Carson. It was a popular show, with two audience favorites; the sexy Heather Locklear who was simultaneously on *Hooker* and *Dynasty,* and William Shatner, the favorite of every "Trekkie."

Aaron Spelling had discovered Heather Locklear and cast her in *Dynasty.* Like a modern-day Alfred Hitchcock who was enthralled with his cool blond Grace Kelly, Spelling found in Heather the perfect American blond beauty and she soon became his favorite. When Spelling was having trouble getting his show *Melrose Place* off the ground in the 1990s he once again turned to his sexy, petite, flaxen-haired Heather. The show's ratings started taking off when Heather joined the cast, and today her career is hotter than ever.

Bill Shatner, the immortal Captain Kirk of *Star Trek* fame, and I had known one another for years, although we had never worked together.

After being assigned the show I went out to location to get acquainted with everyone. As I walked over to Bill he looked me over from head to toe and with an edge in his voice said, "Well, you really look good. . . . You haven't aged at all." His attitude was a combination of amazement and annoyance, and since I wasn't sure if that was suppose to be a compliment or not I just smiled and said, "Nice to see you too, Bill."

Designing Women was one of the smartest and best written shows I had ever worked on at CBS. I knew Linda Bloodworth-Thomason when I was working in development with her first series, *Filthy Rich*, and I was a great fan of her work. Linda had a terrific sense of comedy and delighted her audience with hysterical topical dialogue about current events. In the original pilot the role of Suzanne Sugarbaker was to be played by Lorna Patterson, who had starred in *Private Benjamin*. Delta Burke had been Linda's initial choice, but she was tied up doing a show for HBO called *1st and Ten* and she couldn't get released from her contract. After several days of rehearsal it was clear to everyone that Lorna wasn't going to work out. Following considerable negotiations, Delta was released from her show and before the end of the week had landed in Sugarbaker's decorating business. The chemistry that had worked so well between Delta and Dixie Carter on *Filthy Rich* nearly popped off the screen. Delta was born to play Suzanne Sugarbaker and it was through this flashy, sexy, and thoroughly self-possessed character that Linda could voice every outrageous and "politically incorrect" thought all of us have had and never dared to speak.

Dixie played Julia Sugarbaker, who always had the perfect sharp-tongued response for every situation. Annie Potts's Mary Jo Shively was the classic single working mom who had put her husband through medical school only to be replaced after he got himself established. Jean Smart as Charlene Frazier was simple, honest, and down to earth. Linda had created four women to whom everyone could relate, and through these four very different characters she could view any situation from four funny perspectives. Each one represented a different facet of Linda's personality. Clearly, Linda was the star of *Designing Woman*.

As wonderful as these female characters were, I felt that the show needed a male voice. Linda liked the idea and created Anthony Bouvier, a smart, black ex-con who referred to his time in prison as his "unfortunate incarceration." The role of Anthony had been written as a guest shot, but the actor Meshach Taylor had such a wonderful chemistry with the woman and the role provided such great comedy, that Meshach was being brought back week after week. What could be funnier and provide more comical situations than to have this black man surrounded by four opinionated Southern women. After several appearances on the show, and with his client's part getting bigger by the week, Meshach's agent asked for more money. He said that if we were going to use Meshach every week then he should be paid more than the minimum salary for a guest star who only appears one time.

I felt that it was a very fair request but Columbia Pictures, which owned the show, didn't agree. Their suggestion was to simply replace Meshach with a less expensive actor. I went to my boss, Chuck Schnebel, and together we pleaded our case to Kim Le Masters to keep Meshach. I told them that he had proven himself to be a definite asset and that the idea of having a minority and a male opened up the show and gave it many more story areas to explore.

CBS was convinced, so they negotiated with Columbia and added Meshach's salary into their license fee for the show.

The license fee is the amount of money a network, in this case CBS, pays a studio, like Columbia, for the right to air their show, *Designing Women*. The license fee almost never covers the cost of producing the show each week; that's why you hear about shows running at a deficit. If a show later goes into syndication, then the studio can make up for all the red ink during the years the show is on the network.

Every show on television has a production staff. Usually there are several executive producers, producers, co-producers, and various writers. The network feels more comfortable with several strong writers on a show because if someone gets sick or leaves for one reason or another, it knows that the scripts will still be written and the show will be delivered on time. The network needs the show completed and ready to be aired or it will have to fill that air time with a re-run or anything else sitting on the shelf.

From the beginning, *Designing Women* had an unusually small staff. Linda planned to write the first several scripts so the shows would have a continuity and the characters would be well established. Most creators of shows do this because they are the ones who know the direction they want their show to take. As the weeks clicked by the other writers were getting frustrated because they were not getting the opportunity to script the shows. One by one, the staff quit and went on to other projects, leaving Linda as the sole writer. With the exception of one or possibly two shows, Linda single-handedly wrote the entire first season. The idea of taking on the task of turning out a script every week without a break would be enough to kill most writers, but Linda seemed to thrive on it. And, along with writing, rewriting, and doing last minute polishes on the script, she was also editing the show that had been filmed the week before. There weren't enough hours in the day so I'm sure, to save time, she just gave up sleeping and eating.

The whole idea of this "one-man band" approach to running a show made CBS very nervous, and because I was the program executive assigned to *Designing Women* my job became much more difficult.

Every show is expected to give the network a brief story outline of the upcoming episodes. Usually the producers send over several story outlines, then a few weeks later, a few more, until the season is finally completed. This gives the network an idea of the direction the show is going, but more important, it gives them a sense of security.

Each week my boss, Chuck Schnebel, would call me into

his office and tell me that Linda hadn't sent over any story outlines. Then he'd tell me that I should go over to the production office and talk to Linda and her husband, Harry Thomason, who was also an executive producer of the show, and get the story outlines. I tried each week to explain that Linda didn't work that way, but Chuck didn't want to hear that. So, to make the network happy, I'd call Harry and ask for the outlines and then he'd run interference for Linda, saying he'd see what he could do. Within a few days some story outlines would arrive, but they were few and far between. My guess is that Linda really had no idea what the next five or six shows would be about. Whatever came to her the week of the show was the premise for the script. Even Linda admits that she works best under pressure, and much of it is self-imposed. More than once she told me that she would get to Sunday evening, the day before rehearsal for that coming week's show and she hadn't written one word. Her call to the starting line was hearing the clock ticking on *60 Minutes*, which airs at seven on Sunday night. Then apparently she had the sufficient pressure needed to put pen to paper. She would write all night in longhand on a yellow legal pad then send the pages to her secretary for typing, and sometime after dawn the finished first draft would be off to Xerox. By the ten A.M. rehearsal on Monday the material would be delivered and the cast would sit around the table and read through the script. Linda would hear it, then that afternoon she would rewrite and punch up the scenes that didn't work. If this wasn't hard enough, on several occasions when Linda was back in Missouri visiting family, she'd do her Sunday night writing session and dictate the script long distance to her secretary in Los Angeles. At least when she was back East she gained an extra hour or two because of the time change.

It may have been a heart-stopping, pressure cooker way to write a television show, but it worked for Linda. Even her less-than-brilliant scripts were brighter and funnier than most of the other scripts that were being written for television.

I was always trying my best to keep CBS off Linda and Harry's neck, not to mention my own. No matter how many times I tried to explain that it was best to just leave Linda alone and she would do her best work her own way, my bosses still didn't understand. In fact, my attitude about the problem and theory on how to handle the situation was met with little enthusiasm. CBS was giving me the message that my job was to get the network's demands met and because I couldn't make Linda and Harry conform, I obviously wasn't doing my job. I was reminded on many occasions that I was working for the network, not for the producers of the show.

Little by little I was appearing to be "one of them," the artistic community, and not "one of us," the network mavens. They were probably right, because I understood and sympathized with the problems of producing, writing, and performing more than I understood network rules, policy, or politics.

Designing Women had been a favorite of the critics because of Linda's sharp, witty, and acerbic scripts. With the characters' good natured bitchiness and plenty of sexual innuendoes peppering the dialogue, the audience couldn't get enough. But the first season CBS moved the show all over the schedule and any audience the show was building was being lost with all the time changes and preemptions. It was bad enough when they moved the show from Monday to Thursday night, but when the network announced yet another change to Sunday night, they had no idea that they had come up against an immovable force in Linda Bloodworth-Thomason and Harry Thomason. This decision to move the show to Sunday was interpreted by the producers as a desire on the part of CBS to try and kill *Designing Women*.

With the shrewd strategy of a military general, they marshaled their forces and took their cause to the viewing audience via the press. Between the show's legions of loyal fans and organizations for better television, CBS was losing the battle. In a stroke of genius, Linda had turned this into more than an attempt to save a television show. Now this was a feminist issue and the network was trying to suppress the voice of women everywhere. Suddenly it was CBS vs. Women's

Rights. When a group of female protesters rallied in the CBS parking lot, the president of the network, Bud Grant, came out to face the crowd of angry women. In an attempt to lighten the moment he jokingly told the protesters that they should be at home in their kitchens and off the streets, or something to that effect. Bud is a charming guy and certainly had his tongue firmly planted in his cheek when he made his remark. By the next day every wire service across the country quoted him and the press and feminists everywhere had a field day.

The next morning Bud good-naturedly responded by waving a white flag and announced that *Designing Women* would be back where they belonged, on Monday night. Once again they were in their old time period and *Designing Women's* ratings took off.

There are two very special episodes of *Designing Women* that I will always remember. Linda knew that I was a great fan of her work and if I had any criticism it was the lack of heart in the shows. From all my years' experience doing comedy and working with George Burns and Paul Henning, I learned one important thing. If you touch an audience and they can cry with you as well as laugh with you they'll come back week after week and watch the show. Bantering funny, caustic lines back and forth is great, but unless the audience sees some heart and cares about the characters, you'll soon wear out your welcome and they'll be switching channels.

I guess Linda was sick of hearing me say the same thing over and over, because the next week she wrote what I considered a turning point episode in the series. The show, "Oh Suzannah" dealt with Suzanne wanting to adopt a little Asian girl. Suzanne and Julia have a heart-to-heart talk in which Suzanne, for the first time in her life, must act un-selfishly. She knows that as much as she wants the love and companionship of this child, she must give her up to a family.

The script was brilliant and Dixie and Delta didn't leave a dry eye when they were finished. *Designing Women* had become a different show that night.

The other episode that stands out in my memory not only

had heart, but was the most consciousness-raising and socially important show in the series. The episode, "Killing All the Right People," dealt with AIDS and homophobia.

In it Linda dispelled the rumors about the disease and dealt frankly and honestly about the ways AIDS could and could not be contracted. Then she took it one step further and held a mirror up to the self-righteous members of society who felt that this horrific disease was God's punishment to homosexuals and therefore it was "Killing All the Right People."

Mary Jo becomes embroiled in a debate at the P.T.A. over the distribution of condoms in the high school. My wife, Joan, was cast as Mary Jo's nemesis, representing every parent who wanted to ignore the problem and who passed moral judgment on anyone who disagreed with their homophobic point of view. In the debate Mary Jo explains that this issue isn't about promoting sexual promiscuity in teenagers or unwanted teen pregnancies. The real issue is about dealing with contracting AIDS, a disease that has no known cure, a disease that will kill your child.

It was a breakthrough show, but it made CBS and the Program Practice Department, also known as the censors, very nervous. But when it aired, the show was so well received that the Surgeon General of the United States sent letters of congratulations to Linda and the cast. This was one of those times when a television show was more than entertainment. Linda used her show to raise the consciousness and compassion of her viewers and at the same time educate and entertain them.

Behind the scenes, the private lives of Dixie, Delta, Annie, and Jean were as interesting as the weekly scripts.

Dixie Carter's boyfriend, Reese Watson, was played by her real-life husband, Hal Holbrook. Annie Potts's character of Mary Jo Shively also had a boyfriend in the show, played by the actor Richard Gilliland. But Richard had designs on the tall, statuesque, blond Jean Smart, and by the end of the season they were married. Jean's romance with Richard was only the beginning. Delta's character, the three-times-married former beauty contest winner Suzanne Sugarbaker, was brought back together with one of her ex-husbands, Dash Goff, the writer, played by Gerald McRaney. Mac, as he is known to his friends, was set for a one-time guest appearance on the show. The romantic scenes between Suzanne and Dash Goff were starting to be played for real, and by the end of the week it was obvious to everyone that Delta and Mac were crazy for one another. While filming the show before a live audience, Mac's character Dash gives his ex-wife Suzanne a long lingering kiss, after which Suzanne is supposed to deliver a funny line. The long lingering kiss lingered and lingered and after they came up for air Delta just looked at the studio audience and said "Wow...I can't remember what I'm supposed to say." The audience laughed, whistled and wildly applauded, then several takes later they finished the scene. Unfortunately, Delta's personal aside was edited out of the final cut of the show, so it was never heard on the air. A year later Delta and Mac were engaged.

Dixie Carter and Hal Holbrook, threw an incredible engagement party for Delta and Mac at their home. Strolling violin players serenaded the group of nearly one hundred friends and family as the Dom Perignon flowed. Under the tented back yard overlooking the pool and grounds the guests dined on a five-course meal and toasted the couple. Delta made her entrance down the staircase wearing a royal blue satin dress straight out of *Gone With the Wind*. Dixie was the perfect Southern hostess and no expense was spared.

Hal was on the road that night starring in his one-man show, *Mark Twain*. We all joked that he had to be on the road in order to pay for this lavish and very expensive affair.

If the guests were impressed with the engagement party, they were totally in awe and overwhelmed by Mac and Delta's wedding on May 28, 1989. For those of us who may have been disappointed that we missed out on the marriage of Prince Charles and Diana Spenser, that royal union paled in comparison to witnessing the marriage of Delta Burke to Gerald McRaney.

Joan and I arrived at the Biltmore Hotel in downtown Los Angeles where there must have been several hundred guests waiting in the lobby. At the appointed hour we filed into one of the banquet rooms that had been transformed into a chapel and waited for the royal couple. The music started and the bridesmaids made their way down the aisle, with Delta's sister, Mac's daughter, several friends, and Dixie as matron of honor. Then the doors opened and six trumpeters heralded the entrance of Delta, with the loud fanfare causing a ripple of chuckles throughout the audience.

After the service the newlyweds went upstairs for pictures and the guests retired to another banquet room for cocktails and hors d'oeuvres. Over an hour later the guests were ushered into the grand ballroom where table after table, with grand floral arrangements three feet high, filled the enormous room. A full orchestra played as we all took our seats, then, out of nowhere, the trumpeters returned, blaring the entrance of Delta and Mac.

Course after course of dinner was served as everyone ate, drank and talked about the topic of the day...the cost of this whole incredible extravaganza. Everyone figured that a family of four could have lived very comfortably for maybe five years on the amount of money Delta and Mac spent on this one day.

Security officers roamed through the crowd, speaking into their walkie-talkies in hushed tones, and in the lobby, security men covered the doors. I don't know what they expected to happen. This was the elaborate wedding of two television stars, not the meeting of heads of state. The President of the United States didn't have any more security than Delta and Mac. Rumor had it that Mac was so concerned about security that he hired midgets to hide in the heating ducts of the ballroom, and as bizarre and ridiculous as that sounds, it wouldn't have surprised me. They were also concerned that the supermarket tabloids would crash the affair and take unauthorized pictures. I don't think they were really concerned about privacy. It was probably because they had sold the exclusive rights to cover the wedding to *People* magazine. Anyway, it was a day to remember, and one Joan and I wouldn't have missed.

Working with Linda and Harry and the cast and crew of *Designing Women* was becoming the only bright spot in my job at CBS. I had been at the network for ten years and I had learned a tremendous amount about network television production and, most of all, corporate politics. I had also learned a great deal about myself. As much as I had tried to fit in and be one of the guys, no one would let me forget who I had been. And the more I tried to deny who I was, the more frustrated I became. Every night I'd come home from work and go on by the hour about the latest madness I was dealing with. Joan and I would talk about the situation and the next day I'd go back to my office trying to make what was becoming an unbearable situation bearable.

Times had changed drastically since I had joined CBS as a "suit." At that time the network was still under the strong influence of its founder, William Paley. Now, in failing health, he was passing the control to a businessman, the wealthy, powerful, and very shrewd Laurence Tisch. Tisch was not a broadcaster; in fact, he had no show business background at all. What he did have was a keen business sense. When he took over CBS he found a company that was laden with executives who enjoyed large expense accounts, extravagant parties, and an executive dining room with its own chef and staff. Every perk that could be imagined was available to the executives, from fifty-yard line Super Bowl tickets to all-expense-paid trips to London, Paris, Hawaii, or any other exotic place a show was filming.

But this kind of wasteful spending was not the way Tisch ran a company. He was known for his lean, mean machine approach, and shortly after his takeover entire departments, like Program Practices, disappeared. These were the people responsible for keeping decency in programming and they monitored every profanity and sexual innuendo. Suddenly they were gone, but their job responsibility remained, and it was turned over to each program executive, making them responsible for the content of their individual shows.

I heard from my colleagues that New York was sending in an efficiency team to investigate the program department. Flashes of their cushy jobs going the way of Program Practices struck fear in everyone's heart. The company doing the investigating asked for an outline of the responsibilities and duties of the program executives. From their point of view this appeared to be a seasonal job that could be farmed out to independent contractors instead of the network carrying employees year round. This would save the company an enormous amount in salary and benefits.

They were beginning to ask some of the same questions that I had asked when I first came to CBS. For example, when the shows are completed for the season, what do you do for those three or four months that the production is on hiatus?

All the program executives got together to write up a detailed job description. All, I should say, except me. Apparently my coworkers were afraid that I would tell what the job was really like and blow their cover, so on the day the report was to be turned over and the meeting with the efficiency team was to take place, my boss sent me on some trumped-up trip out to the studio.

At that point I was disgusted by the entire situation. I had been looking for an avenue out and I finally came up with an idea.

In 1987 there had been a flurry of TV reunion shows that had all been ratings winners. Old series were bringing together their original casts and cashing in on the nostalgia that audiences seemed to be craving.

The attempted remake of *Dobie Gillis* at the hands of Jimmy Komack had been such a disaster that I never thought that I would want to take another stab at it. But it had been ten years and I was a lot more experienced and I thought the time had come to bring *Dobie* back. This time I wanted to do it the right way and that meant getting the original team of Max Shulman and Rod Amateau involved, so I invited them to lunch to discuss the project. They were enthusiastic so we began working on the network to give *Dobie* another shot. By this time the network brass had changed; Bud Grant had left CBS to form his own production company, Harvey Shephard had moved on to be president of Warner Brothers Television, and Kim Le Masters, my old boss from my days in comedy development, had scored the ultimate slam dunk and landed in the office of president of CBS Entertainment.

When I pitched the idea of a *Dobie Gillis* reunion movie to Kim, to my surprise he jumped at it. So, with great enthusiasm, I went to work putting all the elements of the project together. In my heart I knew that this was the beginning of the end for me at the network. By producing and starring in a television movie I was starting on a path that would make it not only awkward but nearly impossible to return to my job as a program executive. But I felt that it was time to put into practice everything that I had learned at the network and return to the creative side of the business.

The project started out very smoothly and I was beginning to feel that I would be spared many of the problems that producers experience before they get their shows on the air. Those feelings didn't last very long. Before it was all over, thirty year friendships were nearly destroyed and Dobie Gillis was once again cast into troubled waters.

• FOURTEEN •

WHAT'S IT ALL ABOUT, ALBERT?

I HAD ALREADY SOLD KIM LE MASTERS on the *Dobie* project and he had turned it over to the Vice President of Movies and Mini-Series, my old friend Steve Mills, who was also high on the idea. Max Shulman and Rod Amateau had come up with a story loosely based on a fourth year *Dobie Gillis* episode titled "What's a Little Murder Between Friends?"

In the episode Dobie asks Thalia to marry him and she points out that his total net worth is his G.I. Insurance, which is only good if he's dead. Suddenly Dobie has near fatal accidents and overhears what he thinks are plans to murder him. In Max and Rod's new script incredibly rich Thalia comes back to town and wants to marry Dobie. When he refuses to leave Zelda, she offers money to anyone in the town if they'll "Bring Me the Head of Dobie Gillis." The title was also a steal from Sam Peckinpah's "Bring Me the Head of Alfredo Garcia."

As the weeks went by, both CBS and I were becoming impatient and wanted to see a script. Finally, I called Max to see how he was progressing. I asked him how long it would take to write the script, and he replied, with typical Max Shulman humor, "That's like asking how long it takes to make a blue suit. . . . You want it fast or you want it good?" When Max finally delivered it, neither CBS nor I was very happy. It was a dark, moody piece that had wall-to-wall dialogue with only a few exterior scenes and no action. Feeling that it was like a two-hour dramatic *Dobie Gillis* episode, the network called Max in for a note session and suggested that he lighten up the story, add some comedy, and make the show more visual.

While Max was rewriting I was dealing with Twentieth Century-Fox which was producing the movie for CBS. Harris Kattleman, who was the president of Fox Television at the time, felt that it could be a possible pilot for a new *Dobie Gillis* series. I agreed that, with Max writing, Rod Amateau directing, and the original cast, we had a chance to capture the charm and chemistry of the old series.

When I met with the Fox executives and told them that I wanted Rod to direct and produce, I hit the first of many stone walls. They told me that Rod had directed a pilot called *Six Pack* based on a Kenny Rogers movie and they weren't pleased with it and that Rod was persona non grata at Fox. They were unmoved when I tried to explain that Rod had directed many "Dobies" and that he understood the character, feel, and look that we wanted to capture. Their attitude was getting pro-gressively cooler toward me and by the end of our meeting they told me that if I insisted on having Rod direct, then as far as Fox was concerned, there would be no movie. When I relayed to Max the hard line Fox was taking regarding Rod, he was as upset about the situation as I was. He agreed with me, though, that as much as we hated to lose Rod we didn't want to blow the entire project. As disappointed as I was about losing Rod, I felt that I still had the most important element, Max Shulman, the original creator and writer.

When Max turned in his second draft to CBS several weeks later, Steve Mills sent me a copy of the new script and when I read it my heart sank. I knew CBS would never do this movie. When Steve and I met for lunch he was very concerned about the story and said that people trying to kill Dobie and then Dobie committing suicide was not the network's idea of a Dobie Gillis reunion movie. He told me that Max had taken two passes at the script and neither version was acceptable, so now he'd have to be replaced or the network would drop the project. My worst fears were coming true.

By the time I got to Max he had already received the word that he was off the movie. He was angry and disappointed, and because I was the only one left on the project and because I worked for the network, he felt that somehow I was responsible. When I tried to explain the reason CBS was taking this position about his script, he asked me if I agreed with the network. It was a very awkward question for me to answer. I didn't want to hurt Max, but I also wouldn't lie to him. When I told him that I had to agree with CBS that the script needed a major rewrite, there was a long silence, then Max said, "I see.... Well, good luck with the movie," and he hung up. I was terribly upset. For the first time in our thirty-year relationship I felt that our friendship was damaged beyond repair. I was losing the creator/writer and the original director, who were also my friends, and to make matters worse they both blamed me.

What Max and Rod didn't understand was that the business of making television shows and movies had changed drastically since the original *Dobie Gillis* series had been sold to CBS. In the early days there was little interference from the studio or the network. When Fox Television decided to make the *Dobie* pilot they produced it with their own money, then shopped the finished product around to the three networks hoping to find a buyer. Today it is totally different. The studio won't make a pilot unless the idea has already been sold to a network. Then the concept, writers, producers, director, actors, and finally, the script, must all be approved by layers of people from both the studio and network. Dozens of executives are involved and they all want to put their stamp on the project. After all my years at the network I had watched this "creative process" by committee and the maze of meetings and approvals that producers had to endure in order to get their projects on the air. With this complicated process it's no wonder that there are so few really outstanding shows on television today.

But Max and Rod weren't interested in the network logic or any explanations that I might have; they only knew that they were out of the project that the three of us had started.

Once Max was out of the picture, Fox Studios decided to bring in Don Brinkley, who had produced the series *Trapper John*, to oversee the project. Don was also the father of supermodel Christie Brinkley, and lest anyone forget that fact, the walls of his office were covered with her pictures.

Don turned the rewriting of the script over to two writers from *Trapper*, Deborah Dawson and Victoria Johns. Unfortunately, these women were one-hour drama writers, not comedy writers, and their rewrite was little better than Max's. But, unlike Max, they were very difficult to work with, and it was their antagonistic attitude that put the final nail in their coffin. They were fired, Don Brinkley had moved on to another project, and now *Dobie* was once again adrift. I knew in my heart that with each passing day the project was losing its momentum.

One day I heard a tap on my office door and looked up to see Jay Bernstein standing in the doorway. He had tapped with his signature cane, which he carried at all times. This very colorful character who was producing *Mike Hammer* for CBS had just stopped by to say hello. We chatted and after he left I thought that possibly Jay would have some ideas on how to get the *Dobie* project back on track and moving. Jay had made a name and reputation for himself by discovering Farrah Fawcett, Suzanne Sommers, and Jaclyn Smith, and was very much a Hollywood "mover and shaker." His totally outrageous actions, like kicking down a TV executive's office door when a meeting started without him, had made him the talk of the town. For all his unorthodox behavior, he had the uncanny ability to put all the pieces together and get a project on its feet. I called him to discuss *Dobie* and he asked me to come to his house the next day for a breakfast meeting.

His lavish home in Beverly Hills had at one time been owned by the actress Carole Lombard prior to her marriage to Clark Gable. It was tastefully decorated in what I would describe as "very successful Hollywood bachelor" decor, complete with a trophy room of stuffed animals mounted on the wall and a seven-foot stuffed grizzly bear standing in the corner. Between the bear, the star photos lining the walls, and the breathtaking view, I felt like I was either meeting a Hollywood legend or about to sell my soul to the devil.

The moment I sat down at his dining-room table he proceeded to tell me that no one in the business or the general public knew who I was, or cared a thing about me. But, he quickly added that maybe he could get things going for me. I just sat there and looked at him, not really knowing how to respond. This was like attack therapy. It put Jay in a great position. If he did anything for me it would appear that he was responsible for anything good that happened to me the rest of my life, especially since he was taking on a guy "no one in the world knew or cared about." By the end of our breakfast meeting Jay had laid out a game plan to get *Dobie* moving and, in return, I would give him a percentage of my salary for the movie and on any future deal if *Dobie* returned to television as a series. With my toast stuck in my throat and my head spinning, I shook hands with the flamboyant "star maker" and headed back to my office. As I drove through Beverly Hills to CBS I wasn't sure if I should be relieved or panicked. I must say that Jay went into action and by the end of the week we had a meeting at Fox with all the principal players. Jay took over the meeting, instructing the Fox executives on how to get the project moving and how it would be one of the highest rated movies in television history. I can't speak for them, but he was so excited, dramatic, intense, and in-charge, that I believed every word he said, and from the Fox executives' response, they jumped on Jay's fast-moving bandwagon as well. Suddenly *Dobie* had been given a transfusion and was once again full of life. Had Jay been selling snake oil, I'm sure he could have sold a case that day.

Then Jay headed over to CBS and infused Steve Mills with new enthusiasm for the movie, and within a few days the project had gone from a slow death to a miraculous recovery. Steve decided to turn the script duties over to Stan Cherry, a writer with whom CBS had worked on another comedy TV movie. When he told me that he had brought Stan onboard, I thought that he had made a very good choice since he had directed a few *Dobie* episodes and had studied under Rod Amateau. I felt that at least he understood the characters and had a feel for the old show. The studio gave Stan the okay, which wasn't too much of a surprise since Stan was married to the ex-wife of Harris Kattleman, who was the president of Fox-TV. Stan was a stepfather to Harris's children, so he was very well connected. Stan took the script and amazingly did a complete rewrite in just a few weeks.

In the meantime, we were trying to get all of the original cast members back together. Bob Denver had agreed to return as Maynard, Sheila was taking time from her law practice and running her home for battered women to do the movie, and Steve Franken was once again going to play Chatsworth Osborne, Jr. Bill Schallert also came back as Mr. Pomfritt. The only cast member we were having a problem with was Tuesday Weld. Some things never change.

Before Rod had been fired from the project he had met with Tuesday and talked to her about returning as Thalia Menninger. She had been enthusiastic about the movie and working with Rod, but now that he was gone, the casting director was dealing with her agent at ICM and getting nowhere. Finally I called him and tried to press him for Tuesday's phone number because I wanted to personally speak to her and let her know how much I wanted her to be a part of the project. CBS was prepared to offer her the moon, but her agent wouldn't budge. He not only wouldn't give me her phone number, he wouldn't even give me a straight answer whether or not she was going to do the project. Finally, after fifteen minutes of double-talk I pressed for a definite answer and he told me that Tuesday was unavailable, and abruptly hung up. To this day I don't know if she had any idea what her agent was saying on her behalf or if she really was suddenly unavailable, but the bottom line was...no Tuesday!

Now we had to scramble to replace what I felt was one of the most important elements of the project...having Tuesday Weld play Thalia Menninger. Casting sent over a list of prospective Thalias, which included some possible, but mostly unlikely choices. The list included Teri Garr, Loretta Swit, Sally Kellerman, Morgan Fairchild, Kathleen Turner, Donna Mills, Lindsay Wagner, Sally Struthers, and Connie Stevens. When their agents were approached, some of these actresses were busy, some uninterested, and the few that were interested were either totally wrong for the part or wanted an outrageous amount of money. I was particularly interested in Connie Stevens because I felt she had all the elements to make a perfect Thalia. Glamorous and funny, Connie could play Thalia with the same perfect petulance and sexuality that made the character so appealing. Connie was available and enthusiastic and before the week was out Dobie had a new Thalia.

As the start date for filming approached I took a leave of absence from CBS. The shooting schedule was only eighteen days but I was a producer as well as the star so I would be involved in the pre- and post-production as well as the publicity. It was early October of 1987 and the air date for *Dobie* would be in February 1988.

During my leave, the woman who would be replacing me temporarily was brought over from a different area of the network and had no experience with current programs. I took her around to the shows I was covering, explained the memos and paperwork that had to be turned in each week, and also instructed her that she would have to give notes to the producers on each week's script. She looked at me totally bewildered and asked how she would know if a script was good or bad, and then she asked how she would know how to fix it. It seemed like a fair question, so I tried to explain the typical problem areas and what to look for and the general suggestions that usually helped the producers.

I found it very amusing when I visited the *Designing Women* set several months after the movie was completed and watched this woman in action. Standing on the floor of the stage with script in hand she would look very concerned and serious. If she perceived there was some problem with a scene she'd get a worried look and scribble notes in her script. It was more like she was watching some lifesaving surgery than a half-hour comedy by one of the best writers in the business. Then it came home loud and clear; she didn't have any sense of the creative process, but she had all the corporate moves. Even though behind her back everyone would roll their eyes when she imparted her pearls of wisdom, to her face they would nod and smile because she represented the network. CBS thought she was wonderful because she had learned the corporate moves, played politics, and spoke the company line. She had everything that I never had the heart for; I knew it, CBS knew it, and my replacement knew it.

The usual practice at CBS when a coworker leaves is to throw a farewell cocktail party or, at the very least, all the program executives would go out to a special bon voyage lunch. My last day was not quite what I had expected. Everyone knew, of course, about the project because it was discussed at meetings and covered in office memos. As the press started picking up on the movie and running articles, the attitude of my colleagues was becoming distant, cool, and sometimes jealous and hostile. I had worked side by side with most of these people for ten years and even though I knew we were not the closest of friends, I had always tried my best to get along with everyone. That included ignoring and never responding to some incredibly rude, hurtful, and many times downright stupid comments. But as my last day arrived, even I wasn't prepared for my unceremonious farewell. Lunch came and went as I packed the last boxes in my office. At the end of the day, as I carried out my remaining mementos, I didn't see so much as a cocktail shrimp or a glass of wine. In fact, I hardly got a backward glance or a good-bye as my coworkers sat in their offices, watching the evening news and killing time until the politically correct hour to go home. I was on a leave of absence with my job waiting for me when I completed the movie, but I knew when I drove out of the parking lot and headed west toward the beach and my wife Joan, that my days in the corporate side of show business had come to an end. Actually, it ended as quietly as it had begun.

I had walked through those doors at CBS ten years earlier and had tried desperately to leave any memory of Dobie Gillis or celebrity behind. In those years I had learned an enormous amount about production and the business side of show business. I had also learned that you can't deny who or what you are and that my talents were not in the corporate arena. I would never have the drive, ambition and savvy of a Harvey Shephard or a Kim Le Masters. These guys were masters of a game I never really cared about playing. Who knows, maybe they would like to be a celebrity, though for the life of me I can't imagine why. It looks great from the outside, but, believe me, it doesn't always make your life easy.

The following Monday morning I drove to the production offices of *Bring Me the Head of Dobie Gillis* located on the lot of Twentieth Century-Fox Studios. The actual shooting of the movie wouldn't begin for another two weeks, but I was busy with pre-production and setting up publicity for the show. Jay Bernstein had sent over his old friend, Anita Alberts, to handle the publicity. This woman was a dynamo who started putting together one of the most amazing, comprehensive, and successful publicity campaigns I have ever seen. By the time *Bring Me the Head of Dobie Gills* would air you would have had to be living in the middle of the rain forest not to have seen, heard, or read publicity about the movie.

A few days before we began shooting, Fox decided that they would assign one of their producers to our show to make sure that the director stayed on schedule. This no-nonsense gentleman was a fellow named Stan Hough. Stan, who was married to the former actress, Jean Peters, Howard Hughes's ex-wife, had produced many feature films and was very respected around town. When Stan Hough came onboard our writer-director, Stan Cherry, felt that there were too many "Stans" so he decided to go by his middle name, Zack. Every day he wore a sweatshirt with his new name stenciled across his chest. It was like he had two different personalities. In fact, on his license plate is written "DR. JEKL." The problem with a guy like that is that you never know when he's going to turn into the maniacal "Mr. Hyde."

Zack's idea of making movies was to shoot them as fast and as cheaply as possible. He thought that was the way to impress the studio, although I tried to explain over and over that the studio may seem to be pleased that he saved time and money, but if the finished product looked cheap and if he had missed shots, they would hate the movie and hate him. He ignored my advice and was determined to shoot the movie his way and make a name for himself with the studio. One of his cost-cutting measures was to shoot all of my monologues outside to save the rental of a soundstage. He took his thriftiness one step further and decided that, rather than use another day of the schedule, we would do the monologues at the end of a day's shooting. We would go into overtime, but that would be cheaper than bringing back everyone for another day.

We had been filming the big farewell scene between Dobie and Thalia in a field thirty miles outside of Los Angeles. We had a mock plane setup which was supposed to be Thalia's personal jet, and Connie Stevens looked every inch the character as she made her way up the stairs of the plane. Wrapped in a big fur coat and accompanied by two beautiful Afghan hounds, she bid a touching farewell to Dobie. The scene took most of the day to shoot, and as the moon started to come up and the temperature started to go down, Connie was sent home and Zack informed me that we would shoot all of my monologues that night. The monologues were suppose to take place during the day, so the lighting crew brought out dozens of lights to give the effect of daylight. It's called shooting "day for night." No matter how many lights and reflectors they use it never really looks like the real thing. The crew set up the park scene and wheeled out the *Thinker* statue. It was the original *Thinker* that had been used in the series, and we had rented it from Amy Heckerling, who wrote *Fast Times at Ridgemont High* and *Baby Talk*. She was a big fan of the show and had acquired the statue at a studio auction.

I took my place on the makeshift set and prepared to shoot over twenty monologues. Even my long underwear and the heat from the lights couldn't warm me as I sat in front of the *Thinker* in the middle of this dark, damp, and freezing cold field. With goosebumps all over my body I could hear Max's words ringing in my ears, "You want it fast... or you want it good?"

Aside from some difficult moments, I was really glad to be acting again. Bob Denver could never get over the fact that I seemed so enthusiastic about coming to work every day. More than once he would say, "You're really enjoying all this, aren't you?" The long hours on a movie set may not have been Denver's idea of a good time, but after spending ten years behind a desk at CBS I felt like someone had just let me out of prison.

Although Sheila James had been pursuing her law career, her acting was as sharp as ever... she still knew my lines better than I did. Steve Franken was once again perfect as Chatsworth Osborne Jr. and Connie brought a wonderful energy to the set and was always pleasant and full of fun. Connie gave the impression that her life was one big party and her enthusiasm was contagious.

When we finished filming I went to work publicizing the movie. I did phone interviews from my office with hundreds of radio stations, as well as appearing on television and giving interviews for newspapers and magazines. One day as I was in my office doing a phone interview I heard a flute being played outside my door. As it got louder and louder I was getting more distracted and annoyed. At one point the deejay who was interviewing me said, "Do you hear a flute?" Embarrassed, I told him, "No, I didn't hear a thing." When I finished the interview I headed out of my office to find the person attached to the irritating flute. Outside my door was our director, Zack, who had now turned back into Stan Cherry, merrily tootling away on his flute. He stopped playing long enough to look up and say, "This isn't bothering you, is it?" I gave him an annoyed look and said, "No, I prefer to do all my interviews with background music." He gave me a sarcastic smile then put the flute to his lips, and played his way back into his office and closed the door. The secretaries and I just looked at one another and shook our heads. I didn't realize that "Mr. Hyde" played a flute!

CBS aired the movie in the middle of February sweeps and it was up against some powerful competition. But despite a weak script and the fact that the movie looked like it has been shot on a shoestring budget, *Bring Me the Head of Dobie Gillis* held its own in the ratings race.

The "sweeps" are a four-week period that takes place in February, May, August, and November. During those months the networks bring out their best shows, trying to grab the largest number of the viewing audience. The advertising rates the networks charge their clients are set according to their ranking during the sweeps period.

On February 21, 1988, the night CBS aired *Bring Me the Head of Dobie Gillis*, we were pitted against NBC's mega miniseries, *Noble House* and ABC's coverage of figure skating at the Winter Olympics. Our little movie finished two points behind the multimillion dollar *Noble House* and one point behind the popular Olympic figure skating. The CBS research department later told me that had we been against normal competition we would easily have won the night. *Bring Me the Head of Dobie Gillis* proved once again that Dobie had millions of fans who eagerly tuned in to see their favorite characters together again.

The months of pre-production, shooting, post production, and publicity had been the most satisfying and enjoyable time I had spent in years. Once the movie aired I knew I would have to make a decision about returning to my CBS job. The idea of returning to the corporate world and once again turning my back on acting and producing would be impossible. After ten years at CBS I submitted my resignation, handed them my keys to the building, and closed the chapter on my life as a corporate executive.

During my years at CBS I had been involved in the process of developing television series, one that I felt was more intrusive than nurturing to the creative process. Between the layers of network and studio executives giving their input and the pressure shows are under to be an instant hit, series television, in my view, has suffered.

Most of the classic television shows were not overnight sensations. They needed time to stay on the schedule in the same time period for weeks to build an audience. If series like *I Love Lucy, All in the Family, M*A*S*H,* and *Dobie Gillis* had been placed on the schedule today they would have been gone after only a few episodes because none of these shows were immediate ratings winners. For all the drawbacks in television today, there are still well-produced and well-executed shows. Unfortunately, there are not that many of them. I certainly enjoyed *Designing Women* when Linda Bloodworth-Thomason was writing the series and I felt the women were excellent. *Murphy Brown* is also a polished series as well as *Seinfeld* and *Roseanne.* But no matter how great an actor is in a role, like Alan Alda as *M*A*S*H's* Hawkeye Pierce, or the actresses on *Designing Women,* without well-written scripts a show will never rise above being just another mediocre program. I think many of today's series lack "smartness." When the jokes are obnoxious, the humor crude or tasteless, and the characters cardboard or predictable, that makes for boring television.

Personally, I prefer shows that are "about something" rather than one joke that's played out over and over for a half hour. A believable premise, stories with heart, and characters that you care about, make for classic television shows. The public cared about Lucy, Mary Tyler Moore, Archie Bunker, the troops on *M*A*S*H,* and they also cared about Dobie, Maynard, Zelda, and all of our cast. I believe the common denominator in these, and in all of the classic television shows, was smart writing and vulnerable, likable characters. One of my favorite comedians was the late John Candy. Whether he was doing a *Saturday Night Live* sketch or playing Del Griffith in *Planes, Trains and Automobiles,* he had it all; wonderful comedy timing and, most important, vulnerability. He could make you laugh or cry and you really cared about him.

In thirty years it will be interesting to see what "hits" of today people will still be watching. The year will be 2024; we might be surprised to see that everyone is still looking at *I Love Lucy!*

Several months after *Bring Me the Head of Dobie Gillis* aired I was saddened to hear that Max Shulman had passed away after a long bout with cancer. I knew from our luncheon conversations that he had been ill, but because he was reluctant to talk about his condition and seemed to be in good humor, I was sure that he was recovering. Looking back, I think one of the reasons *Bring Me the Head of Dobie Gillis* had such a dark and brooding premise was that Max had been seriously ill and it was reflected in his writing. I will always regret that we were unable to work together on the movie. Max Shulman was one of the most influential people in my life. He was a comedy genius and by casting me as his Dobie Gillis, my life was changed forever. I have only the warmest feelings toward Max and the most respect for this brilliant, talented gentleman.

During my years on *Dobie* I had been interested in directing, but I was so busy acting in each show that I felt I couldn't take on any more responsibilities. Now I wanted to pursue my interest, so I called Al Burton who produced *Charles in Charge*. I had worked with Al on the show when I covered it for CBS and when I expressed an interest in directing, he offered me an opportunity to do a *Charles in Charge*. The following week I began observing the show and, unlike some aspiring directors who show up for an hour or two then wing it when they get their chance to call the shots, I arrived early every day and was the last to leave when they locked the stage at night. Week after week I would watch and ask questions about everything from setting up camera shots to marking the director's script, so by the time I directed my first show I was confident and relaxed. I thoroughly enjoyed directing. It was a challenge to find interesting ways to shoot the scenes and a pleasure to work with the actors on their performance.

As I observed the shows each week I was always amused by the bevy of lithesome young actresses who appeared on the series. It's hard to imagine that there could be so many gorgeous blond, blue-eyed beauties in one town. Once in a while you will see one of these girls that has that extra something that sets her apart from all the rest. On one particular episode I met, what I considered to be, the ultimate mega-babe. This young girl had an incredible body that had been poured into her sexy top and jeans. She wore her jeans fashionably torn at each knee, along with a strategically placed tear just above her thigh which showed a bit of her lace pantie peeking through. Erika Eleniak was not your average blond bombshell. This young lady knew exactly how to market herself. I was hoping to see more of Erika, and I did, when she became a *Playboy* "Playmate of the Month." The girls on *Dobie* never looked like this!

With the experience of directing *Charles in Charge* I went to Linda Bloodworth-Thomason and Harry Thomason and asked for an opportunity to direct *Designing Women*. They couldn't have been more supportive. I observed *Designing Women* for several weeks, then Harry gave me a show to direct. Unlike *Charles in Charge* where I had my script a few days before the show began production, on *Designing Women* we didn't have a script until the first day of rehearsal. At eight A.M. I stood outside the production offices waiting for the guy from Xerox to deliver the scripts. I grabbed one and started reading and making notes so at least I would be somewhat prepared for our ten o'clock reading. Most shows rehearsed four days and filmed on the fifth, but *Designing Women* worked a short week. They rehearsed half a day Monday, and two full days Tuesday and Wednesday, and filmed Thursday. Basically, they only rehearsed two and a half days.

This particular week the show was having a big press party at the old David O. Selznick studio. It was, appropritely enough, a *Gone With the Wind* party that would take place on the front lawn of Scarlet O'Hara's Tara. It was the original building used in the movie and now it housed production offices. The party was to take place Tuesday night, so the women had to be released from rehearsal at three o'clock for hair and makeup. So much for Tuesday's rehearsal.

The script was also in need of a major rewrite, which was to take place that night, with new pages to be delivered the next morning.

That evening Joan and I arrived at Tara to join in the celebration. As we stood drinking mint juleps, listening to the music and dining on Southern cuisine, I nervously kept looking at the one who was in charge of rewriting the script. By this season Linda had turned over some of her writing duties to another producer. This woman was having a wonderful time and didn't seem to be giving a thought to the work that needed to be done before tomorrow morning's rehearsal. Concerned about the next day's work, Joan and I left and headed home, leaving everyone else to party into the night.

Somehow I wasn't really surprised when Harry told me the next morning that the writer had fallen asleep and hadn't finished the rewrite. Now I had one day of rehearsal left and no script. Miraculously, the show went off without a hitch, due in large part to the professionalism of a wonderful cast and crew.

My directorial debut on *Designing Women* had been a baptism of fire, but I had survived. Linda and Harry were very pleased and gave me several more directing assignments.

While I was busy directing different shows around town, Joan had turned her talents to writing comedy scripts. I was encouraging her to pursue a writing career because I felt she had a great sense of humor and a natural talent for capturing the feel of the characters and turning out witty dialogue. When Joan talked to Linda Bloodworth-Thomason about her writing ambitions, Linda suggested that she do a spec script for *Designing Women*; with Joan's Southern background, she was perfect to write the show. A few weeks later she turned in her script and Linda was so impressed she gave her her first writing assignment and Linda became her mentor.

Later in the season I returned to direct another *Designing Women*. I had always gotten along very well with the cast members, but I discovered that with the success of the show and no doubt the effect of making a large amount of money each week, the women were becoming increasingly more difficult to work with. Jean Smart was unhappy with the quality of the scripts and planned to leave the show. I had to agree with her that the scripts were certainly not the caliber of writing that everyone had enjoyed when Linda was doing the show, but I still didn't believe anyone would quit a successful, highly paid job as a star of a series over bad scripts. It's only a matter of time until the network cancels the show and it's not exactly hard work to collect around thirty thousand dollars a week for twenty-two weeks. I think most of us could put up with almost anything for that amount of money. Apparently Jean couldn't take it and the money wasn't an issue, so as good as her word, she quit the show the next season.

Jean wasn't the only unhappy cast member. Delta was fighting her own battles on the set and, unfortunately, in the press. Every show has some crew member or secretary who leaks inside gossip to the media. Both Joan and I had been privy to information that was suppose to be private and personal, only to read about it two weeks later in a super-market tabloid.

I found Delta to be an enormously talented actress and I was sorry to see her leave. Suzanne Sugarbaker had been the pivotal character in the show and had really held the series together. Nothing was funnier than seeing Suzanne and Anthony together on some escapade. Delta had proved one thing when she left the series, that without "Suzanne," *Designing Women* didn't have the wonderful chemistry of the prior seasons and the show was never as funny.

Dixie Carter, Annie Potts, and Meshach Taylor hung in until the decorating business finally closed its doors and CBS removed them from the schedule.

Annie went on to star in another series, as did Meshach, and Dixie Carter continued to do commercials and her night-club act around the country.

One night when Joan and I were visiting the *Designing Women* set, Harry and Linda invited us to a reception for their old friend, the governor of Arkansas, Bill Clinton. Clinton had just returned from the 1988 Democratic Convention where he had given his now infamous never-ending speech. It was so long that when he finally said, "And, in conclusion..." a roar of relief filled the Convention Center and he nearly got a standing ovation for finally leaving the platform. The press had a field day at Clinton's expense. Even Johnny Carson had made him a staple of his opening monologues. Harry Thomason felt that Bill needed some equal time so he arranged for Clinton to appear on *The Tonight Show* with Johnny. After the show taped, Linda and Harry hosted a reception so that the governor could meet some of their friends.

It was a brilliant move to have Clinton go "one on one" with Carson, and it gave the public an opportunity to see Bill Clinton's self-effacing good humor and charm. After his appearance on *The Tonight Show*, the jokes about Clinton's speech were history and the press and public suddenly were looking at this young, handsome governor in a totally different light.

When Joan and I arrived at the reception, Clinton was shaking hands and chatting with the guests. Making our way over to him, he turned and said, "Oh, my gosh...it's Dobie Gillis...I grew up with you." He asked someone to take our picture together and proceeded to tell me what a big fan he was of my series. *Dobie* was now being rerun on Nickelodeon's "Nick at Nite" and was being enjoyed by a whole new generation of kids; in fact, Clinton's young daughter, Chelsea, was now a fan. As we talked about the show and Max Shulman's wonderful characters, he asked me when I was going to bring *Dobie* back to television.

I had no idea at the time that my loyal fan would become President of the United States. However, he wouldn't be the only President that was a *Dobie* fan. Years before, I had met Richard Nixon, who told me how much he and Pat enjoyed watching the show with daughters Trisha and Julie. Apparently, *Dobie Gillis* was a nonpartisan comedy!

Several years later, at the beginning of the 1992 presidential campaign, Joan and I attended another reception for Bill and Hillary Clinton. Once again he asked when *Dobie* was coming back, and said that it was a comedy the entire family could enjoy. Joan and I told Clinton that many people had thought an updated version would be a great idea. We had even talked about doing a new *Dobie*, with the emphasis on the problems of his teenage son, Dobie, Jr., but I still wasn't sure that I would ever again want to play the role of Dobie Gillis.

The idea of Dobie Gillis having a child was, in a sense, art imitating life. Joan and I had been married for nine years and we wanted to start a family. My son John was now grown and married, and he and his wife, Stacy, lived in San Diego where he was a successful commercial real estate broker. For most men my age the last thing in the world they would want to do is to start a new family. Everyone I knew was talking about retiring, moving to Palm Springs, and kicking back, but my life has never been normal or average. While most men had joined some company fresh out of college, married their sweetheart, bought a house, and raised their children, I had many different jobs, several marriages and divorces, a number of homes, and only one child, who I didn't have the pleasure of watching grow up on a daily basis. My marriage to Joan had been the happiest time in my life. In the years since I had left CBS and began directing, Joan and I had also begun working together developing and writing scripts. We were one of those unusual couples who could spend twenty-four hours a day together and still be happy to be with one another. I knew what a joy it was to have a child and I wanted Joan to experience that joy as well. We had discussed starting a family but, like a lot of couples, the idea was something that would be pursued "next year" after this script or that project was on its feet. Then one day that "ticking clock" chimes an alarm and you suddenly realize that your priorities better change or the most important production of your life will never come to fruition.

Month after month passed and Joan was still not pregnant. At this point we were trying not to discuss the situation for fear we'd be putting too much pressure on ourselves. But the more we tried to avoid the pressure, the more pressure we were starting to feel. We decided to take a long weekend and drive up to Carmel, and during the six hour drive we talked about everything in the world except the one thing that preyed on our minds. Joan and I arrived at our hotel, unpacked, and decided to take a walk around town, stopping at a small drug store. Joan told me that she needed to pick up a couple of items, so we went inside. I was looking at a magazine when I noticed that she had placed a bottle of nail polish and a box on the counter. The box was a pregnancy kit. I looked over at Joan, who smiled and said, "I've got a feeling...but let's not talk about it." Later that night when I was getting ready for dinner Joan walked up behind me and said, "Guess what?" Then she started to cry and told me the wonderful news: the test had proved positive and she was pregnant. Then we held each other and alternately laughed and cried. When we returned to Los Angeles, Joan's doctor reconfirmed what we already knew.

During Joan's pregnancy, I would always accompany her to see her doctor. Unlike when Carol was pregnant with our son John twenty-eight years before, now the father was not only encouraged to participate, he was expected to go through every part of the process just short of actually giving birth to the baby. I think if women could figure out that final detail, childbirth would be a responsibility they might be willing to pass on to some unsuspecting male.

Joan was getting ready for the baby and in the meantime I was about to start filming a movie for Peter Fischer, who is one of the creators of the Angela Lansbury series, *Murder, She Wrote*. Several years earlier I had starred in one of the episodes which Universal Television had intended to be a spin-off of that hit series, but as things turned out the project never got off the ground. The premise of the show dealt with a mystery writer at a major Hollywood studio who had created a popular television series and got involved in real life crimes. I played a vapid, self-absorbed, and very obnoxious studio executive, a role that I thoroughly enjoyed. It was a wonderful satire of Hollywood and I had such faith in the show that I kept trying to convince Peter to put the project back together and see if he could sell it.

After two years he decided to rewrite the movie and retitle it *Cops and Roberts*, the "Roberts" being the last name of the female mystery writer, Maggie Roberts. He assembled a terrific cast: Peter Falk, Dee Wallace Stone, Ron Masak (the sheriff on *Murder, She Wrote*), and Marcia Strassman as the mystery writer. My character, Brian Thursday, was different from any role I had done in a long time and it was great to be playing such a pompous, oily, character. Peter Fischer and I joked that after all my years at the network everyone in town would be wondering exactly who I had based my character on. Peter is a very talented writer, and along with his enormous hit *Murder, She Wrote*, he continues to turn out scripts for his friend Peter Falk's *Columbo* movies, as well as other projects.

A few weeks after I completed the movie, Joan was scheduled for an ultra-sound, which would be our first opportunity to get a look at our tiny baby. As usual, I sat in the lobby of the doctor's office. I always felt self-conscious when I went on these visits. The doctors were women, the patients were women, the only male other than me was the janitor. The nurse came out and told me to go down the hall to the third room on the right where Joan was waiting for me. Between the time the nurse left her and came out to get me, her doctor had moved her into another room. They had just purchased a new higher definition ultra-sound machine and her doctor felt that it would give us a better picture of our baby.

I followed the nurse's orders and headed down the hall, carefully counting the doors so I wouldn't make any embarrassing mistakes. I reached the third door on the right, knocked softly, then opened the door and stepped in the room. I looked up and, to my horror, I saw some strange woman in the most compromising position, on an examining table. She was as shocked to see me as I was to be standing in the room with this half naked woman. I stammered something about her not being my wife and tried to get out of the room as quickly as possible. I started to close the door, and the woman said, "Don't I know you...?" I couldn't bear, that at one of the most awkward moments I had ever experienced, this woman was going to ask me if I was Dobie Gillis or, God forbid, she'd want me to give her an autograph. I mumbled something about never seeing her before, and frantically closed the door.

As I stood in the hallway trying to compose myself, the nurse walked up and said, "I think I sent you to the wrong room." From the look on my face, she knew that she had not found me soon enough. When I told her that I had just walked in on another woman, she laughed and said, "Well, it's no big deal...it'll give her something to tell her friends." Everyone was so blasé. I liked it much better when men stayed at home and didn't get involved in all these personal female activities.

When I finally found Joan and told her about my embarrassing escapade she thought that I was overreacting and being silly. Apparently, everyone was unfazed...except me, but all of that was immediately forgotten the moment I saw the image of our sweet baby on the screen of the ultra-sound machine.

On one of our final visits to the doctor I decided to stay in the reception area. After all, how much trouble could I get into minding my own business sitting on the sofa reading a magazine? In the months that I had been invading this female territory I was constantly amazed at the way these women openly discussed their personal situations. I knew more about these strangers' marital difficulties and "personal" problems than I ever wanted to know. While I sat on the couch, minding my own business, reading my magazine, two women who were total strangers sat next to one another and started to chat. I tried not to listen but it's kind of difficult to concentrate on some article in *Time* magazine on global economics when two women are discussing the different techniques to get pregnant. The more graphic one became, the more the other giggled and then recounted stories about her and her husband's latest sexual gymnastics. They were hysterical, while I hid behind my magazine and tried to disappear into the sofa. I'll never understand women. If a man tells an off-color joke or makes a chauvinistic comment, women get insulted or scream sexual harassment. Yet these same women will sit with a perfect stranger and, in the presence of a male they've never seen before, describe, in graphic detail, their sex life and personal bodily functions!

As Joan's due date approached we knew that she would be having a Caesarean section. Since I had been through this years before with Carol, I felt as least this would be one part of the birth process that I would be familiar with. All that changed when the doctor and Joan informed me that I was expected to be in the operating room during the delivery. In an effort to make the father feel a part of the entire process, we were suddenly allowed to see things and do things only doctors were permitted to do a few years earlier. It was a lot easier in the old days when you could sit in the waiting room smoking cigarettes and watching television. But those days were over and I was going to be a part of this birth process whether I wanted to or not. I reminded Joan that I was the same guy who had ammonia capsules in his pocket during our wedding, but she would not be swayed.

The baby, which we knew would be a boy, was due December 10. We had planned to take him early, but none of us expected him to arrive, on his own, three weeks ahead of schedule. It was one o'clock, the morning of November 23, 1992, when Joan awakened and said that she was going into labor. Half asleep, I told her to go back to bed and phone her doctor in the morning, but she insisted on calling right away. When she returned to the bedroom she told me to get dressed because we were going to the hospital. After all the months of planning, the moment had finally arrived.

The street was deserted as we drove the six blocks to Santa Monica Hospital where we parked and went up to the maternity ward. Knowing that she was about to have the baby, I was amazed at how calm Joan was. When I walked into the labor room, a nurse was asking her questions as she filled out her chart. When she finished, she looked up and said, "Thank you, Mrs. Gillis, I'll be back in a few minutes." When she left Joan and I gave each other a look; it wasn't the first time someone had called her Mrs. Gillis. Then Joan grabbed my hand and said, "Promise that if anything happens to me you won't name this boy 'Dobie'!"

It was 4:30 A.M., Joan was in the operating room and I was waiting in the corridor, when our pediatrician arrived. Bleary eyed, he looked at me and said, "You know, I'm getting too old for this." I quipped, "You think you're too old, you should be in my shoes." I was fifty-eight and starting a new family. They started the C-section, and I found myself standing next to Joan, watching this miracle about to take place. Oddly enough, I wasn't nervous or squeamish, but I was aware of every moment as I tried to burn it into my memory. Then I heard the doctor say, "Wow...big baby." She pulled out our perfectly beautiful screaming baby boy and I felt chills all over my body. Our precious child was placed into Joan's arms and she sobbed with joy. After all the months of despair, wondering if we would every experience this incredible moment, here we were with our darling child.

Our son, Albert Thomas Hickman, had arrived at 5:01 A.M. and weighed in at a robust eight pounds and two ounces. We had named him after Joan's grandfather, Albert Doig, and her father, Thomas Roberts. And, true to my word, there was no reference to "Dobie" or "Gillis" on the birth certificate.

Several days later, on Thanksgiving Day, Joan and Albert came home. That afternoon, our English baby nurse arrived and quickly took charge, helping the Hickman family get settled. I had cooked a turkey dinner with all the trimmings and I couldn't think of a better day than Thanksgiving to start our life with our new baby.

In the year since Albert's birth I've thought many times about the twists and turns my life has taken, and more than once I've looked at my beautiful baby boy and asked, "What's it all about, Albert?" Now, at a time when most men my age are slowing down and thinking about retirement, I've never been busier. Between acting, directing, writing, and, most importantly, helping to raise my precious son, I've also taken up oil painting, something that I always wanted to do. To my amazement my work has been very well received and one day I hope to have a show displaying my art work.

Over the past year I have been approached by creative people in the business, as well as my fans, about bringing *Dobie Gillis* back to television. The idea of *Dobie*, the spokesman for the angst of every teen in the 1950s, now dealing with being a parent of a teen in the 1990s and representing the angst of today's baby boomer parents, certainly has possibilities. I swore that I would never do *Dobie* again, but life can be full of surprises. I never thought I'd experience fatherhood again, and here I am at sixty with a one-year-old child.

When I picked up my mail recently it was like looking at my entire life spread out in front of me; reaching in the mail box I found *Playboy*, *Parents*, and *Modern Maturity* magazines! I felt like a man who had lived many different lives and now I was off in a new direction with my baby son. Sifting through the rest of the correspondence I came across the usual bills, junk mail, and fan letters telling me that *Dobie Gillis* remains one of their favorite shows and requesting autographed pictures. It seems that no matter what direction my life has taken, whether it be working as a hotel executive in Las Vegas, running my own advertising agency, or being with a network, every road seems to lead me back to acting and back to *Dobie*.

Occasionally I have been asked if I had ever regretted playing Dobie Gillis. To be honest, there have been some frustrating times when having played the character seemed more of a curse than a blessing, but I could never say that I ever regretted playing Dobie.

I have been a celebrity for over forty years and have had a life filled with many interesting and really fascinating experiences; experiences I never would have had if I hadn't been cast as "America's Everyman." I have always been treated very well by the general public and I have been enormously flattered by the many fans who have told me that they couldn't have gotten through their adolescence without their friend Dobie Gillis. It is very gratifying to know that through the portrayal of a television character that I have been able to be a positive influence on so many people.

In my personal life I have been blessed by a happy marriage to Joan, a wonderful baby son whom I adore, a terrific grown son whom I am proud of, and a career that continues to lead me into new creative areas.

Fifty years ago, if someone had told that shy little boy hiding behind the scenery what life had in store for him, he would have been overwhelmed.

Even though I have played many different characters and led many different lives, when people hear the name Dwayne Hickman, only one thing comes to mind. So, rather than fight it, I have decided to just go with it and enjoy it because it seems that no matter where I go or what I do, for the rest of my life I'll be...Forever Dobie.

INDEX